SUPERSONIC FIGHTER PILOTS

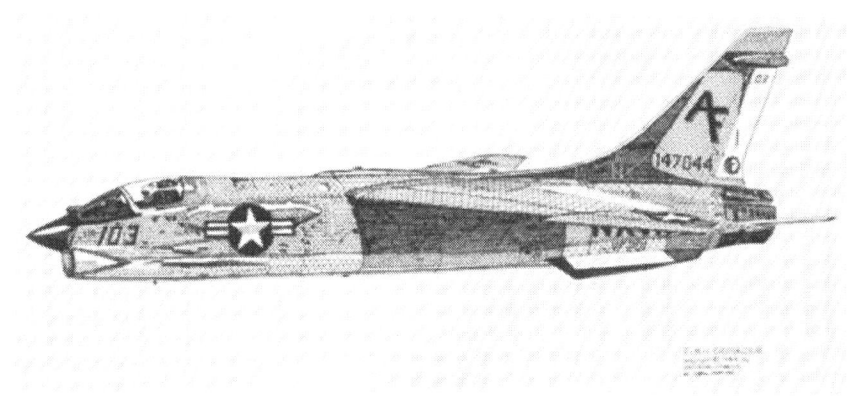

By

RON KNOTT

Copyright © 2011 Ron Knott

All rights reserved. No part of this publication may be reproduced or transmitted in any form or by any means without written permission of the publisher.

Author's note: the following information is believed to be accurate. Material herein is reported in various forms gathered from journals, news releases, magazines, historical records, individuals, Internet, books, LTV, and other sources. However, as one would suppose there are a few inconsistencies over the past fifty-four years of documentation concerning the history of the *Crusader* and its pilots.

Publisher: Ron Knott
700 Knott Ct.
Euless, TX 76039
ronknott1@msn.com

Dedication

It is my pleasure to dedicate this book to all men and women who have served, or will serve in the military of our country. And more importantly, this book is also dedicated to the families of those who have served. Although family members may not wear the uniform they are no less a part of the military team. They are faced with loneliness and loss that accompanies military life. I appreciate your sacrifice. General William Westmoreland said, "When the soldiers came home from Vietnam, there were no parades, no celebrations. So they built the Vietnam Memorial for themselves." How sad! – Ron Knott

A Veteran is someone who at one point in one's life writes a blank check made payable to "The United States of America" for an amount of "up to and including my life." That is honor, and there are way too many people in this country who no longer understand it. – Author unknown.

My Crusader

Like a threatening Eagle, she hunkers down, looking numb with a tight grip on her weapons. Her wing is up appearing detached from the fuselage. Her snout is sucking up air like a Texas tornado. On the deck she is not a thing of beauty. But she is my F-8 and her nest is the steel flight deck of the aircraft carrier: her eggs – four 20mm cannons, four Sidewinder missiles, bombs and rockets, and sometimes cameras. This bird has daggers. She is ready to fight ... and so am I.

I become a part of her – we are one in intention. I connect myself to her with straps, garters and hoses, plugs and connectors. I breathe her air – I communicate through her brain. I see through her eyes.

With a surge of jet fuel, a blast of compressed air, with ignition added she comes alive. We are as one, tied together: the machine is an extension of the man; her hydraulics – my muscles; her radar – my eyes; her mighty engine – my power.

She screams and whines as we taxi along the narrow flight deck. Final checks, her nose pointed down the sharp end of the ship. Resting on the catapult – with her harness attached – we are about to be shot into the air or eternity.

Full power applied – *THUMP!* The afterburner kicks in. An ambient cloud curls in a cyclonic pattern around her nose – she is thirsty for more air.

My salute is her release. She races rapidly toward her freedom – escaping the pitching deck, leaving a roar behind that rattles windows and shakes the onlookers on deck.

"Clean-up; clean-up." This is my mental signal to reduce drag. "Gear-up; Wing-down." She is happy, accelerating and climbing at the speed of heat. I am astonished at the transformation of the ugly duckling into a thing of graceful beauty – yet she is businesslike, threatening, thrusting forward and upward with deadly purpose.

We streak across the oceans below, pushing the Crusader to the limit. We go from 'Feet Wet' to 'Feet Dry' in a matter of minutes. We look and listen for the evil white speck of a SAM rising to kill us. The AAA is reaching out for us. Tracers have the right of way. We evade. That missile is steady on an intercept course, we are the target. Then, on signal – we jinks – it goes stupid. We are saved again.

We search for bogies – they run – they hide. They know the 'Gun Fighter' is deadly. Air superiority is our legend – the word is out. We exercise – man and machine are superior – we train to kill – we don't run from a fight.

We make the sky safe for others – we escort – we strafe – we bomb – some photograph. We claim Air Superiority – Mission Complete – we head home. Low state – we tank – easy goes it – fuel transfer.

All birds return to roost – the big "Bird Farm" pitches and rolls; weaving, moving up and down in the rough seas. It is a dark night – hook down – heart rate up – "A little power, don't climb." *"WAVE OFF, WAVE OFF!"* Foul deck is declared!

We try again – low state – "Sader Ball 1.1 – manual." "Looking good, keep it coming." Salt spray – stack gas – I can do it – meatball – line up – airspeed – concentrate – I can do it – deck is moving – don't look at the deck – meatball – line up – airspeed.

BAM! – aircraft trapped – my body thrown forward – full power – reduce power – find director – taxi clear foul line – fold wings –watch director – easy goes it – still dark – too close to deck edge. Park and shut down – thumbs up – good bird – heart rate down. Brandy time!   Ron Knott

Acknowledgments

Many thanks go out to the following Navy and Marine pilots for submitting their narrative about their flying experiences; Edward Cathcart, Chuck Klusmann, Cliff Judkins, Jim Strawn, Don Jordan, Jim Foster, Tony Longo, Bob Beavis, Bob Shumaker, Bob Hoch, Garnett Haubelt, Bill Rice, Chuck Anderson, Henry Livingston, Hank Smith, Robert Kirkwood, Len Johnson, Charlie Snell, Richard Nelson, Larry Durbin, Larie Clark, Wayne Skaggs, Will Gray, Bill Brandel, Tom Irwin, Peter Michael, David Corbett, Tom Garrett, Tom Myers, Edwin Miller Jr., Don Ressel, David Corbett, Paul Forrest, Jim White, Brooks Dyer, Al Nease, David Johnson, Alan Wright, Peter Michael, Jay Miller, John Miottel, Lou Pritchett, Lynn Helms, Wayne Whitten, and Stewart Seaman. Every *Crusader* story that was submitted is recorded herein.

Thanks to the following authors for sharing information from their publications: Michael O'Connor – *MiG Killers of Yankee Station*, Jan Tegler – *Crusader Chronicles*, John Miottel – *Miottel Collections,* Peter Mersky – *Vought F-8 Crusader*.

Thanks for encouragement from the following to produce this book: Ken Vanlandingham, Wayne Whitten, Mike Long, Ken Jack, Jim Cormack, Robert Scobie, JohnMiller, Dick Atkins (LTV), Len Kaine, Dave Johnson, Stewart Seaman, Jim Carmack, Tommy Thomas, John Allen, Randy Gunnip, Ronnie Cummins, Howard Pierson, Tommy Keeton, Mike Faulkner, Jim Brady and Larry Flenniken.

Thanks to Edward (Mofak) Cathcart for designing the front and back cover of *Supersonic Fighter Pilots* Thanks to George Dubick for the pin & ink drawing of the *Crusader* on the title page, and thanks to editors Roland and Jackie Knott.

"There is no limit to the good you can do if you don't care who gets the credit." General George C. Marshall

Contents

PART I

Dedication i
My Crusader ii
Acknowledgments v
Introduction x

Chapter 1 Training Flights 1
Chapter 2 Recruitment 11
Chapter 3 Flying the Crusader 21
Chapter 4 Over the Rainbow 27

PART II

WHAT IS A FIGHTER PILOT? 35

Chapter 5 The Price of Freedom – Chuck Klusmann 37
Chapter 6 Cold Cat Shangri-La – Jim Foster 53
Chapter 7 I Fell 15,000 ft and Lived – Cliff Judkins 61
Chapter 8 High Speed Ejection – Jim Strawn 75
Chapter 9 My High Dive – Don Jordan 83
Chapter 10 Thunderstorm Flight – Ron Knott 93
Chapter 11 Barricade Engagement – John Miottel, Jr. . . 107
Chapter 12 Rough Sea – Tony Longo 117
Chapter 13 Flight Deck Level Ejection – Terry Kryway . . 127
Chapter 14 A Real Hero – Ed Cathcart 131
Chapter 15 Never Give Up – Bob Shumaker 141
Chapter 16 Navy North Atlantic – Ron Knott 151
Chapter 17 Ejection Over Arizona – Bob Hoch 167

Chapter 18 Saying Farewell Crusader Style –
   Garnett Haubelt 173
Chapter 19 To Kill a Carrier – Ed Cathcart 177
Chapter 20 From the Platform – Bill Rice 185
Chapter 21 Night Photo Mission – Chuck Anderson 191
Chapter 22 My MiG: Almost – Henry Livingston 199
Chapter 23 Cold Cat Midway – Hank Smith. 207
Chapter 24 The Gunfighter – Robert Kirkwood 215
Chapter 25 Cuban Missile Crisis – Ron Knott 221
Chapter 26 Rocky the Flying Photo Squirrel –
   Len Johnson 239
Chapter 27 Crusaders vs Phantom – Charlie Snell 257
Chapter 28 Paddles – Richard Nelson. 261
Chapter 29 Night Carrier Qualifying – Larry Durbin 269
Chapter 30 Cross Country – Larie Clark. 277
Chapter 31 Carrier Qualifications – Wayne Skaggs 283
Chapter 32 Photo Mission – Will Gray 291
Chapter 33 Unexpected Ejection – Michael Hanley 295
Chapter 34 A Nugget's Lucky Day – Tom Myers 299
Chapter 35 Non-Shot Cat-Shot – Bill Brandel 303
Chapter 36 Barricade Engagement – Stew Seaman 307
Chapter 37 Sermon on the Ramp – Dave Johnson 311
Chapter 38 Memories of Nights Gone By – Tom Myer . . 319
Chapter 39 Waste in Space – Ron Knott 327
Chapter 40 Soldier of the Year – Larry Flenniken 337
Chapter 41 The Lost Model – Ron Knott 343
Chapter 42 Fire in Flight – Bob Beavis 349
Chapter 43 Other Courageous Short Stories 355
Edwin Miller Jr., Don Ressel, Alan Wright, David Corbett, Peter Michael, Tom Irwin, Paul Forrest, Jim White, Brooks Dyer, Al Neese, Jay Miller, Lou Pritchett, Wayne Whitten, Ed Cathcart, Russ Longley.

PART III

STATICS

Appendix A Chance Vought Crusader 379
Appendix B Crusaders at War 388
Appendix C MiG Killers 398
Appendix D God and the Military 399
Appendix E Memorial Day 401
Appendix F My Ground Emergency 402
Appendix G About the Author 408

Weapons of Mass Destruction

INTRODUCTION

Supersonic Fighter Pilots is a book of heroes; in fact more than forty heroes are listed herein. And there are many, many, many more. The heroes in *Supersonic Fighter Pilots* were not just a hero for a day, or a one-time event hero. But they were heroes almost every day, day-in and day-out for months at a time for our country. I was honored to serve with the likes of these heroes. We were all one bullet, or one crash away, from eternity. After flying for the Navy for only seven years, more than two hundred of my pilot friends had lost their lives flying Navy aircraft; this is obviously a dangerous profession. In fact, I am the only living pilot left that was in my flight school graduating class. James Michener was quick to recognize and report the heroic actions of Navy and Marine Aviators when he wrote the following statement in *The Bridges at Toko-Ri*, "Where do we get such men?"

Supersonic Fighter Pilots is not a Hollywood story made up to appease the masses, but is rich with true life, courageous stories chronicled by heroic pilots about their lives and near-death, daring experiences. His script was literally written in his own blood, sweat, and tears, no matter if he was on active duty or in one of the Reserve Squadrons. Injury and death made no distinction between the two groups.

Many of the stories in this book have been asleep for more than thirty years. And all too often many such stories are "laid to rest" each year, forever. My motivation for writing these stories is because my kids, grandkids, and associates continue to ask me what it was like flying Navy jets from the decks of aircraft carriers. That is the reason I have included so much detail about some of the normal procedures, abnormal procedures, and emergency procedures. For example, I go into great detail in explaining how an ejection seat works, how it feels to be catapulted off an aircraft carrier, the excitement of flying supersonic speeds, and many more adventures earth-bound people will never experience except through these stories.

All the chronicles conveyed herein are by pilots who are still living at the time of this publication. For each story in *Supersonic Fighter Pilots* there are at least ten other stories where the pilot did not survive. The sad part of this report is the fact that the others may have performed flawlessly, yet they did not survive. They too, were courageous heroes and did their best, but a posthumous recognition is all we can give them now. Yet, we will meet them again in the great "Eternity Fraternity."

You will read in *Supersonic Fighter Pilots* reports of pilots ejecting from their crippled aircraft, crashing on land, boat and sea, being shot down by the enemy, taken captive as POWs, saving airplanes that experienced major malfunctions, and yet, they were usually flying again within a few hours if they did not sustain long term injuries. That takes "real guts," as the old saying goes. These are true tales of real people who overcame fear with courage and valor. These are a very special group of fighter pilots.

Where did these men come from and what were their requirements? First and foremost, they were all volunteers. Most, but not all, were college graduates from the universities and military schools across our nation. They had to be in perfect health with vision of at least 20/20 uncorrected, for each eye. They had to pass a Flight Class I Medical Examination and be in top physical condition.

I chose to publish personal stories of Crusader Fighter Pilots because I was a *Crusader* fighter pilot for about ten years. I know the thrills of flying this machine and the dangers involved as well. And I know many heroic Crusader pilots who risked their lives in this unforgiving machine. This sleek supersonic fighter commanded the respect of all who were fortunate enough to take her screaming through the skies at the speed of heat. This bird would kill you as quick as an enemy missile if you did not stay within her performance envelope. She was a touchy thoroughbred that demanded fair treatment – with it she would give you awe-inspiring performance. Just lead her off the forbidden path and she would throw you into eternity quickly, but she sure was fun to fly!

The accident rate for the *Crusader* was very high. Of the 1261 *Crusaders* built for the Navy and Marines, 517 were lost through accidents or enemy action, with a total of 493 pilots ejecting from their crippled birds. During the thirty-year operational lifetime of the F-8 in the US fleet, there were 1106 major accidents and 186 pilots were killed (not including those lost in combat).

The *Crusader* had quite a deplorable record of the number of ejections. Except for one single month there was at least one F-8 ejection each, and every month during a thirteen-year period from June 1957 to May 1970. A 41% loss-rate may seem a lot, but one has to take into account the eighty-four *Crusaders* lost over Vietnam due to ground fire, plus three or four to MiGs.

The *Crusader* had an extremely high accident rate in comparison to other fighters; the rate was about three times higher than that of the McDonnell F-4 *Phantom;* about four times higher than the A-4 *Skyhawk,* and four times that of the later Grumman F-14 *Tomcat.* The *Crusader's* accident rate in 1957 (number of accidents per 100,000 flight hours) was a staggering 243.9. In 1983, its final year of US Navy service the *Crusader's* accident rate was 68.82 versus an overall Navy rate of 3.34. The F-8s lifetime average was 46.74. By way of contrast, the lifetime average for the F-14 *Tomcat* was less than ten. Nevertheless, the pilots cherished flying the *Crusader.*

I suppose this fighter aircraft provided thrills to its pilots comparable to that of driving a racing car in NASCAR. Even though there are many NASCAR accidents, the driver, if he survives, is quick to get behind the wheel the next day for another racing thrill. And so it was with a *Crusader* pilot. He is quick to jump back in the cockpit for another flight in this awesome fighter.

Crusader pilots were a breed of warriors with a special attitude, aptitude, and spirit. They were fearless, arrogant, and demonstrated a flamboyant personality that exudes confidence and bravado in every minute of flight and every second, at Happy Hour or post-flight activity. The *Crusader* pilot was his own biggest fan, conceited, overconfident, big-headed, and egotistical. I can't argue with that because for the most part it's true – I was a *Crusader* Pilot as well. They've earned their right to swagger by enduring the most intense, rigorous, competitive, and concentrated flight training program their country has ever developed.

In *Supersonic Fighter Pilots* you will read of real life stories written in first person accounts of *Crusader* Fighter Pilots flying this fantastic machine in peace and in war. You will read in this book the *Crusader* was one of the most, if not the most, dangerous Navy fighter aircraft to land on an aircraft carrier. In other words, the airplane was a joy to fly but it would kill you in a second if you did not fly the machine properly. Herein are accounts of flying thrills and adventures reported by a great group of Navy and Marine pilots.

Like Dizzy Dean said, "If you can do it, it ain't bragging."

CHAPTER ONE

TRAINING FLIGHTS

COWBOY

"*Killer*, do you see that simulated tank at 12 o'clock low?"
"Rog, *Cowboy*."
"I'll make an identification pass on the port side and you fly by his starboard side.
"Rog, *Cowboy*."
We let down to the targets altitude, which was about ten feet tall and zipped by him blowing up dust at the speed of heat. There were no electrical lines along this long and lonely stretch of road so we did not have to worry about engaging such hardware. As we passed the target we selected the afterburner, which makes a loud explosive noise like a bomb going off, and made a high "G" pull up toward heaven to avoid the simulated target from getting a fix on our side numbers. As we rolled inverted at 10,000 feet to get a better fix on the target we noted that the target had in fact stopped along side the road and there appeared to be a subject standing beside the target.
Killer and I elected to investigate. We both let down to target altitude about three miles in front of the object, thereby attacking him head on. Again, we were kicking up dust as we approached the object but this time the subject had us in sight. It appeared the subject had a tire tool in his hand and was shaking his fist at us.

"*Killer,* did you see what I saw?

"Rog, *Cowboy.*

The simulated target had the markings of FedEx on the side of his 18-wheeler. Those long lonely roads in the western states sure did make a great TOO (Target of Opportunity). Although this type of training might be a little nerve racking on earth folks it sure was good practice and fun. Of course, the Navy was not debriefed on this mission.

SAM SITE?

On a beautiful Florida morning *Killer* and I were en route from NAS Cecil Field, FL to the Pine Castle Target Range just north of Lake George, FL. As we were slipping across the tall pine trees at 500 mph about eighty miles south of Cecil we noted a big clearing zip under our nose. At first it had all the appearances of a SAM site. I immediately called for a 360-degree turn to investigate the area. On the second pass I noted what appeared to be a large swimming pool and volleyball net. I told *Killer* that it looked like they had tried to camouflage the SAM site.

Killer said, "Rog *Cowboy.*"

We made a few more passes for better identification but could only see the subjects scampering around in what appeared to be skin colored uniforms. The next pass I flew so low that I had to pull up to go over the volleyball net but that allowed me to get a better view of the unusual uniforms. They were skin colored, all right. In fact, skin is all they had on – we had happened upon a nudist camp in the middle of Florida.

Needless to say, we had to make a few more fly-bys to make sure that what we were really seeing was what we were really seeing. Finally, we went on to the target and got a real "bulls-eye," then, went back to our home base and landed. As I was taxiing into the flight line I saw my Skipper approaching and I could tell that he was not a happy camper.

When I got out of my airplane he said to me, "*Cowboy,* did you fly over that nudist camp?"

My first thought was that someone in that nudist camp must have been in the Navy because they knew exactly what squadron to call.

One of the traits of a fighter pilot is to think fast and come up with a quick solution for any problem. I knew that he knew and there was no use in lying about my flight.

I said, "Skipper, I want to tell you the truth. *Killer* and I were not the first ones to fly over that nudist camp."

He said, "What do you mean by that statement?"

I said, "Skipper, someone had already flown over that area and had scared the pants off those poor folks before we got there."

Of course he could not keep from laughing but he went on to say, "*Cowboy,* if you fly over that nudist camp again I will have your wings."

I said, "Yes, Sir, Skipper," saluted him and walked off.

THE FARMER

Killer and I were flying high over a rather large farm in an off-the-record area in northern Florida. We saw what appeared to be smoke rising from the field below. However, upon better intelligence we determined that it was a tractor plowing the dry field and kicking up a tremendous amount of dust.

I said, "*Killer,* let's go down and salute this farmer with our *Crusaders.*"

Killer said, "Rog, *Cowboy.*"

So we let down to the farmer's altitude and came up behind him at the "speed of heat." I noticed in my canopy mirrors that we were kicking up more dust than the farmer before we got to him.

I am sure he was thinking how peaceful and quiet it was in his line of work. He had probably just taken a fresh chew of Beechnut Chewing Tobacco and was relaxing until he had to make a big turn at the end of the row a few minutes ahead. It appeared he had the old tractor at V-max (about 5 mph) when all of a sudden these demons from outer space slipped by him at 500 mph. He could not hear us coming because at our speed we were ahead of any sound from the airplane. I can only imagine what he thought when his world exploded all around him. As *Killer* and I pulled up we noted the farmer dismounted from the tractor very quickly and headed for the tall trees nearby. He was kicking up as much dust running from the tractor as the tractor was making. I am sure that he put a little extra fertilizer on the soil as we passed.

THE SUPERSONIC PASS?

On a lovely Texas day *Killer* and I were out practicing aerobatics, dog-fighting, and flying tight formation. The visibility was great and the air really smooth. One minute we would be at 30,000 feet and the next minute we would be at treetop altitude. It sure was fun taking the *Crusader* to its limits. These are the kind of days you love to be in the air with someone you can trust and just hang on his wing no

Supersonic Fighter Pilot

matter what he does with the airplane. *Killer* was a smooth pilot and a great leader. We had learned long ago that an airplane was no good on earth!

All of a sudden *Killer* remembered he had a handball game scheduled in just a few minutes at the Dallas Sports Club. *Killer* was a great handball player and folks would come in from across the nation just to play against him. He always won no matter who they were or where they came from. He was like poetry in motion on the handball court.

Killer and I were about one hundred miles southeast of Navy, Dallas, when he determined we needed to rush back to the field. We dropped our nose, picked up speed, and headed for Dallas. In just a few minutes we had landed and *Killer* was able to keep his handball appointment while I went on to other activities. Our flight had been breathtaking.

The next day *Killer* and I got a call from the Base Operation Officer to report to Navy, Dallas immediately. Surely they were going to give us some kind of award, but as we approached the Operations Officer it was clear that he was most unhappy.

He started off by saying, "Your flying stunt yesterday may cost you your wings."

Killer and I looked puzzled.

The Ops Officer went on to say, "Don't try to deny what you have done!"

I said, "Sir, what have we done?"

He said, "You and *Killer* were the only *Crusaders* airborne in this area yesterday and you broke $14,000 worth of plate glass windows in a town southeast of here by making a supersonic pass over the city."

I said, "Sir, it is a fact we were airborne yesterday, but I doubt that we went supersonic at anytime during our flight. Do you agree, *Killer?*"

"Rog, *Cowboy.*"

I said, "In fact, we may have seen some Air Force planes in the area where the damage was done. Right, *Killer?*"

"Rog, *Cowboy.*"

This seemed to give some relief to the Operations Officer although he did not believe our story. He was quick to let the Air Force take the blame to get the Navy off the hook, but he was still not happy with *Killer* and me.

You know, that was over three decades ago and some folks still believe that *Killer* and I made that supersonic pass.

THE WATER VESSEL

Killer and I were flying over a certain large body of water and noticed there was a lot of surface activity on this lake. We had to investigate. I dropped down to the surface of the lake until Killer reported that my airplane was making a "rooster-tail" over the water. I figured that was low enough.

I recognized one of the surface crafts as a vessel belonging to my cousin, Julian. As I came across Julian's boat I noted that the subjects on board were enjoying a leisurely day on the lake (they could not hear me coming). On my second pass I noted that the subjects, who had been in the surface craft, were now in the water. For some reason they had abandoned ship.

Killer and I returned to our home base about two hundred miles away, uneventfully, and landed. It had been a great training flight.

Supersonic Fighter Pilot

Later that evening I received a phone call from Cousin Julian.

He said, "You almost killed us today!"

I said, "How is that, Cuz?"

He said, "You flew so low and fast that our chairs were blown into the water and the bathroom door was blown off my boat!"

I asked, "Cuz, do you believe I would do that?"

He continued without a response to my question, "All the other boats on the lake stopped whatever they were doing and just watched you and your friend."

I said, "Cuz, what do you think? Are you mad at those pilots who would do such a thing?"

He said, "No, no, it was the most spectacular flying act we had ever seen and although it scared the water out of us, we loved it." Of course, that made *Killer* and *Cowboy's* day.

LOW LEVEL FLIGHTS

Why do fighter pilots like *Killer* and *Cowboy* like to fly fast and low? Thanks for asking! When you are traveling 1000 mph at 50,000 feet there is very little sense of movement because there is no relative motion of nearby objects. In fact, you appear to be almost standing still because you are so far away from any other mass. For example, if you look at a far away object when traveling fast in your car it seems to move somewhat slowly. But if you look at the ground just in front of the car you appear to be really zipping by. And so it is with flying at low altitudes. A speed of 500 mph at one hundred feet altitude appears much faster that 1000 mph at 50,000 feet.

Ron Knott

Many of our training flights were flown at high speed and low altitude to avoid enemy radar or visual detection. Flying high speed at low altitude is fun because the world just seems to be rolling by below you. It is also extremely dangerous because just a slight wrong input on the flight controls can put you in the dirt and as we commonly say, "this could be church."

The Navy was careful to plan these low-level training flights over unpopulated areas to avoid frightening the earth-people. But no matter how careful you were, you would at times fly over small towns or unknown crowds (like *Cowboy* flew over the nudist camp) slipping along at 500 mph at treetop level.

Another problem we had was chicken houses across the southeastern states. We would be slipping along at 500 mph at low altitude when all of a sudden these big chicken houses would appear under our nose. The extreme noise would cause the chicks to bunch up in a huddle and smother each other to death. The Navy would have to buy thousands of chickens killed by these flights. I think the Navy bought more chickens than Colonel Sanders of KFC. I suppose this is kind of like human beings trampling each other to death trying to get into a soccer game. And of course, some took low-level flying to the extremes. What can I say? It was fun.

Those in command may say this type flying is unethical and dangerous; without a doubt part of that statement is true. But along the same line of thinking those in command put us in "harm's way" many times by launching planes off a carrier when the flying was unnecessary and very dangerous. For example, one carrier launched eight airplanes into a fog bank just to compete with the other carrier in the area. Seven of those aircraft were lost due to weather conditions. This was known as "Black Thursday." Thank goodness, no lives were lost on this launch. Wisdom should prevail by leadership in such conditions, especially, when launching and landing aircraft because the safety of so many people is at stake.

In the next chapter you will read how I became a *Supersonic Cowboy*.

Ron Knott

CHAPTER TWO

NAVY RECRUITMENT

RON KNOTT

As I leisurely strolled through my college Recreation Hall during my senior year, I noticed a booth set up with a large display of Navy posters. As I approached the booth I observed a large poster with a Navy jet flying over some massive mountains somewhere, which stated, "You can be an Executive at 40,000 feet." That got my attention.

I stopped to chat with the two fellows at the cubicle. I noticed they were wearing white britches, white shoes, and white shirts with all kinds of little trinkets attached to them.

The fellow with the black and gold boards on his shoulders greeted me by saying, "Welcome aboard, *Cowboy*, I am Lieutenant Commander Jessie Wood. Let me explain the Naval Aviation Program to you." (I will never know how he knew that I was a cowboy!)

I said, "Please do, but first I have a question. If you are a Lieutenant Commander, will your next rank be a Captain Commander, and then the next be a Major Commander?" (I had been in Army ROTC and knew my ranks very well.)

He said, "No, the Navy does it different. A Lieutenant Commander in the Navy is the same rank as a Major in the Army, and my next rank will be Commander, and then Captain."

That really confused me because I knew that a Captain was below a Major. I just let that bit of confusion slide for a while because I wanted to know more about how to be an "Executive at 40,000 feet."

Mr. Wood continued, "The Navy has implemented a program to recruit college graduates for the Naval Flight School in Pensacola, FL. If you qualify for the program and complete the school you will be a commissioned officer in the U.S. Navy after four months of training. The reason for this program is that the Naval Academy is not able to provide enough officers for flight training."

I asked Mr. Wood how long it took the boys in the Naval Academy to receive their commission.

"Four years," he replied.

That seemed like a super deal. If I could accomplish in four months what it took the Academy boys four years to achieve, I was ready to sign the papers. But first I told Mr. Woods that I might not need much training since I already had my Student Pilot's License.

He said, "Tell me about your flying experience."

I explained to him that I had almost twelve hours in an Aeronca *Champ*, a tail dragger airplane with a sixty-five horsepower engine. I also said, "I would have had more time but the rental prices just went up to $6 an hour."

When he smiled at my testimony I knew right then and there that he had accepted me as a fellow pilot.

"But," he went on to say, "The Navy has developed a lot of flying skills that a pilot like you will appreciate." He said, "It will take about eighteen months to get your Navy *Wings of Gold*."

I was quick to ask, "How many years does it take the Academy guys to get their wings since it takes four years for

Supersonic Fighter Pilot

them to get a commission?" For some reason he did not respond to my question.

Mr. Wood had some beautiful pictures of Pensacola Beach. In fact, he told me this is where I would be receiving my flight training. That really got my attention as well.

But when I asked him about making daily leisurely trips to the beach he said, "The Navy schedule is kind of hectic. You may not want to go to the beach during the first few weeks of training."

Mr. Wood just didn't understand because I knew that I could work around the Navy schedules and be on the beach as much as I wanted. I didn't say any more about that because I didn't want to confuse him.

Mr. Wood continued, "*Cowboy*, the Navy has just developed a new supersonic fighter called the F-8 *Crusader*, and it will go faster than a thousand miles per hour. If you flew that plane you could be called a "*Supersonic Cowboy!*"

"Wow! That would be great, Mr. Wood." I told him that my engineering class had visited the Chance Vought plant while on an industrial tour of Dallas a few months earlier. We were all impressed with this new aircraft.

About that time some of my long-haired friends strolled by the booth and asked what I was doing. I told them I was going into the Navy to become a *Supersonic Cowboy*.

One fellow laughed and said, "The Navy will have you cleaning toilets and swabbing decks.

I looked over at Mr. Wood for some support.

He said, "My program is only for young men with the right stuff, who have an aggressive attitude, and a determination that nothing will stand in their way of reaching their goals. Do you have those qualities, *Cowboy*?"

I said, "Yes, Sir. And I'm going to be a Supersonic *Cowboy* and nothing will stand in my way of being like that fellow on the poster who declares to be, 'An Executive at 40,000 feet.'"

I signed up that day to be a "*Supersonic Cowboy.*" Mr. Wood informed me that the Navy would be sending me a bus ticket to go to the Naval Air Station in New Orleans for testing and for a physical exam.

He said, "It will take a few weeks to process your papers after the testing. If you pass the test you will be given a report date to Naval Air Station, Pensacola, FL a few weeks after you graduate from college."

The trip to the Navy base in New Orleans was interesting to say the least. I thought for sure we would be in the "French Quarters" all night, but no such luck. We had to be on the base for two days to take many tests. They gave us physical exams, medical exams, and psychological exams to determine if we would be able to complete the Navy Flight Training Program. As I recall there were about twenty of us taking the test and only two were selected. I was very thankful to be one of the two.

Within a few weeks after graduating from college, I was on my way to Pensacola for flight training. I was really looking forward to the nice reception they would give me when I arrived.

After all, I was trying to help fill the vacancy for the Naval Academy. It was so nice of the Navy to have a van waiting for me at the airport when I arrived late at night. The fellow with the white hat looked at my orders and drove me straight to a place called Indoctrination Battalion (INDOC).

As I walked in to INDOC I said, "Hello, fellows. I'm *Cowboy*. I shore' do appreciate you all staying up this late for me. If you would be so kind as to show me to my room I will put up my duds, and I would like to see my airplane before going to bed." I noticed right quick that the Marine Drill Instructors and Student Officers sure had a keen sense of humor to say the least.

One of them yelled, "BRACE THE BULKHEAD, CADET!"

I had never heard of a bulkhead and was somewhat surprised that it needed support. Without a doubt they were not aware that I was there to give support to the Naval Academy. There were a couple of other cadets who came in with me and they seemed to understand the need for the bulkhead to be braced. Immediately, they ran over to the wall and placed their backs against it for support. For some reason they had a dead stare at the wall in front of them just across the hallway. I noticed their eyes did not move. Surely, they thought the other wall was about to fall as well.

I said, "Don't worry, fellows, I'll take care of the other wall."

I ambled over to the other side of the hall and gave the wall my support.

One of those fellows, who was wearing a "Smokey-the-Bear" type hat, came over and started yelling all manner of unkind language at me. He was only about 5' 6" tall but his mouth was at least 6' 8." He had to rake his head back to scream up at me. I noticed right off that he had terrible bad breath.

I said, "Mister, you have bad breath." Immediately, his Smokey the Bear hat started quivering and his face turned red as a beet.

He said in a very loud and unkind voice, "CADET, GIVE ME TEN!"

I said, "Mister, I only have eight dollars on me but I'm sure we can get a couple more bucks from the guys holding up that other wall."

Having said that, they got this *Cowboy* straightened out real quick. They never did show me my airplane!

Then these fellows in uniform commenced to yell at us how sorry and sloppy we were and how we had better obey all that they commanded us or we would never even see a jet airplane. Surely, this was a mistake. Surely, the sailor had dropped me off at the wrong building.

I would later learn that this phase of training was designed to distance Cadets from civilian habits and prepare them for taking orders without question. The purpose of the first phase is to psychologically break down the trainee. Civilian thoughts and habits are considered detrimental to necessary military training. The strict discipline is designed to enable Cadets to learn to take orders without question, and to survive in combat or emergency situations.

Even some of the language the civilian is accustomed to had to change. For example the "bulkhead" is a wall, the "deck" is the floor, the "rack" is the bed, the "hatch" is the door, and the "head" is the bathroom. As you will note these terms are used on board ship and land structures as well.

I went from a proud college graduate, a "somebody" to a "nobody," immediately when I walked into INDOC (Indoctrination Hall).

Yes, there were more acts of humiliation that would take place in the next few days. To name just a few; our heads were shaved, our civilian clothes were impounded, we were restricted to the base, we had to march in a group everywhere we went, the cover-alls (poopy suits) we were issued were much too big, we had to spit shine our shoes, polish the brass, make up our racks, and run everywhere we went. And yes, I had to clean the heads (toilets) and swab the decks, as my friend had prophesied when I was signing up for this program during my college days.

In about a week the academic phase was added to our hectic schedule. There we covered subjects in a few weeks that would normally take an entire semester in college to complete. Now I understood why it took the Academy guys four years to get their commission. They rushed us through subjects like, Foundations of National Powers, Aerodynamics, Jet Engine Theory, Mathematics, Meteorology, Navigation, Uniform Code of Military Justice, and many more in just a few weeks. All the while we were up before dawn for uniform inspection and physical training before we went to class. About the only time we had to catch up on our many studies was on the weekend.

We were told when we signed up for this program that we could DOR (drop on request) anytime we wanted to. The Navy wanted to get rid of the weaker ones before spending thousands of dollars on them only to find out that they could not hack the program. Many did DOR those first few weeks. But I was more determined than ever to be an "Executive at 40,000 feet!" I knew if others could complete the training so could I, with a lot of work and help from the good Lord.

The four months passed and I received my commission as an officer in the United States Navy. Then they started treating me like "An Officer and Gentlemen." There were still many challenges ahead but we climbed those hurdles one day at a time.

Our first solo flight was the T-34 *Mentor*. This was a big event. Several students quit (DOR) because they didn't have the courage to fly by themselves. Then the next solo was in my first Navy jet aircraft, called the T-2J *Buckeye* – this was even a bigger event. A few months later I would make my first carrier landing in this airplane. This was even a greater event than the last. In fact, a few friends did DOR when they saw how small the carrier landing area was. They just did not have the nerve to land on the ship. All Navy and Marine pilots fly to the "boat" solo for their first group of carrier landings. One must have the confidence in "self" if he is going to be successful in carrier operations – fear of failure is the father of failure.

T-34 *Mentor*

Landing a jet fighter onto a postage stamp in the middle of the ocean is how the world's best pilots, those of us in the United States Navy and Marine Corps, describe our landings on an aircraft carrier. It is a dangerous but necessary skill to learn. It is very complicated as the pilot negotiates with death and chaos in a controlled crash onto the deck. His heart rate is usually rapid as he maneuvers his plane in an attempt to make an arrested landing by a tailhook attached to his

Supersonic Fighter Pilot

aircraft. The pilot must use his wit and skill to get the airplane on the deck unharmed.

My first arrested landing felt like I had hit a brick wall at 130 mph. It was 500 times more violent than I had ever anticipated. Every part of my body was thrown forward and my arms felt like they were going to separate from my body. The first catapult (take-off) feels like your eyes are being pushed into the back of your head and all the skin on your face is being pulled back. It is a rush!

Navy carrier jets don't just take off. They are blasted off from a seaborne aircraft carrier, shot into the skies by a steam catapult and you accelerate to 140 mph in about two seconds. AWESOME!!!

We then trained in the F-9F *Cougar* and made more carrier landings. The final aircraft we flew in the Training Command was the F-11F *Tiger*.

Finally, after about eighteen months of intense training I received the coveted Navy *Wings of Gold*.

Then came time for the newly designated Navy pilot with his glittering, *Wings of Gold* to be assigned to an aircraft to fly in the fleet. We all had filled out the "dream sheet" that listed our preferences. We had the choice of Fighters (F-8; F-4D; F-3H) or Attack (A-4D; A-3D) and a few others. I wanted the F-8 *Crusader* that would fly faster than 1000 mph and make me an "Executive at 40,000 feet." But these assignments were predicated by your flight grades while in training.

After all my grades were tallied I was assigned to fly the *Crusader* in a fleet squadron. I would be a "*Supersonic Cowboy*" after all. But there was still a lot more training to go through before I was allowed to fly the *Crusader* in the fleet squadrons.

There were several pipelines (ways) to enter the Naval Aviation Flight Training Program. As I noted earlier I came in the Navy under the Aviation Officer Candidate Program (AOC), which required a four year college degree and I was commissioned after four months of Officer School. There was also the Naval Aviation Cadet Program (Nav-Cad) that only required two years of completed college. However, these Cadets did not receive their commission until they received their wings, which was about eighteen months after starting flight training. The Marines had a similar program called the Marine Aviation Cadet Program (Mar-Cad). The Marines also had a Platoon Leader course where the Cadets would spend a couple of summers with the regular Marine Ground troops. They would be commissioned upon graduating from college. The Naval Academy and ROTC supplied many candidates for training as did the Coast Guard.

And that, my friends, is how I became a *Supersonic Fighter Pilot.*

CHAPTER THREE

FLYING THE CRUSADER

RON KNOTT

"Inspector two zero one you are cleared for take off. The wind is down the runway at five knots, and the altimeter is 29.92," the control tower announced.

"Roger, two zero one, cleared for take off," was my response.

However, I was not quite sure I was ready to fly this Supersonic Navy Fighter. This flying machine was capable of exceeding 1000 mph and zooming to altitudes above 50,000 feet. Our first flight in the *Crusader* was a solo flight since there were no two seat F-8s for training.

I looked down the long 12,500 foot runway knowing many things could happen within the next few seconds. If all went as planned the *Crusader* and I would be happily accelerating through the air at a speed of more than 200 mph by the time we reached the end of that strip of concrete.

Could I handle all that power and performance of such a flying machine? Would I be able to raise the gear and flaps prior to exceeding the airspeed limitations for such a maneuver? Had I completed every item on the "check list" before taxiing onto the runway? More importantly was the realization of having to land this monster once I got it airborne.

Ron Knott

Observing my Instructor tucked in tight parade formation on my right wing gave me the assurance I needed. His face was hid behind the sun visor of his helmet, but his thumbs-up response indicated all systems were "go." His gesture gave me the confidence I needed for my first solo flight in the F-8 *Crusader*.

I advanced the throttle to 100% power and held the brakes. The nose strut compressed because of the tremendous amount of power being developed by the J-57 Pratt & Whitney engine. Engine RPM, Exhaust Gas Temperature, Pressure Ratio, Fuel Flow, Oil Pressure, Hydraulic Pressure, Canopy Locks, and all flight instruments were checked by one quick glance through the cockpit. I released the brakes and held on for my first adventurous flight in this awesome machine.

Nose gear steering was an excellent aid in keeping the airplane on centerline of the runway. As the speed increased the aircraft was easily controlled by applying rudder pressure to keep it going straight down the runway. The airspeed was increasing very fast. I was so overwhelmed at this new environment that I forgot to raise the nose wheel off the runway at the calculated speed of 160 knots.

My instructor gave a very simple radio call, "Ease the nose up," to prompt me on that procedure.

I glanced out my right canopy mirror and was pleased to see him locked in tight parade formation on my wing.

The F-8 just seemed to leap off the runway and headed for outer space. Gear up and wing down (flaps up) was the next procedure. I accomplished this with ease. By the time the F-8 had reached the end of the runway we were going the "speed of heat," or so I thought. With full power applied (afterburner) we would be at 30,000 feet in ninety seconds and going faster than the speed of sound.

**Student and instructor
in F-8 *Crusaders***

One of the first things I noticed about this airplane was how hypersensitive, or touchy the controls were. I had noted earlier in the handbook that the roll rate was more than 720 degrees per second. That is two complete rolls in one second. It seemed like I only moved the control stick to the side about one inch and the airplane did a complete roll. "Wow, this bird is going to be a beast in the landing pattern," was my thought.

Another surprise was how quiet the engine noise was once airborne. Before, I could only relate to the thunderous noise the F-8 made on take off when I was observing it from the ground. But in the cockpit all that deafening noise was behind me.

Jet powered aircraft are so much smoother in the air than propeller driven planes. This silky smooth flying was really getting my attention. Flying this jet fighter was a dream come true.

The F-8 *Crusader* was unconventional in many ways. The pilots who flew this supersonic machine loved her with a passion. We admired her reputation with admiration and respect. This sleek supersonic fighter commanded the respect of all who were fortunate enough to take her screaming through the skies.

Others that just observed her in flight with their feet planted safely on the ground had many and varied opinions about her capability. I always felt they were somewhat envious of her breathtaking speed and agility. The earth shaking mega decibels that she produced at full power would get the attention of all within hearing range. The screaming whine that she produced at high speed and low altitude would produce "goose bumps" on the earth-people beneath her path. The unrestricted climb to higher atmosphere was impressive. Other less fortunate airmen who met her in the arena of a well-executed "dogfight" had to admit she had all the qualities of the term, *Air Superiority.*

Air Superiority was the mission of the Vought F-8 *Crusader.* The development and testing of this aircraft was an embarrassment to the U.S. Air Force. The F-8 *Crusader* was faster and more capable than the Air Force fighters with the same power plant at that time.

This slick *Crusader* was a real challenge to bring aboard the boat for many reasons. It came aboard fast. It had a flat power curve at approach speed, thereby making speed control a real task. It took a lot of stick and throttle adjustments to keep it on the correct approach speed. The same power setting would maintain 135 knots or 150 knots.

Supersonic Fighter Pilot

Our approach speed was usually around 147 knots (depending upon gross weight) and we had only 1.5 knots on either side of the approach speed to play with. Hook skip was guaranteed if we exceeded the speed boundaries.

Many F-8 pilots touched down in the landing area aboard the ship, thinking an arrested landing was a sure thing, but were rather surprised to be the world's fastest tricycle going off the angle deck. A "bolter" would throw them back into the arena of flight and instantly they would have to regain their flying sense and do it all over again. This was always embarrassing and down right terror at night. We would say, "A catapult shot at night was like flying in an ink bottle." It was black and dark. There were no visual references outside the aircraft on those dark nights. The instruments in the cockpit were all we had to rely on and many times they were inoperative.

Even after all the good, bad, and ugly characteristics of the *Crusader* the pilots would plead to fly it. In this book you will read of many who found out her greatness, her weakness, and her faults.

My first landing in the F-8 was a little rough, but safe. This first flight was the beginning of many thrilling hours in the *Crusader*.

"If we lose the war in the air, we lose the war and lose it quickly." Field Marshall Montgomery

CHAPTER FOUR

OVER THE RAINBOW

RON KNOTT

After one of our missions I was leading a flight of four *Crusaders* back to our home base. I had elected to take the flight to 50,000 feet to top some thunderstorms in the area. An aviator learns early in his career not to penetrate or even get near one of those massive cumulonimbus clouds. Scientists estimate that one such build-up packs more energy than a large mega-ton nuclear weapon. This day the cumulonimbus clouds were visible in all quadrants, but they topped out at about 40,000 feet. My plan was to stay at 50,000 feet as long as possible to avoid these monsters and start a high dive when we arrived in vicinity of our home base, the USS *Shangri-La*.

The flight leader is not only responsible for his aircraft but he is also responsible for all others in his flight. I well remember another flight a few years earlier, where my Commanding Officer led his flight through an area of thunderstorms, and the result was the loss of two aircraft and one pilot. I was in that flight and was lucky to have survived. The outcome: he was relieved of his command and one family lost their beloved son.

In peace sons bury their fathers: in war, fathers bury their sons. This should not be so!

Ron Knott

As we arrived in the vicinity of the aircraft carrier I pushed over from 50K, as smooth as possible to keep the formation tight, toward an area void of thunderstorms. As our speed increased from subsonic to supersonic (faster than the speed of sound) a vapor donut appeared around the exterior of our aircraft. This was another indication that we were flying faster than the speed of sound because the shock wave was developing around the airframe.

Shock waves become visible in areas of high humidity, which we were entering into around the storm. These shock waves are beautiful but somewhat spooky as it envelops the airplane. Earth-creatures only hear the loud bang that is produced by the compression of the atmosphere at supersonic speed. This is known as the sonic boom. In the cockpit the pilot only hears wind noise around his canopy. And when we are wearing full pressure suits (required above 50,000 feet), as the astronauts wear, you do not hear anything. It is so very quiet. You only hear transmissions from other aircraft.

As we were descending through 30,000 feet I saw something that instantly took me back to my roots in my hometown of Noble, Louisiana, which had a population of only 198 souls. Directly below my flight was the sight of the most beautiful rainbow I had ever seen. It was so colorful and bright, extending from cloud to ground in the majestic arc that only God can form. At once my mind raced back to my high school graduation song, "Over the Rainbow." The lyrics in the song say, *Birds fly over the rainbow, Why then, oh, why can't I?* I was flying over the rainbow at the speed of sound. My dream had finally come true.

The rainbow provides one of the most spectacular light shows known to mankind but as we all know, it packs a

Supersonic Fighter Pilot

powerful promise as well. As recorded in the Bible it was a promise to the earth-people.

Daydreaming was a no-no in my high school but many times when I heard airplanes flying overhead my heart was in that aircraft, not the classroom. When we sang "Over the Rainbow" in high school I would have a mental picture of flying over the rainbow. At that time I had no thought as to what the top of a rainbow would look like. In fact, I often wondered what the top of clouds looked like. I can remember asking my mother, when I was really young, "Mom, what does it look like on top of the clouds?" I don't think I ever received a good answer because I kept asking the question over and over. Others said there was a pot of gold where the rainbow touched the earth. Somehow, I was never able to get to that place. I knew that someday I would find out what it was like "Over the Rainbow!"

Flying "over the rainbow" was a joy and unspeakable for me. My wingmen were not aware of the revelation that was being fulfilled at that moment for their flight leader. We were operating under "zip-lip" conditions (no radio transmissions) so the enemy could not get a fix on our position. During "zip-lip" we only used hand signals to communicate with each other. Fighter pilots are trained to fly tight formations in order to observe signals from their leaders. My wingman would learn about "Over the Rainbow" after we landed and debriefed on the boat.

My dream had come true; my hard work and study had paid off. I was actually flying over the rainbow. *If they could only see me now,* was another lyric that came into my helmet. The other students at my high school had different dreams and ambitions. It took me many years of training and thousands of miles away from Noble to find my rainbow.

While debriefing in the Ready Room I asked my wingman if they saw the beautiful rainbow when were descending toward the ship. Yes, they had because it was so big, bright, and beautiful, and directly in our flight path. I then told them the story of my high school song.

One of the pilots, Bob, asked about my school.

I said, "I was ranked in the top ten of my graduating class.

Bob said, "Wow, I thought I was doing good to be in the top one hundred of my class of four hundred graduates."

I was not too quick to tell Bob and the others that there were only ten graduates in my class, but I finally did. This brought up many questions about being raised in a small rural area. I was not about to let my comrades, who had graduated from some of the nation's largest high schools get the last word about my little town of Noble.

I continued to tell them about my upbringing.

"Gentlemen, I got my education in the barns in Noble, not to be confused with the Barns and Noble book stores. And sometimes I learned a lot out behind the barns in Noble." You see, we country folks did not have a lot of outside activity to mess up our way of thinking and dealing with our fellowman.

Few of us had electricity in our homes in rural northwest Louisiana. Only one old crank telephone was in the town. Emergency messages were sent via telegram to the railroad depot. Indoor plumbing was considered unsanitary. In fact, my grandma used to say, "Anybody that would do something like that in their home must be lower than a snake." We did have an ample supply of Sears & Roebuck catalogs for doing the paperwork and reading in our outside toilet. This multi-tasking was good training for the many jobs a junior officer would be assigned in the Navy. In fact it was considered a luxury to have a two-hole outhouse, although, I never saw one used stereo style.

Most people only had kerosene lamps for night lighting, a wood-burning stove for cooking, and a fireplace for heating. The rub-board was a lot more reliable than those fancy ringer type washers that were to come years later. The dishwashers were the junior kids of the household. The garbage disposal was taking the leftovers to the hog pen out back to fatten these creatures for our pork supply in the winter. The cats stayed on guard for the ample supply of rats that roamed at will through most dwellings. Dogs were our security system that sounded their barking alarm when a stranger approached, or when any other wild creatures invaded our privacy. Chickens produced fresh eggs, cows produced unpasteurized milk, and goats produced more goats. This was a typical home setting in Noble.

My parents owned a little country store in Noble, and it was the duty of my twin brother and I to deliver groceries and cow feed to our customers after school each day. Cow and horse feed came in one hundred pound cloth bags of many different colors and designs. Customers used the cloth bags to make clothing for their families after the feed was emptied. This is where the term "feed sack shirts and dresses" originated. I wore scores of them to school over the years.

Many of our customers demanded we carry the hundred pound bag of cow or horse feed to their barn and unload it in a fifty-five gallon steel barrel. The barrel was supposed to keep the rats from feasting on the feed and the snakes from hiding therein.

Ron Knott

The problem was that the barns were several hundred yards from the nearest road. We had to lug that heavy hundred pound bag to the barn, usually having to open several gates en route, and being very careful not to cut or tear the precious cloth bag. And you can believe that the 'Mama' of the house followed us every step of the way to make sure that her new dress material would not be damaged. She barked out severe warnings like a Marine drill sergeant of what would happen if we ripped her feed sack. Every now and then, when she got really rough on us, we would catch a little ole snake, by hand, and offer it to Mama. That usually put great distance between us and Mama.

Were we underprivileged? No, absolutely not! Our wealth was not measured in dollars and cents or the rise and fall of Wall Street. Prosperity in our town was measured by the best coon dog, the fastest horse, the best milk cow, the fattest pig, the tallest corn stalks, or the best tasting watermelons. The women folk liked to brag about how many jars of peas, corn, and jelly they had canned. The local stock market was just that; the price of the local stock, such as, pigs, cows, horses, hay, and eggs. This was our stock market. This was our standard of living for that day and time.

Every now and again a little airplane of some denomination would fly over us earth-people at Noble. I would watch it as long as it was visible, from horizon to horizon. I was determined to find out more about flying.

After Noble and graduating from college I headed for Pensacola for flight training in the Navy.

At a recent college homecoming a group of alumni was testifying about how the University had spring boarded them into their profession.

Supersonic Fighter Pilot

When it came my time to speak, I said, "The smartest thing I did while in college was to skip classes and take flying lessons." They did not expect such a statement. I had made more money, had more fun, been to more places than most of them, and more importantly, I was the happiest professional in the group.

I was a fighter pilot.

Ron Knott

PART II

FIGHTER PILOTS

What is a fighter pilot? My fighter pilot friend, Ed *"Mofak"* Cathcart, retired Marine LCOL, says it best, "The name fighter pilot can be attached to any of the following pilots if he flies a *Skyraider*, a *Skyhawk*, a *Crusader*, a *Warthog*, a *Super Saber*, a *Tomcat*, an *Intruder*, an *Eagle*, a *Super Hornet*, a *Cobra* Gunship helicopter, and many other fighting military aircraft.

"A fighter pilot is *always* a fighter pilot even when he is grounded, in hack, hospitalized, retired, and even when he is deceased. Some pilots flew fighter aircraft, but were not *fighter pilots.* They were afraid of the mission, canceled night flights, downed airplanes in poor weather, turned back before crossing the bomb line in combat, called in sick when scheduled for a night carrier landing, and often heard night noises during day flights. We branded these pilots, cowards. We knew we were a breed apart from those who let fear of accident, injury, or even death in flight, guide them astray from the dauntless spirit borne in the brave heart of a real fighter pilot."

True fighter pilots are courageous. Who is the best fighter pilot? They all are. If pilots don't exhibit that attitude then they are a drawback to the group.

Movies are made about fighter pilots because people are awed and inspired by the skill and coolness of fighter pilots under stressful and near death situations. Even within the fighter pilot ranks there's a hierarchy, at least in the mind of the fighter pilot. Not to belittle the missions of other military pilots, the airline pilot that ferries your family, the crop duster speeding low over fields, the daring acrobatic pilot, or any other aviators who earn their living flying. But it's simply a fact – fighter pilots are at the top of the heap. Most fly alone and face the enemy many times, far beyond friendly lines, and often right in their face.

And yes, that includes the brave photo fighter pilot flying alone, unarmed and unafraid, to go to the very spot where armed fighter pilots have just attacked the enemy, and have them stirred up like a swarm of mad hornets. They get the battle damage pictures knowing that the enemy will be trying their best to knock them out of the air. Nothing in life is so exhilarating as to be shot at without result.

Fighter pilots learn early in combat that bullets and missiles fired at them have the right of way and they must avoid a collision with them at all cost.

Being a true fighter pilot – *it is a state of mind.* You can always tell a fighter pilot, but you can't tell him much.

The following chapters are true life reports of heroic fighter pilots revealing their stories of survival and excitement when flying the Supersonic *Crusader*. – Ron Knott

CHAPTER FIVE

THE PRICE OF FREEDOM

CHUCK KLUSMANN

THE OPERATION

The U.S. Government had been requested to provide a show of support to the Royal Laotian Government. No one had flown over North Vietnam and the air war in the south was still in the early stages of getting organized. The request of the Laotian Government would provide the catalyst, which would lead to the most intensive air war ever conducted by anyone. The beginnings were relatively minor on a worldwide scale; but the events were very real for those who were assigned the missions.

The aircraft carrier USS *Kitty Hawk* was about to return home after an eight-month cruise. While cruising off of Okinawa, the *Kitty Hawk* received orders to proceed to a geographic point about 100 miles east of Da Nang off the coast of South Vietnam. This point was to be designated "Yankee Station."

En route, there was considerable discussion regarding how the show of support for Laos was to be implemented. The options being considered ranged from an air group fly-over of a large number of aircraft, or to just fly six to eight fighters and bombers. Finally, it was decided that the fly-over would be only two unarmed RF-8 *Crusader* photo reconnaissance aircraft.

There was very little coordination between those at the command level. For example, the Navy knew that the Air Force and the Marines were operating at various locations in South Vietnam, but they did not know their exact location. We had been briefed that there was an organization called Air America (CIA) operating in Laos as well. Their main job appeared to be delivering food and supplies to the friendly civilian and military forces.

We knew approximately where the good guys and bad guys were located but very little detail of their operation was known. Air America had only VHF radios and we had only UHF radios so we could not communicate directly with them. Our messages had to be relayed via other means if we needed to communicate with each other. Search and Rescue (SAR) was limited. If a plane went down it might take two days to get to the crew, especially if they were in northern Laos.

We were not concerned about this SAR dilemma because we pilots thought we were invincible in the *Crusader*. That concept met some serious challenges over the next few weeks.

The decision was made to make a show of force. The reconnaissance aircraft would fly to Plain of Jars in northern Laos and from there over the road to North Vietnam. We were ordered to get some low level photos of the area to see what was going on. LCDR Ben Cloud and I were the two pilots who were assigned to fly this mission. The distance was approximately 500 miles from the carrier to the target area. This was well within the range of the Photo *Crusader*.

[Author's Note: "The Plain of Jars" is in Xieng Khouang Province, Laos, and is one of the most enigmatic sights in

Supersonic Fighter Pilot

the world. Here, in this forgotten corner of Asia, is a highland plains about 1000 meters above sea level, where you find giant-size stone jars, created and left behind by a civilization that has now disappeared.]

As we reached the target we spread out to improve our coverage of the area, but we were still in sight of each other. Ben called out, "I think we're being shot at!" Then I noticed some white puffs around my aircraft and some red streaks coming up from the ground. About that time several red lights came on in my cockpit. I also saw fuel pouring from my left wing. Ben told me to make a quick turn to avoid the AAA (Anti-Aircraft-Artillery) that was tracking up my tail.

I had to make many rapid turns to get away from the intense AAA. As I was clearing the target area I noticed that my left wing was on fire. I decided quickly that it was time to get out of this hostile area.

I started a rapid climb to a higher altitude in hopes that the fire in my wing would go out. A few minutes after reaching 40,000 feet the fire did in fact stop. I was a happy camper to say the least.

On the flight back to the ship I noticed pieces of my wing falling off.

Ben said, "Don't worry everything is okay." After all, it wasn't his plane that was in trouble! The flight back to the ship was a bit tense. I had lost a considerable amount of fuel due to the holes in my wing. I did not know if I had enough gas to make it back to the ship.

The weather was great en route to the *Kitty Hawk*. I started an idle descent from 42,000 feet to conserve fuel. I had to use emergency procedures to configure the airplane for landing due to the fact I had lost most of my hydraulic fluid. I landed with only 600 pounds of fuel. That means the plane would have flamed-out in about ten minutes had I not landed.

Crusader

After landing it was noted that the left wing was a mass of melted metal and the aileron was completely burned away. There were many bullet holes all over the aircraft. It was only then that I realized just how fortunate I had been on this flight.

SHOT DOWN

The reconnaissance missions would continue, both day and night, for the next several weeks. Many requests from the ship's Captain and the Seventh Fleet Admiral were made for these reconnaissance flights, to be provided with armed fighter escorts. They were all denied.

Supersonic Fighter Pilot

The flying was difficult. Nothing changed with regard to the rules of the game. We still had no escorts and no good SAR plans in case a pilot had to eject over this area. This continued until early June. We had been deployed for more than eight months and were due to rotate back home. We had only one more mission remaining and that was on the 6th of June. "Piece of cake," I thought. "We fly this mission and we're on our way home tomorrow." Little did I know!

I was assigned to fly this last mission with LT Jerry Kuechman that memorable day. The launch was normal. Jerry and I proceeded toward the target by flying down along the Mekong and taking a heading for the Plain of Jars. As we were approaching the target area the AAA got really intense and I took some hits in the wing. I was losing a lot of fuel from the hits.

I called Jerry and said, "Pull up; we're getting out of here!" During the pull up, I took a good solid hit on the fuselage. This was the first out of four times being hit, that I could actually feel the impact of the ammunition. I knew that I was in deep serious trouble. The plane was climbing and flying very fast, but I was losing my flight controls. The F-8 has a fully powered hydraulic system and I was losing this precious fluid quickly. In just a couple of minutes the controls system froze. I had to get out of the airplane or die in it.

I called Jerry and said, "Adios." I actuated the ejection system. The ejection was a violent ride. Fortunately, the parachute opening was as advertised, but I was floating down into enemy territory.

I took my body inventory and noted that all the parts seemed to be properly attached and in working order. GREAT! I saw my plane crash in a ball of fire not too far away. I sure hated to lose that aircraft. I could hear a lot of shooting from the ground. It dawned on me that I was their target. I could hear bullets whizzing by my body. Thank goodness I was not hit. I was about to land into a really deep ravine and the ground was coming up fast. There was only one tree in the clearing and I was heading directly for it. I landed in the top of the tree and fell to the ground, making a hard landing.

My right hip, knee, and foot were badly wrenched. I could hardly stand up. I did manage to wedge my foot in a bush and pulled until something popped. That procedure helped and the pain somewhat subsided. I surveyed the situation and gathered my survival gear. I had to get out of that area quickly because I knew the enemy was coming after me.

Jerry remained circling overhead until his fuel got low. After he departed it got really quiet. I started walking up the hill. The grass was high and I was leaving a significant trail that could be noticed easily by the enemy. I couldn't walk very well due to my injuries. I could only half crawl and half drag myself through the rough terrain. Soon I heard another aircraft. I jumped with joy when I spotted a *Helio Courier* aircraft overhead. There was no radio in our survival package to communicate with the SAR pilot. There was only an electronic beeper that would automatically send out a distress signal. I assumed that it was working and hoped that the battery would last for a long period. In addition, I set off a smoke signal to let the pilot know my exact location. This probably let the bad guys know where I was as well. When I signaled the plane with my signal mirror they spotted me immediately. The pilot responded by rocking his wing and revving up his engine. I thought, "Great! Now at least, someone knew I was alive."

Supersonic Fighter Pilot

Two additional aircraft, a C-123 and a *Caribou*, soon joined the *Helio*. I was almost sure that these aircraft were from Air America (CIA).

Jerry later confirmed that after the first MAYDAY (distress) call; Air America responded with, "Where are you, and what do you need?"

Aviators, like seamen, are quick to respond when one of their clan is in trouble. These aircraft remained overhead for a couple of hours. I still had not seen or heard any of the ground troops during this period.

Finally, I heard the sound of helicopters in the distance. I thought for sure that I would be rescued in no time. I confirmed my position with them by my signal mirror. Then I crawled up a small hill, to a clearing on the ridgeline, to make my rescue much easier. Soon the H-34 helicopters approached my position. I was to learn later that Tom Moher flew the first helo that started in after me. (I will always be grateful for the heroic effort of all the pilots and crewmen who placed themselves in danger during all my rescue attempts.)

As the first helicopter started toward my position all hell broke out with intense ground fire from the enemy. They were trying to knock the chopper out of the air. It seemed like gunfire was coming from everywhere. Tom pulled up and struggled to get away from the hostile area. (I later learned that his co-pilot was hit in the head and the helicopter had more than eighty hits from the enemy.)

Then the *Caribou* made a low pass for ground fire suppression. Crewmembers in that airplane were shooting and throwing out hand grenades on the bad guys. This was particularly exciting since one of the grenades went off about fifteen feet from me. The ground troops responded with more gunfire during these fly-bys.

In spite of the enemy's barrage of bullets, Bill Cook, the second helicopter pilot, started in to make an approach for me. As he flew near, it became obvious to me that there was no chance for a safe rescue. If he continued his crew would be injured or killed. I did not want other people hurt that were trying to rescue me. These guys had pulled out all the stops and made every possible effort to liberate me. I really appreciated their heroic effort, but I could not let them continue and be slaughtered. I signaled them to leave the area. This placed me in a lonely and desperate situation. My world as a jet pilot had abruptly changed that day. I prayed!

THE CAPTURE

Within a short time, I could see the Pathet Lao troops closing in on me from all sides. They were all heavily armed with automatic weapons. I only had my trusty .38 handgun for defense. They captured me. My hands were tied behind my back and a noose was tied around my neck. Then they took me to a nearby small village. They noticed that I couldn't walk very well so they untied my hands and made a crude crutch to assist me in walking. It was almost dark when we reached the village. I was offered some rice, cooked greens, and a small can of stewed pork. It was not tasty, but it was all the nourishment I had for a while.

The next morning, after a sleepless night, I was taken to a nearby cave. I was kept there most of the day. During that day a T-28 aircraft made bombing raids on the village. This old Navy trainer aircraft didn't do much damage and no one seemed too concerned about the raids. I assume that Laotian pilots were flying these aircraft.

In late afternoon we started walking toward the village of Xieng Khouang. It took us three days to get there. After arriving I was given a bucket of water to clean up a bit. My hotel for the night was one of the infamous tiger cages. They tied me down and latched the door. The following day, I was loaded into a truck and we headed toward the Plain of Jars.

All of a sudden the sky was filled with United States Air Force F-100 fighter/bombers. The guards looked apprehensive and I was quietly cheering for the Air Force. They hid me under an old farmhouse during the raid.

After the raid we continued on the journey. We walked through the Plain of Jars for a while. Then they headed us into the mountains past Khang Khay along Route 7, finally arriving in a small village. The next day I met the 37mm AAA crewmembers who were given credit for shooting me down. They were heroes and I was the caged enemy. I was on display, in a tiger cage, for all who cared to observe me. (I will never like going to a zoo again to see caged animals!)

That night I was taken to a high-ranking civilian. I think he was Prince Soupanouvong. There was an officer in uniform who spoke English and acted as the interpreter. He became my interrogator and indoctrinator for the next couple of months. His name was given as Captain Boun Kham. He claimed to be a Laotian, but I believe he was North Vietnamese. Nothing much came of that meeting and I never saw the Prince again.

They then moved me to an area of small huts. I was placed in a small room in a hut that had no windows, a dirt floor, walls of mud plastered over woven bamboo, and a thatched roof. Furnishings consisted of a few boards between logs for a bed, a mosquito net, a grass mat, blanket, a metal table and chair, a cup and a canteen. The guards that captured me stayed in the other part of the hut 24/7.

The daily routine was much the same each day. I would be escorted to a latrine nearby and then down to a stream to wash-up. The morning and evening meals usually consisted of a small bowl of rice, some soup, and some boiled greens. Occasionally the guards would share some of their food which was a fiery sauce made with fish, salt, and roasted peppers. Occasionally they would have a raiding party on nearby caves to catch rats. They also caught stray dogs. They would then cook these creatures into some kind of stew and call it a "special meal." Yes, I ate it. I made up my mind that it was T-bone steak. In a situation like this one will eat whatever he can get to survive. I went from 175 pounds to 125 pounds in a very short time.

The interrogator came nearly every evening. He was more interested in talking about politics than in seeking military information. He was well informed about the military and said that they knew what they needed to know. He had a copy of a book similar to *Jane's All the World's Aircraft*. He also had a very recent copy of the *CINCPACFLEET* (Commander In Charge Of the Pacific Fleet) organization manual. I wondered how he got a copy of that classified document. This document listed all the US Navy ships. It also listed all squadrons aboard each ship and who was in command of each unit. He said that he knew that my ship, the USS *Kitty Hawk*, had passed through the Bashi Channel north of the Philippines on a particular night in May while en route to Vietnam – he was correct on the date!

Supersonic Fighter Pilot

This all seemed a bit incongruous to be sitting in a mud-walled hut deep in the jungle with only a kerosene lantern for light, and listening to him talk about world politics. His primary effort, I later determined, was to get something for publicity purposes and political influence.

He frequently mentioned that the radio had announced that I had been killed in the crash and that no one knew that I was alive. He said I could write letters, but later said that he couldn't deliver them for one reason or another. He suggested that I make a radio broadcast, just to let everyone know that I was alive and being treated well. I replied with reference to a well-known phrase about the probability of frigid temperatures in Hades. He never asked again. He did continue to encourage me to write a letter to the Prince requesting my release.

I was constantly bothered by diarrhea. Sometimes it was not so bad and other times it was severe. I had a serious attack with fever that lasted about two weeks. This left me terribly weak and unable to concentrate. The guards kept a fire going in the hut and the smoke caused me to cough almost continually. This lasted the entire two months that I was in solitary confinement.

In my weakened condition and after considerable coercion I wrote a brief note asking to be released. My letter was rejected. Then, I was compelled to sign a dictated letter. I did not have the strength to resist and was not coherent at the time. I really didn't comprehend what I was writing.

Days later the interrogator proceeded to read the letter that I had written to the Prince. I was shocked and mortified at what was in the letter. Only then did I realize that they had set me up. That was a big mistake on their part, because from that moment on I was determined to escape or die trying.

About a month earlier I had tried to escape by digging under a wall. That is when I discovered that they had driven bamboo stakes about three feet deep around my room. This was their way of making it impossible for me to dig out. I would find another way out of that POW camp. The false letter they tricked me with gave me more willpower to get back at them by escaping.

A few days later I was moved to another prison compound about a half mile away. On the way there we passed a two-story wood frame building with many antennas on the roof. I recognized the building. I had taken photographs of it on an earlier photo mission. This let me know my exact location in that foreign country and it would be helpful knowledge in my escape.

The new POW location was in a group of buildings that was isolated from the main road. It was, in fact, the location of Pathet Lao Headquarters. The building they put me in was long and divided into three rooms. They placed me in a small room in the center part of the building.

There was a three-foot gap between my building and a barbed wire fence. I had access to that area. There was another barbed wire fence about five feet beyond the first one. The area between the fences was filled with matted barbed wire making an escape impossible; so they thought.

Soon they placed about thirty-five Laotian prisoners in the other two rooms. I had learned a few words of Lao, but my communication ability was limited with these new prisoners. One of them had worked in Vientiane and had an English/Lao dictionary. This really helped us in communicating with each other.

Supersonic Fighter Pilot

THE GREAT ESCAPE

About a week after the new prisoners arrived, one of them approached me about the possibility of trying to escape. At first I was somewhat apprehensive about this fellow. I pretended not to know where we were. Then he proceeded to draw a map in detail about our location. The map was very accurate so I began to have trust in him.

Over a period of several weeks we discussed the escape plan and where we should go once we got out. After much planning we decided that our best escape route would be through the two fences. We activated a plan to work the nails loose that held the barbed wire to the posts. Wiggling the nails for hours freed them so they would easily slip out of the post. The inside fence did not take long to convert for our purpose. However, the outer fence was much more difficult.

We were occasionally allowed to wash our clothes in a nearby stream. They allowed us to hang our wet clothes on the outer fence to dry. When we did that, we managed to work on the nails of the outer fence as well. We took our own good time and were very deliberate where we hung our clothes. This frustrated the guards but they did not have a clue why we were so slow.

Eventually, we were ready to give it a try. There were six Laotians who intended to go out with me. The group was large but we all had a right to make a go of it. My escape partner was Boun Mi. The conditions were just right. It was about 9 PM on a dark rainy night and the guard had gone to his shelter to get out of the rain.

I changed into the dark trousers and shirt that we were given. I asked God for help and guidance. Then I eased around to the rear of the building where we had loosened the nails. The guards were busy talking. Boun Mi gave me the signal to go. I raised the wire and crawled under the loosened section. I was out of the compound in seconds as planned. We had about two hundred feet to go to a tree line to hide from view. Boun Mi was right behind me. Two others quickly joined us. We were concerned about the others. One of our group said he would wait for the others and join us later. We never saw him again, nor do we know what happened to the others who had planned to go.

The three of us worked our way around some Russian built tanks that were being guarded. We then had to cross a wide clearing in order to get to the mountains covered with trees. We dashed across the clearing and made it to the woods safely. We found a well-worn trail and followed it for several miles. We stopped for about twenty minutes waiting on the others. They never came. We had to keep going. It was still very dark and we needed to travel as far as possible before daylight.

After daylight we saw a farmhouse at the upper end of the valley. The third man in our group wanted to try to get some food from the farmers. I had a really uneasy feeling about this endeavor. I told Boun Mi that we needed to take cover and watch him approach the house. My gut feeling was correct. In just a few minutes he emerged from the house with his hands tied and a rifle at his back. He had walked into a guerrilla outpost. Soon a large group of soldiers were heading our way with the intent to re-capture the escapees.

This caused us several hours of excitement as we fled through the forest. The soldiers did fire some shots in our direction but I don't think they ever actually saw us. We managed to double back on our course and lose them. We made the decision to never approach anyone unless we were positively sure that they were friendly.

The remainder of our trek was just pure drudgery; going up over one mountain and down the next. The terrain was very rugged and steep. It was slow going, for sure. I prayed for strength to continue. It came. Surely the "Unseen Hand" was watching over me. I didn't want to ask for too much so I prayed for God to get me over the next hill and I would climb the following hill on my own. It worked. We ate bamboo shoots, corn stalks, sweet potatoes, wild berries and fruit that we found along the way. Finding water to drink was not a problem since this was the rainy season.

Leaches were one of the worst pests that we had to tolerate. They seemed to be everywhere. When possible we used animal trails to make travel easier. We had to stop occasionally to remove the leaches from our bodies. They were drinking way too much of our precious blood. They would always go back to the same wound and start feasting again. This caused some really bad wounds on our bodies. Our motivation kept us going even though our capabilities were lagging.

Three days later we were crossing a high mountain. All of a sudden we heard voices coming from a small hut. We were very cautious. Boun Mi indicated that they were friendly forces. I wasn't so sure and wanted to keep going. He indicated that he was so sure that he would go in by himself. He agreed for me to watch from a safe distance. As he approached the small hut two men came out with guns and met him. They talked for a few minutes. Then I noticed that they shook his hand and lowered their guns. Boun Mi turned and waved and for me to join them. I did.

Ron Knott

We had reached an outpost of the village of Baum Long, or better known as Site 32 to Air America. A man was dispatched to the village to telegraph the authorities about our arrival. After a short rest we walked the last two kilometers of our ordeal to the village Baum Long.

At Baum Long we received a very warm welcome. We were given food and treatment for the many cuts, scratches, and leach bites that we acquired along the ordeal. About an hour after we arrived I heard the sound of an aircraft. The villagers hurried us toward the landing site.

It was an emotional moment for me when I saw the airplane land. This was truly the sound of freedom, at last! I heard an American voice calling my name. Terry Burke, who was one of the CIA representatives, greeted me as a long lost brother. He helped me up to the aircraft where I met Dr. Jiggs Weldon and pilot Lloyd Zimmerman. After a few pictures were taken they flew us back to Udorn. It was hard to believe. My prayers had been answered. I was finally on my way to true freedom.

About two months later we learned from intelligence sources that the two men, who initially escaped with us, were recaptured and executed. This let us know, "That the price of freedom is *never* free."

To quote an anonymous inscription on a wall of the Hanoi Hilton, "Freedom has a taste to those who fight and almost die for it that the protected will never know."

CHAPTER SIX

COLD CAT SHANGRI-LA

JIM FOSTER

The grand finale of a long cruise on a Navy carrier is the fly-off when the ship is approaching homeport. This is a really exciting day for the pilots on board the "big boat." They may have been away from home for six months or longer and might have completed many heroic flights, but nothing compares to getting home a couple of days ahead of the ship.

Normally, at a distance of about 300 miles from homeport, the Air Group will launch every available aircraft in the fly-off. Do the math. The ship is sailing along at 15 knots and the departing airplanes head for home at 300 + knots. So the aircrew members can arrive home early and take care of some domestic thrills a couple of days before the ship finds the port.

It is amazing how sick airplanes, airplanes that have been unable to fly for days, will all of a sudden be ready for this launch. And this is where seniority really comes into play. As the old saying goes, "RHIP" (Rank Hath It's Privileges)!

The fly-off order is by rank. In other words, the Commanding Officer has the first choice of a ready airplane and the junior officers are assigned airplanes accordingly. For example, if you have 12 flyable aircraft in the squadron, the first 12 pilots, in seniority, will get to fly them home. If you have 16 pilots, four of the junior pilots would have to ride the ship home.

And to top off the early fly-off, there is a big party awaiting the pilots at the home airbase. The wives and family members of those arriving early are eagerly awaiting the sound of jets overhead. Their honeys are home! It is a wonderful event, to say the least.

In early 1965 the USS *Shangri La* (CVA-38) was returning from a six month Mediterranean cruise with Air Group 10 on board. As described above when the *Shang* arrived near the 300 magic mile point from home, the Air Group was to be launched. Every pilot that was assigned an airplane to fly-off was very excited.

Commander Jim *"Fearsome One"* Foster was the Commanding Officer of Fighter Squadron 13. Of course, he would have a plane if no one else did. Now the story gets a little more traditional. Not only do the officers have seniority status but the airplanes have seniority status as well. The side numbers on the aircraft, and the pilot's name painted on the canopy rail designates the so-called "Primary Responsible Owner" of the aircraft. This designation has little meaning during the cruise because it is impossible to only fly your so-called "own aircraft" due to the operation. But on fly-off day, the side number of the aircraft reveals destiny. Typically, the Commanding Officer's aircraft would be numbered, in this case AK-101. AK designating the symbol for Air Group 10 and aircraft 101 would be the CO's bird. Aircraft AK-000 would be the aircraft designated for the Carrier Air Group Commander (CAG). The Air Group Commander is senior to the Squadron Commander.

Supersonic Fighter Pilot

Commander Foster did not like the tradition of placing certain side numbers on the aircraft, especially the number "101." (I will explain why later.) However, Commander Tom Hayward, the Carrier Air Group Commander, suggested that the numbers be placed on the aircraft for the fly-off. This was a simple request but that is all it takes from a senior commander for proposals to be put into action. VF-13 mechanics placed the side number of "101" on the CO's aircraft the night before the fly-off.

Crusader **ready for launch**

The anxiously awaited fly-off time was at hand. Commander Foster manned his aircraft (AK-101) and Commander Tom Haywood mounted his flying machine (AK-000). Since CAG was the senior pilot on the fly-off he would be launched first, followed by Commander Foster. The plan was for CAG to circle overhead the ship until all the fly-off aircraft were launched and had joined him in formation. They

55

would then make a fly-over the ship as a salute to the shipboard crew and then head for the home port.

The following is a narrative from Commander Foster about his "Cold Cat Shot.

Commander Jim "Fearsome One" Foster

As planned, Commander Haywood in AK-000, was launched from the starboard catapult. Seconds later I was to be launched from the port catapult. Excitement was in the cockpits from all those on the fly-off.

The "Shooter" (Catapult Officer) gave me the signal to advance my engine to full power. As I did, I checked my engine instruments and determined that all systems were "go." My signal back to him that I was ready to fly was to give him a normal military salute with my right hand. I had to get that hand back on the flight controls quickly because in a couple of seconds I would be going down the flight deck as the world's fastest tricycle.

I completed my entire checklist and gave a snappy salute to the Shooter. I was ready to go flying off the sharp end of his ship. The Shooter went through his normal ballet movement, in a low squat (similar to a female goat giving birth to a kid) as he pointed to the bow of the ship. This was his signal to the catapult crew to activate the launch control switch. I waited for the 300 pounds of steam to accelerate my aircraft to about 160 mph in less than two seconds. The catapult fired, but due to a catapult launch valve problem, the shot only supplied about 30 pounds of pressure. This was not enough pressure to get my airplane to flying speed at the end of the ship. However, it was too much pressure for me to stop the aircraft before going overboard.

Supersonic Fighter Pilot

"What in the heck is going on?" I thought. "Here I am in my trusty Supersonic F-8E *Crusader* on my way to Florida, but it looks like I am about to make a high-dive into the Atlantic Ocean!"

Immediately, I went through every emergency procedure known to man to stop the airplane. First I shut the engine down and then I applied full brakes. I even tried to turn the airplane to the right with nose gear steering. All the while I was headed for the end of the ship. Sure enough, the F-8 and I made a high plunge (about 68 feet) into the wet Atlantic Ocean.

Obviously, hitting the water in a 26,000-pound aircraft from a 68 ft. fall made for a rough landing. Instantly the airplane started to sink. Water was rushing into the cockpit very fast. I tried to blow the canopy off to exit the sinking aircraft. It would not budge because of all the water pressure.

I was rapidly sinking and had to do something quick to survive. I was at least 40 feet deep in the now dark ocean. My last choice was to eject but the ejection system would not fire until the canopy was off. I remembered that there was a 'canopy interrupter' that would allow the pilot to eject through the canopy in just such cases. The interrupter was hard to reach, but I finally found it. I pulled it with one hand and the ejection curtain with the other. Immediately, I was shot out of the cockpit by the ejection seat through the thick canopy. They said I looked like a *POLARIS* missile coming out of the water as I popped about 20 feet in the air along the port side of the ship. That was one rough but happy ride for me. The five-inch rocket motor on the ejection seat burns in about eleven seconds. This placed tremendous pressure on my body but I am not complaining because it saved my life.

I made another mini-dive from twenty feet back into the ocean. My ejection seat separated automatically and my parachute deployed, as it is designed to do, after I ejected. Now, I had to attend to that big nylon rag. I got it off just in time, because the parachute got caught in the ship's big propellers. I was only a few feet from certain death. The ship's screws could have chewed me to bits. Thank God I remembered to deploy my Mae West flotation gear. Staying afloat is very difficult with the 30 or 40 pounds of flight gear that pilots must wear.

The *Angel* (helicopter) was right on top of me as I floated aft of the ship. They dropped me a rescue collar and hoisted me on board their craft (I can never thank that crew enough). From the time I went into the water until I was back on board the carrier was less than four minutes.

This secured the fly-off operation for a while. CAG was orbiting overhead wondering where all the airplanes were. As soon as I got back on the carrier deck I went to one of the aircraft that was manned by a junior pilot. I beat on his canopy and said, "I am the Skipper. Give me your airplane." Of course, this was not about to happen. There I was in my wet flight gear, Mae West deployed, and not in any shape to fly. About that time the Flight Surgeon said, "Skipper, we need to check you over in sickbay." And when they did I was pleased to learn that I had no injuries.

I was pleased to see the fly-off resume, even without me, so my squadron could see their awaiting families and friends. They did fly me home a few hours later in a COD (Carrier-On board-Delivery [mini-transport aircraft]) as a passenger only.

I can honestly say that I never got frightened during the entire ordeal. I was really surprised how calm I was. Yet,

Supersonic Fighter Pilot

within a few hours my hands were shaking so badly that I could not hold a pencil to write up the accident report. I got over it and was flying the *Crusader* two days later.

In retrospect, the Navy survival training, such as the *Dilbert Dunker*, prepared me for this disaster. And I must give credit to the Almighty for His mercy that dreadful day.

[Author's Note: The reason that Commander Foster did not want AK-101 painted on his aircraft is because the squadron had lost several aircraft in the past with the side number AK-101. After that accident AK-101 was never painted on another squadron aircraft. Also, Jim Foster had experienced two other "Cold Cats" in the past, but was able to stop the aircraft on the flight deck before taking a high-dive. In addition, during the Korean War, the enemy shot up two Corsair (F-4U) aircraft that he was flying. By his flying skills he was able to save both of these planes. Jim is a true survivor.

It is also interesting to note that in 1953 during the Korean War, these same two pilots were flying off the USS *Valley Forge* (*HAPPY VALLEY*). Both were LTJGs at the time and were flying the F-9F *PANTHER*-5. However, LTJG Jim Foster, in VF-53, was on the starboard catapult and LTJG Tom Hayward, in VF-51, was on the port catapult. Foster had a normal launch. However, it was Tom Hayward who went into the water that day due to a "Cold Cat" shot. This is just the opposite position that the same two pilots had years later when Jim Foster experienced the "Cold Cat" shot and went into the water. Tom Hayward came up in the wake of the ship, having bitten his tongue almost off, and almost unconscious. His *PANTHER* jet went through the big propellers of the carrier, just in front and just behind the cockpit, without injuring Tom. The *VALLEY* finished the line period of combat but had to have the propellers repaired in Japan when relieved on station.

It is a well-known fact that Tom Hayward later became CNO (Chief of Naval Operations), which is the most senior rank in the navy. He was a great leader.]

CHAPTER SEVEN

I FELL 15,000 FEET AND LIVED

CLIFF JUDKINS

"Jud, you're on fire! Get out of there!"

That startling command obviously got my attention. As you will read in this report, this was just the beginning of my problems!

It had all started in the brilliant, sunlight sky 20,000 feet above the Pacific Ocean, as I nudged my F-8 *Crusader* jet into position behind the lumbering, deep-bellied refueling plane. After a moment of jockeying for position I made the connection and matched my speed to that of the slowpoke tanker. I made the graceful task of plugging into the trailing fuel conduit so they could pump fuel into my tanks.

This in-flight refueling process was necessary and routine, because the F-8 could not hold enough fuel to fly from California to Hawaii. This routine mission was labeled "Trans-Pac," meaning, Flying Airplanes across the Pacific.

This had been going on for years. Soon, after plugging-in to the tanker, my fuel gauges stirred, showing that all was well. In my cockpit, I was relaxed and confident. As I was looking around, I was struck for an instant by the eeriness of the scene: here I was, attached like an unwanted child, by an umbilicus to a gargantuan mother who was fleeing across the sky at 200 knots as though from some unnamed danger.

Far below us was a broken layer of clouds that filtered the sun glare over the Pacific.

In my earphones I heard Major Van Campen, our flight leader, chatting with Major D.K. Tooker who was on a Navy destroyer down below. Major Tooker had ejected from his aircraft in this same area the day before, when his *Crusader* flamed out mysteriously, during the same type of refueling exercise.

Crusaders in-flight refueling from a C-130 Tanker

At that time no one knew why his aircraft had flamed out. We all supposed it had been some freak accident that sometimes happens with no explanation. One thing we knew for sure, it was not pilot error. This accident had to be some kind of mechanical malfunction, but what? Our squadron had a perfect safety record and was deeply disturbed because of the loss of an airplane the day before.

"Eleven minutes to mandatory disconnect point," the tanker commander said.

I checked my fuel gauges again; everything appeared normal.

Supersonic Fighter Pilot

My thoughts were, "In a few hours we'll all be having dinner at the Kaneohe Officers Club on Oahu, Hawaii. Then after a short rest we'll continue our 6,000-mile trek to Atsugi, Japan, via Midway and Wake Island." Our whole outfit – Marine All Weather Fighter Squadron 323 – was being transferred to the Far East for a one-year period of operations.

"Nine minutes to mandatory disconnect."

My fuel gauges indicated that the tanks were almost full. I noticed that my throttle lever was sticking a little. That was unusual because the friction lock was holding it in place and was loose enough. It grew tighter as I tried to manipulate it gently.

Then – *thud!* I heard the crack of an explosion.

I could see the rpm gauge unwinding and the tailpipe temperature dropping. The aircraft had lost power – the engine had quit running – *this is a flame-out!*

I punched the mike button, and said, "This is Jud. I've got a flame-out!"

Unfortunately, my radio was already dead; I was neither sending nor receiving anything via my radio.

I quickly disconnected from the tanker and nosed the aircraft over into a shallow dive to pick up some flying speed to help re-start the engine. I needed a few seconds to think.

I yanked the handle that extended the air-driven emergency generator, called the Ram Air Turbine (RAT), into the slipstream, hoping to get ignition for an air start. The igniters clicked gamely and the rpm indicator started to climb slowly, as did the tailpipe temperature. This was a positive indication that a re-start was beginning. For one tantalizing moment I thought everything would be all right. But the rpm indicator hung uncertainly at 30 percent of capacity and refused to go any faster. This is not nearly enough power to maintain flight.

The fire warning light (pilots call it the panic light) blinked on. This is not a good sign. And to make matters worse, jet fuel poured over the canopy like water from a bucket. At the same instant my radio came back on, powered by the emergency generator, and a great babble of voices burst through my earphones.

"Jud, you're on fire! Get out of there!"

Fuel was pouring out of my aircraft – from the tailpipe; from the intake duct; from under the wings, and igniting behind me in a great awesome trail of fire.

The suddenness of the disaster overwhelmed me and I thought, "This can't be happening to me!"

The voices in my ears kept urging me to fire the ejection seat and abandon my aircraft.

I pressed my mike button and told the flight leader, "I'm getting out!"

I took my hands off the flight controls and reached above my head for the canvas curtain that would start the ejection sequence. I pulled it down hard over my face and waited for the tremendous kick in the pants, which would send me rocketing upward, free of the aircraft.

Nothing happened! The canopy, which was designed to jettison in the first part of the ejection sequence did not move. It was still in place and so was I.

My surprise lasted only a second. Then I reached down between my knees for the alternate ejection-firing handle, and gave it a vigorous pull. Again, nothing happened: this was surprising. Both the primary and the secondary ejection procedures had failed, and I was trapped in the cockpit of the burning aircraft.

The plane was now in a steep 60-degree dive. For the first time I felt panic softening the edges of my determination. I knew that I had to do something or I was going to die in this sick airplane. There was no way out of it. With great effort I pulled my thoughts together and tried to imagine some solution.

A voice in my earphones was shouting: "Ditch the plane! Ditch it in the ocean!"

It must have come from the tanker skipper or one of the destroyer commanders down below, because every jet pilot knows you can't ditch a jet and survive. The plane would hit the water at a very high speed, flip over, and sink like a stone and they usually explode on impact.

I grabbed the control stick and leveled the aircraft. Then I yanked the alternate handle again in an attempt to fire the canopy and start the ejection sequence, but still nothing happened. That left me with only one imaginable way out, which was to jettison the canopy manually and try to jump from the aircraft without aid of the ejection seat.

Was such a thing possible? I was not aware of any *Crusader* pilot who had ever used this World War II tactic to get out of a fast flying jet. I had been told that this procedure, of bailing out of a jet, was almost impossible. Yes, the pilot may get out of the airplane but the massive 20-foot high tail section is almost certain to strike the pilot's body and kill him before he falls free of the aircraft. My desperation was growing and any scheme that offered a shred of success seemed better than riding that aircraft into the sea, which would surely be fatal.

Ron Knott

I disconnected the canopy by hand, and with a great *whoosh* it disappeared from over my head never to be seen again. Before trying to get out of my confined quarters, I trimmed the aircraft to fly in a kind of sidelong skid, nose high, and with the tail swung around slightly to the right.

Then I stood up in the seat and put both arms in front of my face. I was sucked out harshly from the airplane. I cringed as I tumbled outside the bird, expecting the tail to cut me in half, but thank goodness, that never happened! In an instant I knew I was out of there and uninjured.

I waited ... and waited ... until my body, hurtling through space with the 225 knots of momentum started to decelerate. I pulled the D-ring on my parachute, which is the manual way to open the chute if the ejection seat does not work automatically. I braced myself for the opening shock. I heard a loud pop above me, but I was still falling extremely fast. As I looked up I saw that the small pilot chute had deployed. (This small chute is designed to keep the pilot from tumbling until the main chute opens.) But I also noticed a sight that made me shiver with disbelief and horror! The main 24-foot parachute was just flapping in the breeze and was tangled in its own shroud lines. It hadn't opened! I could see the white folds neatly arranged, fluttering feebly in the air.

"This is very serious," I thought.

Frantically, I shook the risers in an attempt to balloon the chute and help it open. It didn't work. I pulled the bundle down toward me and wrestled with the shroud lines, trying my best to get the chute to open. The parachute remained closed. All the while I am falling like a rock toward the ocean.

I looked down hurriedly. There was still plenty of altitude remaining. I quickly developed a frustrating and sickening feeling. I wanted everything to halt while I collected my thoughts but my fall seemed to accelerate. I noticed a ring of turbulence in the ocean. It looked like a big stone had been thrown in the water. It had white froth at its center; I finally realized this is where my plane had crashed in the ocean.

"Would I be next to crash?" were my thoughts!

Again, I shook the parachute risers and shroud lines, but the rushing air was holding my chute tightly in a bundle. I began to realize that I had done all I could reasonably do to open the chute and it was not going to open. I was just along for a brutal ride that may kill or severely injure me.

I descended rapidly through the low clouds. Now there was only clear sky between me and the ocean. This may be my last view of the living. I have no recollection of positioning myself properly or even bracing for the impact. In fact, I don't remember hitting the water at all. At one instant I was falling fast toward the ocean. The next thing I remember is hearing a shrill, high-pitched whistle that hurt my ears.

Suddenly, I was very cold. In that eerie half-world of consciousness, I thought, "Am I alive?" I finally decided, and not all at once, "Yes, I think I am ... I *am* alive!"

The water helped clear my senses. But as I bounced around in the water I began coughing and retching. The Mae West around my waist had inflated. I concluded that the shrill whistling sound that I had heard was the gas leaving the CO_2 cylinders as it was filling the life vest.

A sense of urgency gripped me as though there were some task I ought to be performing. Then it dawned on me what it was. The parachute was tugging at me from under the water. It had finally billowed out (much too late) like some Brobdingnagian Portuguese man-of-war. I tried reaching down for my hunting knife located in the knee pocket of my flight suit. I had to cut the shroud lines of the chute before it pulled me under for good.

This is when I first discovered that I was injured severely. The pain was excruciating. Was my back broken? I tried to arch it slightly and felt the pain again. I tried moving my feet, but that too, was impossible. They were immobile, and I could feel the bones in them grating against each other.

There was no chance of getting that hunting knife, but I had another, smaller one in the upper torso of my flight suit. With difficulty, I extracted it and began slashing feebly at the spaghetti-like shroud line mess surrounding me.

Once free of the parachute I began a tentative search for the survival pack. It contained a one-man life raft, some canned water, food, fishing gear, and dye markers. The dye markers colored the water around the pilot to aid the rescue team in finding a downed airman. All of this survival equipment should have been strapped to my hips. It was not there. It had been ripped away from my body upon impact with the water.

"How long would the Mae West sustain me?" I wondered.

I wasn't sure but I knew I needed help fast. The salt water that I had swallowed felt like an enormous rock in the pit of my gut. But worst of all, here I was, completely alone, 600 miles from shore, lolling in the deep troughs and crests of the Pacific Ocean. And my *Crusader* aircraft, upon which had been lavished such affectionate attention, was sinking thousands of feet to the bottom of the ocean.

At that moment I was struck by the incredible series of coincidences that had just befallen me. I knew that my misfortune had been a one-in-a-million occurrence. In review, I noted that the explosion aloft should not have happened. The ejection mechanism should have worked.

The parachute should have opened. None of these incidents should have happened. I had just experienced three major catastrophes in one flight. My squadron had a perfect safety record. "Why was all of this happening?" was my thinking.

In about ten minutes I heard the drone of a propeller-driven plane. The pot-bellied, four-engine tanker came into view, flying very low. They dropped several green dye markers near me and some smoke flares a short distance from my position. They circled overhead and dropped an inflated life raft about 50 yards from me.

I was so pleased and tried to swim toward the raft. When I took two strokes, I almost blacked out due to the intense pain in my body. The tanker circled again and dropped another raft closer to me but there was no way for me to get to it or in it, in my condition.

The water seemed to be getting colder and a chill gripped me. I looked at my watch but the so-called unbreakable crystal was shattered and the hands torn away. I tried to relax and surrender to the Pacific Ocean swells. I could almost have enjoyed being buoyed up to the crest of one swell and gently sliding into the trough of the next, but I was in such excruciating pain. I remembered the words W.C. Fields had chosen for his epitaph: "On the whole, I'd rather be in Philadelphia."

In about an hour a Coast Guard amphibian plane flew over and circled me as though deciding whether or not to land. But the seas were high and I knew he couldn't make it. He came in very low and dropped another raft; this one had a 200-foot lanyard attached to it. The end of the lanyard landed barely ten feet from me. I paddled gently backward using only my arms. I caught hold of it and pulled the raft to me. Even before trying I knew I couldn't crawl into the raft due to my physical condition. I was able to get a good grip on its side and hold on. This gave me a little security.

The Coast Guard amphibian gained altitude and flew off. (I learned later that he headed for a squadron of minesweepers, who were returning to the United States from a tour of the Western Pacific. He was unable to tune to their radio frequency for communications. But this ingenious pilot lowered a wire from his aircraft and dragged it across the bow of the minesweeper, the USS *Embattle*. The minesweeper captain understood the plea, and veered off at top speed in my direction.)

I was fully conscious during the two and a half hours it took the ship to reach me. I spotted the minesweeper while teetering at the crest of a wave. Soon, its great bow was pushing in toward me and I could see sailors in orange lifejackets crowding its lifelines. A bearded man in a black rubber suit jumped into the water and swam to me.

"Are you hurt?" he asked.

"Yes," I said. "My legs and back."

I was now desperately cold and worried about the growing numbness in my legs. Perhaps the imminence of rescue made me light-headed for I only vaguely remember being hoisted aboard the ship. I was laid out on the ship's deck as they cut away my flight suit.

"Don't touch my legs! Don't touch my legs!" I screamed.

I don't remember it. Somebody gave me a shot of morphine and this erased part of my extreme pain.

An hour or so later a man was bending over me and asking questions. (It was a doctor who had been high-lined over from the USS *Los Angeles*, a cruiser that had been operating in the area.)

He said, "You have a long scar on your abdomen. How did it get there?"

I told him about a serious auto accident I'd had four years earlier in Texas, and that my spleen had been removed at that time.

He grunted and asked more questions while he continued examining me. Then he said, "You and I are going to take a little trip over to the USS *Los Angeles;* it's steaming alongside."

Somehow they got me into a wire stretcher and hauled me, dangling and dipping, across the watery interval between the *Embattle* and the cruiser.

In the *Los Angeles's* sickbay they gave me another shot of morphine, thank God, and started thrusting all sorts of hoses into my body. I could tell from all the activity and from the intense, hushed voices, that they were very worried about my condition.

My body temperature was down to 94 degrees; my intestines and kidneys were in shock. The doctors never left my side during the night. They took my blood pressure every 15 minutes. I was unable to sleep. Finally, I threw-up about a quart or more of seawater. After this my nausea was relieved a bit.

By listening to the medical team who was working on me, I was able to piece together the nature of my injuries. This is what I heard them saying. My left ankle was broken in five places. My right ankle was broken in three places. A tendon in my left foot was cut. My right pelvis was fractured. My number 7 vertebra was fractured. My left lung had partially collapsed. There were many cuts and bruises all over my face and body, and my intestines and kidneys had been shaken into complete inactivity.

The next morning Dr. Valentine Rhodes told me that the *Los Angeles* was steaming at flank speed to a rendezvous with a helicopter 100 miles from Long Beach, California.

At 3:30 that afternoon I was hoisted into the belly of a Marine helicopter from the USS *Los Angeles's* fantail, and we whirred off to a hospital ship, the USS *Haven,* docked in Long Beach, CA.

Once aboard the *Haven*, doctors came at me from all sides with more needles, tubes, and X-ray machines. Their reaction to my condition was so much more optimistic than I had expected. I finally broke down and let go a few tears of relief, exhaustion, and thanks to all hands and God.

Within a few months I was all systems go again. My ankles were put back in place with the help of steel pins. The partially collapsed left lung re-inflated and my kidneys and intestines were working again without the need of prodding.

The Marine Corps discovered the cause of my flame-out, and that of Major Tooker the day before; it was the failure of an automatic cut-off switch in the refueling system. The aircraft's main fuel tank was made of heavy reinforced rubber. When the cut-off switch failed, this allowed the tank to overfill and it burst like a balloon. This then caused the fire and flameout. We will never know why the ejection seat failed to work since it is in the bottom of the ocean. The parachute failure is a mystery also. Like they say, "Some days you are the dog and others you are the fire-plug."

Do I feel lucky? That word doesn't even begin to describe my feelings. To survive a 15,000-foot fall with an unopened chute is a fair enough feat. My mind keeps running back to something Dr. Rhodes told me in the sickbay of the *Los Angeles* during those grim and desperate hours.

He said that if I had had a spleen, it almost certainly would have ruptured when I hit the water, and I would have bled to death. Of the 25 pilots in our squadron, I am the only one without a spleen. It gives me something to think about. Maybe it does you as well.

[Author's Note: Amazingly, Cliff Judkins not only survived this ordeal but he also returned to flight status. He was flying the F-8 *Crusader* again within six months after the accident. After leaving the Marine Corps he was hired as a pilot with Delta Airlines and retired as a Captain from that position.]

Ron Knott

CHAPTER EIGHT

HIGH SPEED EJECTION

JIM STRAWN

On 16 October 1961, I was the Squadron Duty Officer (SDO) for Marine Fighter Squadron VMF-333. I was not scheduled to fly that day.

My squadron was stationed at Marine Corps Air Station (MCAS) Beaufort, SC and we were equipped with the F-8U2 *Crusader*. We were undergoing our annual Operational Readiness Inspection (ORI) of ground controlled, supersonic intercepts. I was a First Lieutenant with about 700 total flight hours and 450 of those hours were in the *Crusader*. I had carrier-qualified on the USS *Saratoga* (CVA – 60) the previous month and had completed the F-8 training syllabus.

I was temporarily relieved of SDO duty so I could go to lunch. When I returned the Operations Officer addressed the Lieutenant who was temporarily standing in for me and informed him that he was to keep the SDO duty. He then informed me that he wanted me to suit up as a Ready Room standby pilot for the last ORI sortie.

Well, the ORI chief administratively downed the airplane of the scheduled flight leader. This meant that the original wingman was launched as the lead pilot and I got scrambled to be his wingman. This was a natural extension of the exercise because part of the ORI tested the squadron's ability to rapidly regenerate aircraft.

75

Ron Knott

The flight leader, First Lieutenant Joe McDonald, had taken off about fifteen minutes ahead of me. I could see his aircraft making contrails (which normally appears above 30,000') and I accelerated to join him and complete the intercept. His speed was about 1.4 Mach. So I had to accelerate to 1.55 Mach to join up with him at 34,000 feet.

All of a sudden I heard a loud noise and felt a tremendous windblast. Immediately I had severe tunnel vision and I was only able to discern thousands of glass fragments flying around in the cockpit. My canopy had broken, and at that high speed glass filled the cockpit. I leaned forward in the seat to avoid the awesome windblast and at the same time I reduced power to slow the aircraft. I then reached up to raise my helmet visor and discovered it had been ripped off by the wind. I put my hand back on the throttle to reduce the power even more and deployed the speed brakes. Immediately and with no action on my part, the F-8 and I parted company. I was ejected involuntarily out of the airplane at supersonic speed.

From the time that the canopy shattered until I was ejected from the aircraft was only about five seconds. I learned later that the windblast had pulled out the ejection seat face curtain initiating the normal ejection seat sequence. The aircraft accident board, with the help of Chance Vought engineers, determined that my speed at ejection was 1.45, which indicated Mach number or 565 knots indicated airspeed at an altitude of 34,000 feet.

Some folks have experienced a 100-knot wind in a hurricane and report that it is almost unbearable. Instantly, I experienced five times that force in an atmosphere that was about 50 degrees below zero. This was not a fun high-dive.

I don't have any memory of actually leaving the cockpit. My first semirational thought was that I was caught in a gigantic pinwheel as I violently tumbled head over heels. My vision was blurry. I soon became aware that the two dark objects in front of my face were the bottoms of my flight boots.

I made some feeble attempts to stabilize my body by holding out my arms and then noticed that I was still attached to the ejection seat. I also noticed that something was blocking my vision, and I wasn't breathing too well. I managed to move my flight helmet back into position. The entire assembly had rotated backward until the part of the oxygen mask, which was normally close to my throat, was across my lower teeth.

I knew that I would be better off out of the ejection seat, as I was still rotating briskly around all axes. Then the parachute suddenly opened. I attempted to visually check the parachute canopy condition, but I could not get my head through the straps while wearing the helmet. Accordingly, I removed the helmet to gain a better perspective of the condition of the chute. What I saw was far from comforting. The riser cords, starting from just above my head to around twelve to fifteen feet below the parachute canopy, were tightly wound into about a 1.5" bundle, and the canopy itself was only 3/4 inflated.

Because of the condition of my legs, I had some concern about landing hard on top of the raft assembly. I knew that I was not going to land in any body of water. So, I jettisoned the whole mess including the hat and mask. By this time I was getting close to the ground but I did not have the sensation of dropping too fast. Luckily, I was drifting slowly backward and hit the ground with my heels dragging and landed on my butt. No further injuries were incurred during the landing.

I had landed behind a small farmhouse where a young boy was playing. He saw me hit the ground and ran over to where I was laying. I gave him instructions and got him to start the Sea Air Rescue effort.

I was on the ground about 45 minutes before a helicopter from Shaw AFB arrived with a flight surgeon. He splinted my legs, and I was then flown to the Shaw AFB hospital.

When I was examined by the Air Force flight surgeon, he informed me that I had dislocated my left shoulder. I was somewhat surprised as I had removed the harness Koch fittings as I usually did, with my right hand on the left one and my left on the right one and had not noticed anything wrong with my left shoulder. Anyway, the doctor proceeded to put his foot into my left armpit and began pulling on my arm to reduce the dislocation. After a few minutes, he gave up and said they would fix it when they fixed my legs. Then they promptly put me to sleep. This was fine with me as the doctor on the helicopter wouldn't give me anything for pain because I had several lacerations on my face that precluded it. (Side note: It's little wonder that all enlisted Navy Corpsmen serving with Marines are called "Doc" as a sign of respect for their services and most of the commissioned physicians are called "Quacks.")

Upon waking up from the dislocation procedure I found that I had dislocated knees rather than broken legs as I had initially thought.

Also upon awakening there were two USN Captains in my room who informed me they were from the Navy Aviation Safety Center. They told me: one, I was the first person to

Supersonic Fighter Pilot

have survived a supersonic ejection. Two, they wanted to know all the details. They may have been my first visitors but they surely were not my favorites.

I spent a week at the Shaw AFB dispensary and was then taken to the Naval Hospital in Beaufort, SC. I spent the next seven months there undergoing physical therapy and rehabilitation after surgery to both knees. I had sustained superficial face wounds from flying glass, a dislocated left shoulder (most likely from my arm striking the canopy railing on the way out of the cockpit). Both of my knees were dislocated from hyper-extension and flailing around in the extreme air pressure.

After my rehabilitation I returned to flight status in November 1962 and found there had been some interesting developments in the accident investigation.

The F-8 aircraft was equipped with a leg restraint system designed to prevent the lower legs from being damaged in a high-speed ejection. The accident investigation board concluded that the leg restraint cord had functioned properly and was loosened by something hitting the tension release knob during the initial ejection sequence. The knob was located on the right front corner (facing the seat) of the seat and in just the right location to have been hit by my left hand as the seat went up the rails, because I was holding on to the throttle at the time of the ejection. The leg restraint system in the F-8 was modified as a direct result of my ejection to preclude a similar incident from happening.

The Martin-Baker ejection seat that was in my aircraft contained a drogue chute that was connected to the main personnel chute. During my ejection the controller drogue deployed normally and did withdraw the stabilizer drogue. However, the stabilizer drogue failed. This was due to the fact that seventeen of the twenty-four shroud lines parted and the stabilizer chute completely shredded due to the extreme forward momentum of the seat after ejection.

The purpose of the stabilizer drogue is two-fold: first, to prevent the seat from tumbling. And secondly, to slow the fall of the seat until main chute deployment altitude is reached. Since this chute failed the seat was free to rotate and to continue falling at a high rate of speed. These factors led to my knee injuries and resulted in the "candlestick" appearance of the main parachute shroud lines.

After our unpleasant separation the aircraft continued to fly for approximately 55 miles and impacted the ground on the artillery range at Fort Jackson, SC. According to eyewitness statements the airplane was going almost straight down and still supersonic when it hit the ground.

The Aircraft Accident Board (the official investigating body) determined that the primary cause of the accident was the design deficiencies of the Martin-Baker face curtain assembly, with a contributing cause to be the canopy glass failure. As the board pointed out the loss of a canopy shouldn't result in loss of the aircraft.

Interestingly, most of the hardware including the canopy, seat, hardhat, mask, and raft were found due to some excellent detective work by the accident board. The only items not recovered were the kneeboard and my flight gloves that were lost during the ejection.

My next F-8 flight was in the spring of 1967. It was in preparation for a Vietnam tour with VMF – 232 and VMF – 235. I was a little nervous on that first supersonic run but managed to complete the flight without being shot out of the cockpit again.

Supersonic Fighter Pilot

I attribute my survival to two things: the day before the accident I had gone to the flight equipment division and had the flight helmet nape strap tightened (I think there had been some safety article about it; I know I wouldn't have thought of it on my own), which kept the helmet on my head, and secondly, I only weighed about 150 lbs, which allowed the ejection seat to blast me high enough to avoid a collision with the vertical stabilizer.

Second thoughts: after completing the prescribed physical therapy I had 0 to 130 degree flexion in my left leg; and 5 to 50 degree flexion in my right knee. I shudder to think what would have happened to my right leg if I had to have ejected a second time. I should not have passed a flight physical but somehow managed to do so. After another twenty years of quarterly physical fitness tests, which included a three-mile run, my knees were in pretty bad shape. I had a knee replacement operation in 2006 and things have been much better since.

Ron Knott

Supersonic Fighter Pilot

CHAPTER NINE

MY HIGH DIVE

DON JORDAN

"Crash! Crash! Crash! Eject! Eject! Eject! Man-Over-Board! Man-Over-Board! Pilot in the water!" was the deafening report that was broadcast from the public address system on board the flight deck of USS *Bonhomme Richard* (CVA-31).

I could not hear those announcements since I was the one who was going off the angle deck in my Navy Jet Fighter. I would soon be struggling to stay alive in this, my high dive into the Pacific Ocean. I will never forget that frightful day of the 10th of October, 1962.

Why was I in this situation? That is a good question. I was only obeying orders and they almost killed me. My Navy F-8U *Crusader* squadron, VF-191 was aboard this big ship 100 miles off the coast of Hong Kong in the Pacific Ocean. (V stands for heavier than air aircraft, F identifies this as a Fighter type aircraft and 191 is the squadron number.) We had been in the Port of Hong Kong the day before and had to make an emergency departure due to forecasted typhoons entering the area.

Wisdom should prevail by the leadership in such bad weather conditions, especially when launching and landing aircraft because the safety of so many people is at stake. The Commanding Officer of the ship decided to conduct air operations that lousy weather day. The flight deck of the carrier was pitching and rolling like a cork in a washtub on washday. The storm was near, yet the order was given, "Launch the aircraft!"

The leadership often told us junior pilots, "You can't buy experience like this on the outside." And we would often reply, "And you can't give it away either!" There is an old military saying, "Never ask the reason why; yours is to do and die," adapted from Alfred Lord Tennyson's poem, *"The Charge of the Light Brigade."* And that day I almost did die.

Please don't get the wrong impression about my desire to fly. I would be eager to launch in any type of weather or other hazardous conditions to protect my ship, or my country. That is what we are trained for and why we were there. But just to fill up squares on a chart at the risk of losing a pilot, aircraft, or deck crewmen is nonsense. I feel I can make these statements because it almost cost me my life.

Our mission that day was to "run the deck." This means that flight operations are conducted with the sole purpose of achieving as many takeoffs and landings for each pilot as possible. This is a task that every Navy carrier pilot will eagerly accept; even when conditions are not the best. The accumulated number of carrier landings, which are recorded in a pilot's logbook, is the most highly sought status symbol of a Navy pilot. It is his bragging rights. It is a well known fact that landing on the flight deck of an aircraft carrier is one of the most difficult procedures any pilot can ever experience. Add bad weather and/or night flying to the operation and the risk factor is increased exponentially. As a note of interest the US Navy pilots are the only pilots in the world who land on an aircraft carrier at night. We are proud of that fact.

Supersonic Fighter Pilot

Carrier pilots are taught to advance the throttle to full power immediately when the wheels touch the deck when landing. This will give them maximum thrust to "go around" in case they miss the wires. If you catch a wire the cable will hold the aircraft even at full power. If you miss the wire full power will give you the necessary thrust to get airborne again. All Navy pilots have missed a wire, called a bolter, when attempting to land on the ship. It's kind of like playing any sport; some days you're right on, some not. Landing on the carrier takes one's full concentration.

The secret to a successful approach and landing aboard the aircraft carrier is to follow the visual information presented on the Optical Landing System called the "mirror." A beam of light is projected from the deck of the ship on a pre-determined glide slope, which will guide the pilot to the landing area of the deck.

The LSOs are located on the aft part of the flight deck to better observe and communicate with the pilot on each approach and landing.

In many cases the LSO can tell what corrections the pilot needs to make before he is able to notice his error. For example, the LSO will radio the pilot if he is low, slow, fast, left, or right of the desired path. In fact, an aircraft is not allowed to land on a carrier unless a LSO is on the duty platform. The LSO's job becomes even more important when the ship is bucking and rolling in heavy seas. The ship's movement has cycles of pitching and rolling. The LSO's job is to judge those cycles and "wave off" (don't allow a landing) the pilot if the deck is pitching too much for a safe landing. The pilot's job is to look at the information presented on the gyro stabilized mirror system. He is to rely 100% on the LSO to guide him to a safe landing.

Ron Knott

Due to the rough seas that fateful day, the ship was bucking and rolling like a dirty sock in a washing machine. When my aircraft was about to touch down the ship rolled hard to the right. This put the entire weight on the left main landing gear and caused the left main wheel to separate from the aircraft.

As per standard operation procedures I applied full power to the engine when touching down on the deck. (This procedure should accelerate the aircraft to flying speed if an arresting cable is missed. If the pilot failed to apply full power he may take a swim in the ocean due to lack of flying speed when leaving the ship.) My tailhook engaged the # 3 arresting cable on that landing but for some unknown reason the hook disengaged from the wire. In seconds I was airborne again. Primary Flight Control (tower) advised me to make a fly-by so they could make a visual inspection for damage. They noted that my left landing gear was in fact damaged.

Primary Flight Control announced that I would be making a barricade engagement when landing. In other words I would fly into the "net." Having observed a successful barricade engagement several weeks prior involving a different jet aircraft on our ship, I elected to bring her aboard in the barricade.

This procedure is simple and relatively safe most of the time. The only harm that normally occurred from such a landing is minor damage to the leading edge of the wing, which would require only a little work to repair. The flight deck crew can erect the "net" (barricade) in just a few minutes.

There are two tall steel stanchions recessed into the flight deck on both sides of the ship. These can be raised

Supersonic Fighter Pilot

when needed to trap an aircraft that is having a problem such as mine. After they are raised a steel cable is attached from one side to the other, both at the top and the bottom. Between these two cables are nylon straps, which are now vertical and are designed to collectively entrap an aircraft. This net arrangement is about twenty feet tall. The pilot makes a normal approach and landing, and flies into this net. The aircraft will be caught by these vertical nylon straps and will be stopped in an efficient manner. This is the way it is supposed to work. The guarantee is like that of a parachute: "If it doesn't work bring it back and we'll give you another one." The barricade didn't work for me that day.

Line up, speed, and glide path were established on a long final approach. My touch down was perfect. The tailhook caught the #1 wire as was planned. However, the tailhook released the cable again after slowing the aircraft slightly and about that time I engaged the barricade.

The cable attached to the top of the stanchion is supposed to release when engagement is initially made. That did not happen. As a result two of the nylon straps were caught on the engine intake and they snapped. On the left side several straps snagged the *Sidewinder* missile launch rack and they broke as well. Several more straps were caught on the leading edge of the wing where there was a sharp joint, severing them. The *Crusader* and I were about to be in deep serious trouble.

I had been briefed that the barricade arrestment would be much gentler than a normal arrested landing. So, as I approached the end of the angle deck I was still expecting to stop. But the aircraft did not stop, nor did it have enough speed to fly. This supersonic Navy jet and I did a big belly flop in the water 60 feet below.

Ron Knott

I was dazed after the hard impact but realized that I was still alive (Records indicate that very few pilots survive a water landing in a jet airplane). The first thing I noticed was the tail of the airplane was in front of me. The aircraft had broken up when it hit the water. The cockpit, of which I was attached, was floating but the canopy was gone. As I tried to exit the cockpit it rolled over and started sinking. I released my two top shoulder harness fittings that connected me to the ejection seat. I was working as fast as I could to exit this death trap. I had always planned to use the ejection seat for egress if I found myself in this situation. However, firing the ejection seat with my body in an awkward position would have probably broken my back.

As I sank I discovered that the fitting on one side of my oxygen mask had broken, requiring me to hold the mask to my face so I could breath underwater. With my free hand I released the two lower restraining straps that held my body to the seat. Then I attempted to exit the cockpit. That is when I discovered that my left foot was jammed under the rudder petal and I was sinking rapidly.

Somewhere, I had read about a guy who was logging and a large tree fell across his leg. This poor fellow cut his leg off at the knee to free himself.

Part of our flight equipment was a large hunting knife. The thought flashed through my head that I might have to cut off my jammed foot. I know I probably would have drowned or bled to death long before completing that operation.

With all my effort I lunged upward and the wedged foot popped free. I was somewhat relieved until I realized that my fighting to release my foot had resulted in tearing loose the oxygen hose. Now, I was without air to breathe and at a depth of about 40 feet below the surface of the salty ocean. It was dark but I could see what I assumed were aircraft parts floating down around me.

Suddenly I saw a huge object off on my right. It was rotating and throwing off thousands of bubbles.

"What the heck is that?" I thought. Then I realized it was one of the ship's four massive propellers. If I had been just a few feet to the right that propeller would have made shark bait out of me.

It is normal procedures to turn the ship into the crash site, thereby swinging the stern of the vessel away from the pilot. In this case, the crewman at the helm in all the excitement ordered full right rudder. This caused the stern of the ship to swing toward the wreckage. In so doing, that big propeller almost got me!

It seemed like I had held my breath for an eternity. I desperately needed to get to the surface for air. Finally, I remembered I had a floatation device known as a "Mae West" attached to my body. I actuated the pull-tabs of the Mae West and popped up out of the water like being shot from a cannon! Those first few breaths were so sweet! I will never take free air for granted again.

All Navy pilots have to go through the *Dilbert Dunker* training before they received their wings. The *Dilbert Dunker* is composed of a simulated cockpit. This cockpit is placed on rails about 30 feet above the swimming pool. The student is fully clothed with helmet, flying suit, boots, and is strapped into this cockpit. The instructor trips a switch and the *Dunker* races down the rails in a 40 degree dive and impacts the water. The *Dunker* becomes submerged and flips over (upside down) with the trainee strapped in the cockpit. This is to simulate what a pilot might experience in a real ditching.

The trainee is to orientate himself, unstrap, and swim clear. Panic is usually overcome by the will to survive. Safety swimmers are hovering underwater to assist the student if necessary.

All my fellow students were apprehensive when facing this necessary event. In my real cockpit that horrible day, it sank, flipped over, and I saw thousands of bubbles just like in the *Dilbert Dunker*. As you can tell the water survival training was outstanding although some of us student pilots feared it. This training was definitely an aid in my survival.

The "Angel" (duty helicopter) was directly over me when I popped to the surface. The crew lowered a horse collar and winched me up into the waiting arms of the crew. I was back on the ship in just a few minutes. (During all flight operations the "Angel" is hovering near the ship to recover a pilot in case he goes into the ocean.)

My Commanding Officer, LCDR Merle Gorder, my Executive Officer, LCDR Jack Snyder, and the squadron Safety Officer, LT John Harker, met me on deck as the helicopter brought me back on board. There was a lot of jubilation and joy from the entire ship that I had survived. I was definitely the happiest man on board that day. I had faced death several times during this ordeal but had survived.

The entire event had lasted no more than five minutes. I only required a stitch on my elbow and one on my chin. In fact, I was flying again two days later but there was a big investigation about the failure of the barricade.

Three years later I returned to civilian life and flew for American Airlines.

In review, I had a lot of malfunctions on that October day in 1962. First of all the ship was bucking and rolling, which caused my left landing gear to fail. Second, the tailhook spit out the # 3 arresting wire on landing. It should have held the aircraft. This failure allowed me to become airborne again. Third, on my second approach and landing the tailhook again spit out the target # 1 arresting gear wire. This caused me to engage the barricade. Fourth, the barricade malfunctioned and the plane crashed in the ocean. Fifth, my foot was caught under the rudder pedal. Sixth, my oxygen mask was ripped from my face making it difficult to breathe underwater. Seventh, the ship almost ran over me. Surely, Admiral Almighty was looking over me that extraordinary day!

CHAPTER TEN

THUNDERSTORM FLIGHT

RON KNOTT

"DIAMOND ONE FLAMED OUT!"
"DIAMOND TWO FLAMED OUT!"
"DIAMOND ONE EJECTING – STAY WITH ME IF YOU CAN!"
"DIAMOND THREE FLAMING OUT!"
"DIAMOND TWO EJECTING!"

It was a beautiful Florida Saturday morning in August 1962, when a flight of seven Navy F-8 *Crusader* jet fighters took off from Cecil Field, near Jacksonville, FL. We were heading for Guantanamo Bay, Cuba.

I well remember LTJG Tom Malloy laughing and pointing to his new flight suit as we briefed for the long flight early that morning. He had been issued the flight suit the day before and had not tried it on. It was about three sizes too big and he looked lost in that tent-sized costume. There was no way to exchange the flight suit for another one since it was Saturday and the Naval Supply Office was closed. Tom had a wonderful sense of humor and accepted our kidding with a big smile. That is the way I remember him until this day. Just a few hours later he would be gone from our sight forever.

Ron Knott

As you may recall this time and date was just prior to the Cuban Missile Crisis. Our mission was to demonstrate a 'show of force' at the small Naval Base on the southeastern side of Cuba. I had joined Fighter Squadron 62 just a few weeks earlier and this was my first major deployment with the squadron. I was a 'Nugget' as they call the new pilots fresh out of flight school.

Fighter pilot's gear (LT Ron Knott)

Two Divisions (a total of eight airplanes) were scheduled to deploy that morning but one of the airplanes had mechanical problems. LCDR Paul Gillcrist was scheduled to be the second division leader but due to a mechanical problem he was not able to take off with the flight. Therefore, we only had a flight of four F-8s (*Diamond Flight*) and a flight of three F-8s (*Blue Flight*) heading for Cuba.

We went "Feet Wet" (flying over water) just north of Miami, FL at an altitude of 39,000 feet. The flight leader adjusted our heading to a southeasterly direction so we would fly just north of Cuba to stay out of their protected air space. About 150 miles southeast from Miami over the Caribbean we entered an area of low visibility at our cruising altitude. Our forward visibility was one mile or less. We had no weather radar. In fact the radar on board the older *Crusaders* only had a maximum range of 16 miles and most of them never worked.

We received a weather briefing before the flight and there was no mention of severe weather along our route of flight. We were completely unaware that huge thunderstorms were hidden in the haze ahead. Nevertheless, these cumulonimbus demons were in our flight path and they were about to inflict major damage to our flight.

The Skipper of our squadron was CDR John Brozo (*Diamond Flight*). He was leading the first division of four airplanes that consisted of LTJG Tom Malloy (*Diamond Two*), LT Dick Oliver (*Diamond Three*), and LTJG Ben Walker (*Diamond Four*). Navy pilots establish a call sign early on in their training and usually keep that 'handle' for the rest of their time in the Navy.

CDR Brozo's "handle" was *Diamond One* therefore all members of his flight would be *Diamond Flight*. My flight leader was LT Al Wattay and his call sign was *Blue Flight*. As a result, I was *Blue Two* and LT John Nichols was *Blue Three* as we only had three birds in our flight. *Blue Leader*

(LT Wattay) positioned our flight about five miles aft and two miles abeam *Diamond Flight*. Although the visibility was low the ride was fairly smooth as I recall, and we could occasionally see the vapor trails ahead from *Diamond Flight*.

Vapor trails, or commonly called contrails, can be seen most any clear day from aircraft flying high overhead. They usually start around 30,000 feet altitude, depending on the temperature. The moisture in the exhaust from the jet engine freezes at about 52 degrees below zero Celsius and produces a beautiful white stream behind the aircraft. These ice crystals usually last for several minutes. The colder the temperature the longer the contrail will be. These tale-tale contrails are visible for miles on a clear day and can reveal your position to the enemy. The wingman is usually briefed to call "marking" to his flight leader when climbing out so he will know the exact altitude that the vapor trails start. The leader will mark that altitude and usually fly a few thousand feet below, where the temperature is warmer to keep from revealing his position.

Everything was going great until I heard the Skipper say in a loud and frantic voice, "*DIAMOND ONE FLAMED OUT!*"

And as my heart was elevating up into my throat I heard his wingman LTJG Tom Malloy saying with even more fear in his voice, "*DIAMOND TWO FLAMED OUT!*"

Before I could suck up more oxygen I heard the Skipper say, "*DIAMOND ONE EJECTING – STAY WITH ME IF YOU CAN!*"

Just seconds later I heard LT Dick Oliver say, "*DIAMOND THREE FLAMING OUT!*"

Nothing was heard from *Diamond Four*. We thought he had flamed out as well.

Supersonic Fighter Pilot

WOW! This was my first major cross-country with the squadron and the airplanes were falling out of the sky. I was anxiously waiting for my engine to quit as well. We were only seconds away from their position. I was very tense to say the least. My heartbeat was louder than the jet engine. However, our flight of three flew through the same area, basically at the same time, without any problems. It took many months and numerous accident investigations to determine how our flight made it through this area without difficulty. I'll explain why later.

The F-8 was a great airplane to fly as long as the engine was running. However, an engine flameout causes instant electrical and hydraulic power loss. In addition, at the higher altitudes the canopy fogs over almost immediately, and you lose all pressurization and heat.

We were at 39,000 feet and the pilots who lost engine power experienced all of the above instantaneously. This makes the great *Crusader* not too "user-friendly," to say the least. All flight instruments go ape, the airspeed decreases rapidly, and the flight controls freeze since there is no hydraulic power. In a situation like this the pilot is just along for the ride, but he is frantically trying to regain control of that hunk of metal falling through space by instant recall of his emergency procedures. All the while he is being slammed around in the cockpit like a sock in a washing machine.

The Navy had a term called "Over Learning." All pilots had to go over and over emergency procedures time and time again until they could respond automatically, in any situation without thinking. This rote memory of learning emergency procedures saved many pilots and planes.

One of the undesirable characteristics of the F-8 *Crusader* was when the indicated airspeed reduces below

170 KIAS it will automatically enter into a spin with just a little aileron or spoiler input. Due to the conditions of this flight listed above, these flamed-out *Crusaders* automatically entered into a spin.

It was really tough to recover the F-8 from a spin in day VFR conditions. Add a big bad thunderstorm to the equation with the engine flamed-out, the flight controls frozen, the airplane spinning, and the canopy iced over makes recovery from a spin nothing short of a miracle.

The F-8 was equipped with an emergency air driven electrical generator/hydraulic pump that provided some AC & DC electrical power and regain of primary flight controls in case of an engine failure. The pilot was required to pull a lever in the cockpit to extend this Ram Air Turbine (RAT). This wind driven generator/hydraulic pump was designed to windmill in the air stream and recover part of the electrical power and part of the hydraulic power as well.

Electrical power was needed to re-start the engine after a flame-out. These aircraft had no batteries to supply this needed electrical power. The emergency generator switch had to be turned on after extending the RAT, or no electrical power would be supplied to the aircraft. This procedure was easy to omit.

The RAT restored hydraulic power automatically for primary flight controls. It was impossible to move the flight controls without the hydraulic pump working since the system needed 3000 pounds of pressure for operation. The control stick would be frozen until power was restored.

It takes a few seconds for the RAT to come up to speed after deployment. Sometimes, like in this case, those few seconds can seem like an eternity.

Supersonic Fighter Pilot

As I recall, LT Oliver said later in the accident report, "The airplane was spinning before the RAT became effective."

Yet, with all this adversity *Diamond Three*, LT Dick Oliver, did recover from the spin and went through the in-flight restart procedures to get his engine running again. This was by no means an easy task. He first had to extend the RAT to regain flight control and then he had to recover from the spin. A spinning F-8 may go from 10 degrees nose up to 190 degrees nose down, while pulling plus 4 to minus 3 Gs, all the while rotating rapidly like a west Texas twister. This short paragraph does not do justice for the superb airmanship that LT Oliver demonstrated that awful day.

Spin recovery procedures in the F-8 were very different and extremely difficult on a clear day. While experiencing the violent maneuvers noted above, the pilot had to move both hands to the left console, and unlock the pneumatic switch for emergency extension of the leading edge landing droop. This extended droop changed the aerodynamics of the wing and served to get the stalled wing producing lift again. In addition, full aft stick and full aileron into the rotation of the spin was required. (That is a correct statement of full aileron into the rotation of the spin.) At the same time full opposite rudder into the spin was essential. This condition was held until the rotation stopped and only then could the nose be brought up to pull out of the dive.

I don't know of another aircraft that required these type procedures to recover from a spin.

If the airplane was still in uncontrolled flight at 10,000 ft. altitude the pilot was required to eject. After recovering from a spin the leading edge landing droop could not be retracted in the air. This placed speed and "G" restrictions on the airplane. In addition, the maximum range was reduced consequentially as well. Spins were to be avoided – if you got in one it left you with a crippled airplane.

When my flight leader, LT Al Wattay, heard the radio transmissions from *Diamond Flight* flaming-out he advanced power by selecting the afterburner. We accelerated to Mach One and climbed to 50,000 feet. LT Nichols and I were hanging on his wing as best we could. Little did we know at the time that the extra speed and altitude is what saved our flight and possibly our lives!

It was determined in the accident report that the Skipper of *Diamond Flight* had allowed his flight to slow below Mach .70, which is slow at that altitude. They also determined that it was a good possibility that vertical wind shears/or engine icing could cause a flame-out during such conditions. In addition, the older model F-8s were not equipped with engine anti-ice. The engines could have quit due to icing conditions. This was also a factor considered in the accident investigation.

Due to the fact that LT Wattay accelerated our flight to a much higher airspeed the wind shear had no effect on our engines. In addition, climbing to a higher altitude removed us from the icing area. Thanks, LT Wattay, for great airmanship that day.

We radioed *MAYDAY* reports to the Search & Rescue Squadron that was based in Miami. We could only give them an approximate position of the emergency since our navigation aids were useless that far from a land transmitter. There was no way for us to locate the downed pilots since the weather was clogged in all the way to sea level. And besides that we just barely had enough fuel to fly to Guantanamo.

Supersonic Fighter Pilot

There were no *Texaco Tankers* available that day for in-flight refueling. We continued on to Guantanamo with only three out of seven airplanes that we started with; that was not a very pleasant flight.

After landing in Cuba we assumed that all four aircraft had been lost. We still had no word from *Diamond Four*. Suddenly, we heard an F-8 coming into the area at the speed of heat. We were thrilled to see *Diamond Four*, LT Ben Walker, overhead. Later he told us that he had lost his generator in the midst of all the excitement, dropped his RAT for electrical power, but never regained his radio. All that he knew was that his flight had disappeared in the clag.

A few minutes later, LT Oliver, *Diamond Three*, appeared for landing. As stated above he had flamed-out, got into a spin, recovered from the spin, got a re-light and headed toward GITMO. We were sure glad to see those two squadron mates come through that ordeal. But two were still missing.

The Skipper, *Diamond One*, was found two days after the accident by an Air Force rescue team that answered our *MAYDAY* call. These courageous Air Force pilots flying an amphibious aircraft landed in very rough seas to retrieve CDR Brozo. He was in the supplied one-man life raft that was bouncing around in the ocean like a rubber ball.

Emergency radios were placed in the survival pack that was attached to the life vest. The life raft was attached to the pilot's ejection seat. CDR Brozo was able to direct the rescue aircraft to his position by using this radio. He had suffered a broken back due to the tremendous forces placed on his body during ejection.

The F-8 had an explosive cartridge in the ejection system that hit you in the butt with mega "Gs" when ejecting.

This type exit was necessary from a high-speed jet aircraft to keep the pilot's body from striking the tail when he ejected. A 35mm cartridge would actually shoot the pilot out of the airplane when he activated the ejection handle. A spin produces a lot of negative Gs causing the pilot to rise slightly out of his seat. If the seat fires during such a procedure it can really damage the pilot's back. CDR Brozo said that he was in a negative G flight when he ejected. He was later relieved of his command for taking his flight through a thunderstorm. Yet, he had no way of knowing that severe weather was in his flight path.

Diamond Two, Tom Malloy, was never found. About two years after the accident his helmet washed ashore on one of the small islands in the Caribbean. He was reported missing until that time. We never really knew what happened to him after he called "Ejecting." The Skipper said that his ejection was very rough. And after landing in the water he almost drowned by his parachute pulling him under. The wind on the surface was very strong. Under those conditions a parachute in the water can be deadly. If Tom was injured during ejection as the Skipper was, his survival would have been in jeopardy.

The following is what a pilot may experience when ejecting from a fast flying airplane at high altitude. As you can imagine it is a hazardous experience. As stated above the explosive charge in the ejection seat can give you a kick in the butt. This big kick is necessary to insure that the pilot clears the vertical tail of the airplane during an ejection. The first sequence in an ejection is for the canopy to separate from the airplane. If it does not separate the pilot is shot through the canopy.

Supersonic Fighter Pilot

For example, if the pilot ejects at 40,000 feet he is quick to feel the cold rushing wind hitting his body at the speed at which he ejected; let's say 400 knots, for example. It may be 60 degrees below zero at that altitude and with very little oxygen to breathe. This is not too good for the boys in summer flying suits. The pilot cannot survive in that environment very long because he would freeze to death and or die from hypoxia (lack of oxygen).

The ejection system is designed so that a small drogue parachute about the size of an umbrella extends immediately after ejecting at high altitudes. This small chute prevents the pilot from tumbling during descent but he is still falling like a brick. The ejection seat is equipped with an emergency oxygen bottle that will last about ten minutes for just such high dives. This system can be used under water as well. That is, if your mask has not been ripped from your face during the high-speed exit of the airplane.

The pilot is still strapped in the ejection seat at this time and will free-fall, in this case 30,000 feet, before the main chute opens. He is falling straight down. (Disney World or Six Flags can't compete with this feat.)

The sequence is for the main parachute to open automatically, by a barometric release, which is normally set at 10,000 feet above ground level. When that altitude is reached a bladder in the seat inflates pushing the pilot out of the seat and then the main parachute deploys.

If the automatic system does not work the pilot can manually push the ejection seat aside and pull the "D-Ring" for the chute to open. How does the pilot know when he reaches 10,000 feet? He can only estimate his altitude by visual references. In a thunderstorm that is impossible. In a storm such as this there would be limited visibility, which would make it impossible to estimate your altitude. In addition the pilot may be in heavy rain, or hail, severe turbulence, and possible heavy lightning. This is not the best flying conditions.

Let's assume that the pilot gets a good parachute opening at 10,000 feet and floats gracefully down to the waiting ocean and sharks. He still has a lot of emergency procedures to accomplish to insure his survival.

First, and most importantly, he must unhook from the life saving parachute, which now becomes a death trap once it hits the water. When a parachute is filled with water it will sink like a rock taking the pilot down as well. If the pilot's hands or arms are injured it may be impossible to release the parachute. This can quickly turn into a critical situation. In addition, once the parachute is released from the pilot's harness shroud lines from the chute may entangle the pilot. These lines may snare him and take him under as well. For that reason all Navy pilots carried an open knife, with a hook blade, attached to their harness to cut the shroud lines if necessary.

If all of the above is accomplished without incident the pilot still had a lot of work to do. He must inflate his life vest to keep him afloat, since he is burdened with about fifty pounds of flight gear. At this time he needs to deploy and inflate his one-man life raft that is stored in a packet, which is attached to his harness. In this parcel are such items as shark chaser, a radio, dye marker, signal mirror, fishhooks, a small salt-water distillery to convert seawater to fresh drinking water, and a host of other small things including a New Testament, in case all else fails.

Boarding the one-man life raft is no easy task in a calm swimming pool. It becomes even more difficult to board the little boat in rough seas or if one is injured. Once onboard the little rubber raft, a big wave can dump you back in the water quickly and totally mess up your command at sea. You must re-board the little "private yacht" or the sharks may eat you for dessert. This could go on for days. These were the conditions that *Diamond One* and *Diamond Two* were faced with that awful day.

The news media in our city broadcasted that all planes in our flight were lost at sea. "They were lost in the Bermuda Triangle," so some said. That needlessly placed undue stress on our families and friends. Communications back then were comparatively antiquated. It took hours for the facts, as we knew them, to get back to our home base. Thereafter, this story was told many times in pilot training. The point was made loud and clear to never fly into a thunderstorm.

The positive aspects of this tragedy were the findings in the accident investigation. The main statement made was never to fly into a thunderstorm. The aircraft were fitted with engine anti-ice systems that would prevent the engine from flaming-out in such conditions. The radar was improved and could detect weather as far as sixty miles ahead of the flight path. And last, but not least, this incident gave us more respect for our fellow pilots. One day they are here and the next day they may be gone.

I record this account in tribute to my fallen comrades. CDR John (*Diamond*) Brozo, deceased; LT Dick (*Smooth One*) Oliver, deceased – killed with the Blue Angels; LTJG Tom Malloy, killed on this flight; LT Ben (*Bugger*) Walker, deceased; LT John (*Pirate*) Nichols, deceased. LT Al Wattay and I are the only living souls out of that flight of seven.

Ron Knott

(Note: the rank indicated in this story is the rank these officers held at the time of this accident.)

In this narrative I was amazed at how many emergency procedures I could recall forty-five years later. This information is 100% from my memory and not from documents or other sources. This again proves the point that the military drilled into all pilots about the "Over Learning" process. My dear wife wonders why I can't remember birthdays and anniversaries.

And so it was back in the mid-sixties. We F-8 *Crusader* pilots have annual conventions and share many such stories that are never forgotten.

CHAPTER ELEVEN

BARRICADE ENGAGEMENT

JOHN "CRASH" MIOTTEL, JR.

In early 1957 the *Crusader* became operational and that was the start of the real test of this airplane. Our squadron, VF-154, was the first Pacific Fleet fighter squadron to receive the revolutionary new Navy jet. VF-154 was assigned to the doughty USS *Hancock*.

The modifications for the old *Hancock* were the addition of the angle deck, the Mirror Landing System, and the Steam Catapult.

Our awareness of the seriousness of the business at hand was reinforced by the fact that we quickly lost three of our new aircraft and two squadron-mates during carrier qualifications.

FIRST PILOT TO CARRIER QUALIFY

Somehow, in spite of my own inexperience, I had the good fortune of being the first pilot in VF-154 to carrier qualify in the new jet. This meant that in the first squadron ever to deploy flying a truly supersonic operational carrier aircraft, I was the first pilot to carrier qualify.

An observer of our carrier qualifications (carquals) was a young Marine Major. He had been assigned to the office responsible for the development of the *Crusader*. He had also just completed *Project Bullet*, a supersonic coast-to-coast speed record run in an F-8 at an average speed faster than the muzzle velocity of a .45 caliber slug. He went on to garner a bit more than the allotted 15 minutes of fame. His name was John Glenn.

FIRST PILOT TO HIT THE BARRICADE

A month or so later I captured another somewhat less enviable record, during the work-up for our Operational Readiness Inspection (ORI). We were at sea somewhere south of Oahu when I suddenly found myself facing the challenge of becoming the first *Crusader* pilot ever to attempt a shipboard landing using a carrier's fearsome barricade recovery system.

The objective of the barricade recovery is to snare some poor soul who has no tail-hook, no fuel left, and no "bingo" (no alternate land-based field). The barricade is explained in other chapters in this book but I would just like to add that the aircraft in this case, is like a multi-ton tennis ball on a 150 mph bad serve. Once a pilot is committed to a barricade recovery there is no turning back.

At this juncture, like all first tour pilots, my only prior tailhook experience consisted of six traps (carrier arrested landings). These traps were made two years earlier during flight training in the trusty and extremely forgiving SNJ; a bright yellow propeller-driven WWII trainer. Amazingly, none of us nuggets (first tour pilots) in VF-154 had any jet carrier experience whatsoever prior to joining our operational fleet squadrons.

Obviously, as a recovery option, the barricade is not highly relished by carrier pilots. The result of the *Crusader's* first tangle with the "net" under my supervision did nothing to dispel that prejudice. Among the adverse circumstances that prefaced my predicament were rapidly deteriorating weather conditions due to the sudden onset of what turned out to be Hawaii's worst storm in fifty years.

Two prior landing accidents had not only fouled the deck and caused critical delay but also resulted in the removal of two of the five cables available for an arrested landing. Add to that my broken tailhook (the result of materiel failure on an otherwise "picture perfect" earlier attempt to trap). And just enough fuel remaining for my first (and last) shot at the barricade – it was a nasty situation exacerbated with every passing second.

You might ask, "Why not 'ditch' the aircraft or use the ejection seat?" The ostensible answer was that it was your duty to exercise your best efforts to save the multi-million dollar aircraft (and your own posterior) if at all possible. The other reasons were even more compelling. The ditching maneuver (crash landing the F-8 in the water) was always climaxed by a spectacular explosion as the cold seawater swamped the red-hot F-8 engine or by the *Crusader* otherwise disintegrating on impact with the water. Even at stall speed this was just like hitting a ten-foot thick brick wall.

Out of five attempted semi-controlled collisions with the water the aircraft were instantly torn apart; only one pilot survived. And this instance was not a true ditching, a landing F-8, slammed down on the carrier deck as usual but its tailhook broke and the plane was only partially arrested. It was too slow to fly and too fast to stop before going over the side. Nasty business! The pilot jammed full power on including afterburner but the decelerated *Crusader* ran off the angled deck at low speed. Somehow the wings stayed level as the shuddering *Crusader* flopped down into the water. The lucky pilot was able to scramble out of the cockpit just before the engine exploded. The rescue helicopter quickly plucked him out of the briny. Hence, ditching definitely was not a viable option.

Oh, by the way, what about in-flight refueling, a standard and vital component of today's air operations? Forget it! It was strictly an Air Force luxury in the late 50s. Except as a rare training exercise, for us sea dogs it was nonexistent.

Consequently, in a situation where the fates had dealt the carrier jet pilot a low fuel state, no tailhook, and no divert field, the only possible ace in the hole was the barricade.

My roommate, Chuck Ramsey, had confirmed that ugly reality as I prepared for my *Crusader's* debut with the barricade. I watched in horror as his F-8 touched down on deck and WHAM! His port main landing gear disintegrated. Unfortunately, this was an all too common occurrence at this stage of the *Crusader's* career. It was even more distressing because the landing gear struts also served as the reservoir for the hydraulic fluid necessary to operate the *Crusader's* flight controls. Chuck poured the coal to the crippled *Crusader*.

He was trying to nurse it up to speed and to get to an altitude high enough to eject. The F-8 staggered up to about 700 feet when one of the control officers on the ship apparently mistook the streaming hydraulic fluid for smoke. He thought that Chuck's aircraft was on fire and frantically squawked over the radio, *"BAIL OUT! BAIL OUT NOW!!"*

Before I could even key my mike to warn Chuck otherwise, he ejected. He was just able to disengage himself from the ejection seat. He tumbled in free fall and his parachute only streamed. But the chute did not have time to blossom. He dropped like a sack of rocks and hit the water at terminal velocity. The chopper was busy trying to pick Chuck's body out of the sea as I was turning on final approach.

For me, the suspense of my predicament was now further heightened by the realization that because everyone was operating in new and untested territory, fatal mistakes like Chuck's abortive ejection were more than a remote possibility. And hell, I had never even seen a picture of a barricade before this flap I thought, "Watch out, Buster, or you'll be next!"

As I came onto glide path I saw my first barricade, ever. But, what I DID NOT SEE was the mirror, the pilot's only guide to a successful carrier landing. I finally realized that the mirror was obscured behind the huge port barricade stanchion. In the few instants that it took me to figure this out and to get to a point where I could see the mirror I was both off alignment and very low. This was not a pretty picture!

I was correcting as I skimmed a couple of feet over the ramp end of the ship. I drove the F-8 into the net at about 150 mph. Everything seemed okay until the force of the engagement with the lower horizontal load strap of the barricade suddenly tore off my port landing gear. The F-8 instantly pivoted on the wing tip. I hit the afterburner but it wasn't doing any more flying that day. I was truly snagged and was skidding to the port edge of the carrier deck. I was on my way to an unanticipated and highly unwelcome salt-water immersion.

As the *Crusader* careened into the deck edge catwalk and started to roll over the side of the ship, a little voice advised me to jettison the aircraft cockpit canopy.

"Better blow your lid now. Don't get trapped in the cockpit by water pressure as you sink. Forget about an underwater ejection through the canopy unless you want to end up three feet tall and shredded."

The canopy exploded away from the F-8. Now I could enjoy a more unfettered leisurely exit one way or another once things settled down a bit on my impending voyage to the bottom of the sea. In short, I was trying to figure it all out, to improvise at least as rapidly as the situation was deteriorating.

My interest in expeditious preparation for underwater survival was sharpened by my acute awareness that during the past few months two roommates, another squadron mate, and a fourth air group pal had not been able to extricate themselves in similar aquacades.

Supersonic Fighter Pilot

My F-8 lurched over the side and rolled inverted. I looked "up" and saw the tumult of the ship's wake approaching pretty rapidly. As the F-8 plunged into the water, and the sea boiled into the cockpit, and engulfed me, I reached down to my right and yanked the "ditching handle." This released me with my parachute from the ejection seat. I waited thirty feet under water for ten tons of *Crusader* to come down on top of me.

It's pretty obvious that I made it so I won't burden you gentle readers with all of the ensuing gory details. Suffice to say that my problems weren't over yet.

Anyway, the upshot of this little fandango was that the old aviator's maxim that goes, "Any landing you can walk away from is a good landing," was amended to incorporate the words "or swim."

ANOTHER FIRST

Aside from the above records I went on to capture several other dubious distinctions. Notable among these was an incident at Atsugi, Japan US Naval Air Facility.

After extensive study and assiduous preparation I was able to garner laurels as the first and only Naval Aviator in history to retain his wings and flying status subsequent to execution of a very precise and deliberate four point slow roll on take off. What made this performance really special was that the base commander was gaping out of his office window in stupefied disbelief as this $2 million *Crusader* snapped into an inverted attitude and disappeared below tree level off the end of the duty runway. My justification? Pretty obvious to any thoughtful person: having completed testing the undersea capabilities of the *Crusader,* it was

Ron Knott

obviously necessary for the VF-154 safety officer, me, to thoroughly explore the extremes of the *Crusader's* high speed low-level acrobatic performance envelope. There was the obvious salutary effect on squadron morale of doing so in this auspicious setting. Any rational, objective observer would certainly stipulate to the fact that this type of maneuver had substantial pertinent precedent. After all, Atsugi had been the main base for the Kamikaze. Furthermore, although some may think that this was an unintended consequence, I believe that the direct result of my Atsugi aeronautical endeavor was that I was substantially better prepared for my record-shattering return engagement with the Hancock's barricade three months later.

Well, as it turned out, I didn't lack for company. During our post-Korean pre-Vietnam war work up and deployment we never fired a shot in anger. Nevertheless, during this less than two-year cycle VF-154 lost a full squadron complement of fourteen aircraft in major accidents as well as something like 40% of our pilots. We had a 20% fatality rate, not including the unfortunate death of one of our crewmembers. Of something like fifteen or nineteen of us *nuggets*, only two were still flying by the end of the '58 cruise. An old squadron mate, CDR Dave Winiker, was one of them. He went on to be a flight instructor and to fly hundreds of combat missions. Dave tells me that, in terms of pure hazard and pure flying thrills nothing ever compared to those pioneering *Crusader* days.

However, the *Crusader* was dubbed the *MiG MASTER* in honor of achieving the highest kill rate of any fighter in the Vietnam War. The *Crusader* was in active service for over forty years, which is a record for a jet fighter. There are no more single engine, single pilot, gun-toting fighters left. So it

Supersonic Fighter Pilot

is truly *The Last of the Gunfighters*. I've never met a fighter pilot who didn't love (and respect) the *Crusader*.

Supersonic Fighter Pilot

CHAPTER TWELVE

ROUGH SEAS

TONY LONGO

In August 1961, VF-142, the *World Famous Fighting Falcons*, (CO CDR Jack Stetson) flew our F-8s to Norfolk to board the USS *Kitty Hawk* (CVA-63) for a shakedown cruise at Guantanamo Bay, Cuba.

After this inspection we were to take the ship "around the horn" to her new homeport of San Diego, CA. Our squadron had been reassigned from CAG-14 to CAG-11 to replace VF-111, who was not yet operational. VF-142 swapped their F-8U2s with the Marines for their F-8U1s. The squadron flew to Norfolk via Naval Air Station Dallas, TX.

While in Dallas Chance Vought gave the squadron a great party at one of the big downtown hotels. The next day we flew to NAS Norfolk, VA, loaded our squadron aboard the *Kitty Hawk,* and sailed for GITMO.

I still remember the exciting landing on the short (5000') runway at NAS Norfolk. You had to really be on your toes (literally) to get the *Gator* stopped on such a short runway or off the end you would go.

The shakedown cruise on the *Kitty Hawk* was without incident and the ship departed GITMO for Rio de Janeiro, Brazil. We crossed the equator the before entering Rio and the ship held the usual *Pollywog* ceremonies. We all became *Shellbacks.* The ceremonial haircuts were curtailed due to our next day arrival in Rio. Rio was a great liberty port as was noted by the number of senoritas being off loaded and boated ashore even as the ship was leaving port. We called the ladies who followed the Navy ships, *Seagulls*.

A few days from the "Horn" the Commanding Officer of the *Kitty Hawk* decided that the VIPs taken on board in GITMO, needed to observe shipboard carrier operations. There had been no flight operations since departing Cuba. He directed that an aircraft from each squadron would be flown in the demonstration. I don't know why they chose me but I was selected to be the F-8 pilot from my squadron.

I thought, "What the heck, this should be fun." Little did I know!

The operational flight conditions were as follows: visibility at least fifty miles – GOOD; 30-35 foot swells – BAD; only the # 1 and # 4 wires were operational – VERY BAD; nearest divert field was Terra del Fuego and not a desirable option – BAD; the mirror landing system would be useless – VERY, VERY BAD!

I'm only a LTJG and besides, I had never landed on any carrier in such rough conditions. The Ready Room received the "go" signal and I headed for the flight deck. Of course, I had felt the ships movements in the Ready Room, but once on the flight deck I saw what a challenge I would be facing.

I thought to myself, "This should be interesting."

My *Crusader* was parked near the center of the flight deck. I strapped in the cockpit, started the engine, went through all the checks, and started taxiing to the catapult. I again noticed how much the deck was pitching. I remember looking at the ocean staring up at me and then disappearing below the flight deck. My aircraft was slipping on the non-skid deck as the ship turned into the wind. Somehow I arrived at the catapult without sliding over the side. As I looked out of the cockpit all I could see was the ship bucking in the heavy seas. The bow would be in a 30 degree dive; it would stop momentarily, and then slowly start moving up to a 30 degree climb above the horizon and roll in both directions at will. This reminded me of a bucking horse trying to get rid of the cowboy.

The Catapult Officer gave me a turn-up signal to select full power for the launch. I advanced the throttle, selected afterburner, and saluted the Cat Officer that I was ready to go. But was I?

The ship's bow was below the horizon. I prayed that I would not be shot off until the bow was on the rise. As the bow started up I was fired off the ship. I was finally safely airborne: little did I know that this would be the easiest part of the flight.

I entered the landing pattern with approximately 3000 lbs of fuel. The Commander Air Group (CAG) Landing Signal Officer (LSO), Jesse Reed, would be verbally controlling the approach because the mirror was useless due to the pitching deck. The position of the flight deck in it's up and down gyrations, would determine if I could safely land. Only the LSO could make the decision for me to land.

On my first pass I called ball and was told by the LSO, "Keep it coming."

I could see that the A-4 ahead of me had landed. Everything looked good except the unusual view of the flight deck and my inability to see the glide slope. I was not allowed to land on this approach because the A-4 was still in the arresting gear. I had to go around and try for it again. Now the fun really begins.

Ron Knott

On my second pass I called ball and the LSO said, "Keep it coming," then, "WAVE-OFF, unsafe deck position!"

My third pass I called ball and the LSO said, "Looking good, keep it coming." I landed in the vicinity of the # 3 wire, but got a hook skip and boltered.

My fourth pass I got another WAVE-OFF for unsafe deck position.

On my fifth pass everything looked good. I landed near the # 2 wire and got another hook skip and a bolter. This was starting to become a pain in the butt. I was now the only plane flying and my fuel state was about 1500 lbs.

On the sixth pass I got another WAVE-OFF due to the pitching deck. I'm now getting a little "pucker factor."

My seventh pass looked good all the way and I felt this was going to be a good landing. I landed short of the # 1 wire and sure enough I got another hook skip and bolter. To add to my problems the low level fuel light came on. "S- -t! Now I have a much bigger "pucker factor" to deal with.

My eighth pass (with only 900 lbs of fuel remaining) I called ball and the LSO said, "Keep it coming, don't go high."

I started going high. I had to get aboard on this pass. I shook the stick left to right to kill the lift and landed extremely hard just short of the # 4 wire. Thank goodness I caught a wire and was safely on board. I hit the deck so hard on this landing that I almost ate the control stick. It felt to me like a 15 G landing. The plane director tried to taxi me out of the landing area but the plane wouldn't move. I was then directed to shut down the engine and get out of the airplane.

I noticed that the maintenance crew was diligently checking the landing gear. On this hard landing I had blown all three tires and that is the reason I could not taxi the aircraft. It is a wonder the landing gear did not collapse. At this point I could give a rat about the condition of the airplane. I was put in a terribly dangerous position and had survived. I expected to get the usual ribbing from my comrades about my air show but was amazed there was none. I guess they were glad to have me back. I don't remember the LSO's remarks.

I still question the "powers that be" on their decision to fly that terrible day. I hope the VIPs understood just how dangerous our flight demonstration had been. If I had known better … oh, well, it all turned out okay. Our maintenance crew dropped checked the landing gear and no damage was found. All that my *Crusader* needed was three new tires. Obviously there was no more flying on that trip until the air group flew off at San Diego.

[Author's Note: In the U.S. Navy, when a ship crosses the equator a time-honored ceremony takes place. This is a Navy tradition and an event no sailor ever forgets. With few exceptions, those who have been inducted into the "mysteries of the deep" by Neptune Rex and his Royal Court, count the experience as a highlight of their naval career. Members of Neptune Rex's party usually include Davy Jones, Neptune's first assistant, Her Highness Amphitrite, the Royal Scribe, the Royal Doctor, the Royal Dentist, the Royal Baby, the Royal Navigator, the Royal Chaplain, the Royal Judge, Attorneys, Barbers, and other names that suit the party.

Officially recognized by service record entries indicating date, time, latitude and longitude, the crossing of the equator involves elaborate preparation by the "Shellbacks" (those who have crossed the equator before) to ensure the "Pollywogs" (those who are about to cross the equator for

the first time) are properly indoctrinated. All pollywogs, even the Commanding Officer if he has not crossed before, must participate. Below are just a few of the harassment tactics for the Pollywogs.
- Wearing heavy weather gear for hours in the sweltering equatorial heat.
- Walking, crawling, rolling, sliding, or being pulled, pushed, or dragged through, or simply being doused with a stinking miasma of rotting food, spent and new machine lubricants, elements of laundry duty gone bad, anything that fit the label "disgusting," including a large amount of substances whose origins were never revealed.
- Getting a custom haircut by the Royal Barber.
- Being stationed in a Gig for a few hours dressed in a Pea Coat and watch cap.
- Being flogged by socks filled with who knows what.
- Getting the Royal Electrocution by the electric prod of the Royal Electrician while lying prostrate on a salt water saturated mattress atop the steel deck or sitting in a chair in similar condition to assure good continuity.
- Kissing the Royal Babies' grease-filled navel.]

J-57, A GREAT ENGINE

As noted above we were en route to San Diego, CA on board the USS *Kitty Hawk*. However, Captain Walker, Commanding Officer of the USS *Constellation* (CVA-64) entered our Ready Room and announced that most our squadron would be assigned to his ship in the newly formed Air Group 13 and we would be based at NAS Cecil Field, FL.

Supersonic Fighter Pilot

It was quite a surprise knowing that as soon as we arrive in San Diego we would have to move to the East Coast. Since I was a bachelor this would be an easy move for me.

I reported to VF-132, *Peg Leg Pete's*, in December 1961. The squadron had new F-8U2NEs. Our Commanding Officer was Herk Camp and our Executive Officer was George Monthan. Our CAG was the famous CDR *"Gorgeous George"* Watkins. He was a bachelor and had a suite of rooms in the BOQ at Cecil Field, FL. Fortunately, or unfortunately, Tom Scott, John Holm, Mac Lupfer, and I lived directly across the hall from *"Gorgeous George."* That's another story.

Our new F-8s were all-weather fighters. So it was deemed by the powers that be that we should be night carrier qualified on the ship. After flying many night FCLPs we were scheduled to make our night landings aboard the USS *Independence* (CVA-62) operating off the coast of Norfolk, VA.

We hoped for a bright night with a full moon and smooth seas. But this was not to be. The January nights were cold, cold, cold, with no moon, and it was dark, dark, dark. Besides these conditions it was decided that because of this extreme weather they would require the pilots to wear cold weather survival gear called 'poopy suits.' These rubber suits looked like a cloth flight suit but it was waterproof. They would extend your life a few minutes if you had to land in the cold water. They were somewhat uncomfortable but not hard to put on or take off. However, we learned that there were no poopy suits available for our squadron. Well the "can do" Navy resolved that problem by commanding us to wear the high altitude full pressure suits.

I thought to myself, "You have got to be kidding."

Ron Knott

These "Moon Suits" as we called them took at least an hour to put on. They restricted the pilots' movement in many ways. Not only that but they muffled the customary cockpit sounds you normally hear during flight. In addition, the pressure suit tended to inflate and deflate with engine power changes. Mike Denham said, "It made you feel like the Michelin Tire Man." This was not going to be fun.

When the big night arrived for the first night carrier qualifications, all pilots on the schedule put on the awkward full pressure suits. I was in the first flight. Our F-8s were parked near the center of the ship. The aircraft were light loaded with fuel because we only needed a few thousand pounds for the landings. The lightweights caused the nose gear to extend higher than normal. That elevated the first step on the side of the aircraft several feet. There was no way that I could get my leg high enough to reach that first step, because the "Moon Suit" was so rigid. I had to have assistance. Thank God for my plane captain's support. By the time I had strapped in the cockpit, I was sweating like I'd just gotten out of a sauna. Man, those pressure suits are wickedly hot.

The start-up, taxi, and catapult were normal (if one can say night carrier operations are normal). Now it was time for me to earn those wings. My first approach was so high that all I saw was the WAVE-OFF lights.

"Wow, this is not going to be a fun night," I said. I finally settled down and completed five landings even though my knees were shaking. I had to give up my airplane to another pilot so he could get some landings as well. I would fly again later for that one last landing that I needed.

I promised myself to complete this last landing on my first approach. Once again the plane captain had to help me

Supersonic Fighter Pilot

reach the first step and strap me in the cockpit due to the clumsy "Moon Suit." I was sweating profusely again. The start-up was normal and I began to taxi forward to the catapult.

I heard a transmission over the radio from Mac Lupfer (bless his soul) say, "F-8 taxiing, you have sparks coming out of your exhaust!"

Full Pressure Suit (Ron Knott)

That really did not identify which airplane had the problem since there were six of us taxiing. Huh?

The flight director gave me the shutdown signal. I had to again un-strap and exit the aircraft in this full pressure suit. I got to the flight deck sweating buckets and was told to report to Flight Deck Control.

I was advised that I must have taxied over an electrical cable and this is what caused the sparks. My F-8 was checked by maintenance and they noted nothing wrong so I was cleared to fly the airplane.

Again, I had to have the plane captain's assistance to get into the cockpit. I was soon shot off the ship and came around for my final required landing. I only needed one more arrested landing and I would be night qualified. Although my knees were still shaking I made that critically important final landing and got out of the airplane so the next pilot could get his landings.

Guess who the next pilot was for my airplane was? It was none other than GAG himself, *"Gorgeous George,"* waiting impatiently for me.

He said, "I got it, Dongo."

CAG proceeded to make two A/B launches and two traps in this airplane.

When he got out of the airplane he said, "It sounded like all hell was breaking loose in the engine section of this *Crusader*."

The aircraft was taken below and the engine removed and inspected. Maintenance found parts of a one-quarter inch socket wrench in the turbine section that had destroyed the engine.

That Pratt & Whitney J-57 engine again proved itself to be the most reliable engine in its day. It had propelled the aircraft during five take offs and landings with major internal damage. Without question, I bet my life on the J-57, as we all did.

CHAPTER THIRTEEN

FLIGHT DECK LEVEL EJECTION

TERRY KRYWAY

LTJG Terry Kryway is photographed making a low level ejection from the deck of the USS *Roosevelt*. This famous ejection, in 1961, has been displayed, and rightly so, many times over the years. This ejection was the first, or one of the first, deck level ejections from the *Crusader*. And what is so renowned about this ejection is the fact it was caught on camera, in a series of very detailed photographs.

Note the explosion in the right wheel well

Rough seas prevailed that October day. This led to the right main landing gear strut exploding upon a hard landing, due to the pitching deck. The wheel broke off, went into the wheel well, and ruptured the main fuel line that caused an instant fire. This fuel-fed fire can be seen in the pictures. It is reported that the tail hook caught a wire, but parted from the shaft due to the excessive strain.

Kryway's hands are on the ejection face curtain

LTJG Kryway was considered an excellent pilot of Fighter Squadron 11 (Red Rippers), but the pitching deck was more than the Crusader's landing gear could handle. After the fire started Kryway was just along for the ride. However, due to his quick thinking he was able to escape the damaged aircraft before it crashed into the ocean.

The fire is intensifying. The engine has flamed out. The pilot must eject to survive.

Supersonic Fighter Pilot

The canopy is leaving the aircraft

**Note the pilot is ejected
clear of the plane**

Ron Knott

The canopy can be seen just aft of the aircraft. The pilot is inverted in the ejection seat overhead the Crusader.

**The Drogue chute is deployed
just prior to impact**

Terry hit the water and was rescued quickly by the helicopter. He only received a small abrasion on this neck from the incident. Needless to say, he was a very lucky pilot.

CHAPTER FOURTEEN

A REAL HERO

ED "MOFAK" CATHCART

The D6C was the 2,000 pound general purpose bomb with a chemical fuse. The Marine Corps used the big bombs for interdiction/road cuts on the Ho Chi Minh trail and the many routes that split off into "I" Corps and other Provinces of South Vietnam. The chemical fuses were designed to activate upon impact. The chemical would detonate the huge bomb between forty minutes and eight hours after the fuse was activated. These types of bombs had the purpose of discouraging overnight road repair on the Ho Chi Minh trail.

Death Angel Crusader aircraft carried two of these 2,000 pound bombs, one on each wing. One worry with the chemical fuse was the possibility that a bump while flying would activate the chemical fuse and could detonate the bomb before it impacted the ground. This was not just a theory, it could happen!

I was orbiting with a flight of two F-8s overhead the Brasserie just north of the Cambodian border waiting to drop our load of four D6Cs on the Ho Chi Minh Trail. Norm Marshall was leading the section and called off on his bomb run. I watched his bomb flight for contact with the road but noticed the bomb detonate in a fireball about 2000 ft. above the target. Since the bomb was dropped from about 6000 ft., there was safe separation between the F-8 and the explosion.

**Marine *Crusader* and "Mofak"
ready for an attack**

Premature detonation became a cause for concern by all pilots scheduled to drop these chemical bombs. However, no *Death Angel* pilots ever refused to take them on a mission.

A particularly dangerous situation occurred when one of the *Death Angel* pilots could not release a D6C from his *Crusader*. We knew that the fuse could have been activated and could explode somewhere between the forty-minute and eight-hour time after fuse activation. No one knew for sure when, or if the bomb would explode.

The pilot was ordered to land with the bad bomb and taxi to the end of the runway where another *Crusader* was parked. The ground crew would take the bomb off the incoming aircraft and place it on another F-8 that would transport it over the South China Sea for a safe drop, time permitting.

Finding a pilot willing to risk his life to fly the standby *Crusader* was another issue. Assigning a pilot to fly the potentially deadly mission was a tough call. Many troops and equipment could be seriously damaged if the bomb exploded on the air field.

Norm Marshall, *"The Animal,"* had a reputation for stepping up for risky assignments. Without hesitation Norm volunteered for the dangerous flight.

The duty bound ordnance crew quickly downloaded the D6C and attached it to the right wing of Norm's *Crusader*. Within seconds Norm was rolling down the Da Nang south runway on takeoff. He climbed out at maximum rate and headed for the Tonkin Gulf.

Rocket City

We all breathed a sigh of relief as he crossed the beach south east of Da Nang, but kept our fingers crossed for the safety of Norm. A few minutes later Norm called that the bomb was jettisoned safely and had detonated upon impacting the water. Norm was met upon his return by his squadron mates and treated like the hero he was.

Da Nang carried the nickname of "Rocket City" for good reason. The Viet Cong, with the arms and assistance from the North Vietnamese Regular Army, frequently launched Soviet manufactured 140mm rockets into the Air Base from positions within six miles of the runways.

The rockets were almost always launched at night which provided the greatest surprise and the most damage to both equipment and troop morale. I personally was a target of three night rocket attacks at Da Nang in 1967 when assigned to the *Death Angels* of Marine All Weather Fighter Squadron 235.

It was 3:10 AM on February 27, 1967 that I was first introduced to Soviet surface to surface rockets. Following a 2 AM diarrhea run to the ten-hole outhouse, I was lying awake on my cot in our four man hootch (building) at the Marine Air Group Eleven compound. We were located about 100 yards west of the Da Nang dual runways. My thoughts were on my wife and three small kids back in Pensacola, FL carrying on life without me.

A shrill whistle got my attention. Multiple loud whistling noises joined the original sound. The whistling was overhead!

I jumped off the cot and shouted, "Incoming! Hit the bunker! Incoming! Move it! Move it!" I grabbed my .38 revolver and ran for the bunker adjacent to our hootch.

My roommates, "Eagle" Ridings, "Rocky" Plant, and Colin Ruthven mumbled, "Crazy nuts!" and remained in the security of their bunks.

Supersonic Fighter Pilot

The whining rockets were really loud by the time I cleared the hootch door, and as I dove into the bunker. They were impacting the runways and taxiways just east of our hootch. WHOOOMP, WHOOOMP! WHOOOMP! Security sirens commenced wailing, and more rockets exploded. WHOOOMP! WHOOOMP!

My three hootch buddies suddenly were landing on top of me as they dove into our sandbagged bunker. I was nearly crushed by the pile of pilots. Being the first into the four-by-six bunker had its drawbacks. The rockets continued to walk up the runways. WHOOOMP! WHOOOMP! WHOOOMP!

Destroyed Marine F-8 by rocket attack

When the explosions stopped I commandeered the duty officer's jeep and hurried to the east side of the runways. East of the runways was commonly referred to as the Air Force side even though our hangar and flight line were located on the north end of Air Force side.

Six of our VMF (AW) 235 *Crusader* aircraft had shrapnel damage. One Marine was killed at our refueling site.

The Air Force did not fare as well with fourteen reported killed and thirty-five wounded. About 300 Vietnamese civilians were killed by several rockets that overshot the Air Base and landed in the adjoining village. And this is why we named the place *Rocket City*.

WINGS FOLDED TAKE-OFF

This is a story of a young Lieutenant who was transferred to the "Grunts" (ground troops) as a Forward Air Controller because of his reluctance to fly with his Squadron at night. He would down any airplane he was assigned to fly at night due to an apparent fear of flying in the dark. The Squadron had to get rid of him, and they did.

About three weeks later the Lieutenant called the squadron from the boondocks and requested a combat mission on the day flight schedule. He was placed on ten minute scramble alert duty with the Air Group.

Here is what happened: when the alert bell rang the pilots ran for their previously prepared *Crusaders*, jumped in the cockpits, started the engines and commenced taxiing for take-off. The flight leader hurriedly taxied onto the duty runway at Da Nang, waved a thumbs up at his wingman, and took off.

The "day only" Lieutenant was his wingman, and commenced rolling a few seconds later. *Boom!* Afterburner lit, the wingman took off with his wings folded.

So, the world's day land speed record for the *Crusader* was probably set that day. Before the plane reached the overrun separating the runway from the old French minefield, the pilot pulled the streamlined *Crusader* from the runway. He flew around the base in day VFR weather conditions thereby letting all the Vietnamese, Viet Cong, DOD civilians, Army, and Air Force personnel see how clever the pilots were in VMF (AW)-235. The ordnance was jettisoned and he made a safe landing but his flying days were over in the *Crusader.*

There were two successful flights in the F-8E with the wings folded in the same VMF(AW) 235 *Death Angel* squadron at Da Nang. The first such wing folded flight occurred less than a year prior to our FAC's daylight demonstration and was a night all weather spectacular.

The 1966 flight was at night and in the rain. The pilot folded his wings to taxi around a Pan Am 707 for takeoff. He forgot to spread the wings. He took off in the black rain probably setting the night land speed record in the *Crusader*. He yanked the aircraft into the air before entering the minefield at the end of the runway.

F-8 flying with wings folded

The pilot raised the gear after becoming airborne. Having no idea what was wrong with the *Crusader*, he turned downwind and declared an emergency on the Tower radio frequency. With all the flashing yellow and red lights, warning horns, black night, rain, soiled underwear, and uncontrollable urges for terra firma, the pilot forgot to put his gear handle back down.

Being a combat flight he had a box fin two thousand pound bomb on each wing station. The anguished pilot landed on the two 2000 lb. bombs with a mighty "Crash!" but nothing detonated except the Commanding Officer after he discovered what had happened to one of his valuable aircraft.

The pilot was medevaced (medical evacuation, usually by air) to the states with a fractured vertebrae and a tooth-shredded rectal orifice. Not exactly a hero's departure out of Da Nang Air Base.

USS SARATOGA (CVA 60)

She was a ship – not a boat! I can close my eyes and feel the screaming, electrifying, accelerating boot of the catapult launch. And then relive the harsh slam and chest crushing deceleration upon catching a wire on arrested landing. The many hours between the two moments of intense excitement during a sortie from the carrier have faded from memory. But, not the exhilarating seconds at the beginning and at the end of each launch. Many nights I relive the pure joys I experienced with *Sara'*.

Sara' loved rum goodies! That was why she kept a huge juice machine going all night in the wardroom. We carried large quantities of spirits aboard after each liberty run. Having booze aboard a Navy ship was against all regulations. If one was caught with liquor on board he would be in deep serious trouble to say the least. But the rum

Supersonic Fighter Pilot

goodies and other drinks of choice flowed in the secret parts of the ship.

The empty liquor bottles were accumulated until we had a 30-gallon garbage bag full. Then a gold bar, low on the pecking order, would be assigned the dangerous mission of launching the empty bottles off the fantail.

Our "grunt" ordnance officer was given the job one night about midnight, to launch the empties overboard. He was called Turk because of his closely cropped black hair and his handle bar mustache. Turk was briefed precisely how to make his way up to the flight deck, aft to the fantail, and told exactly how to launch the bag into the ocean.

We hit our racks. Next morning there was hell to pay!

It seems that the aft elevator was down. Turk went to the edge of the elevator barrier that dark night, thinking he was at the back of the ship, and launched his thirty-gallon bag of empty rum bottles onto the hangar deck of the elevator sixty feet below. The Officer of the Day was supervising movement of ordnance and support equipment in that area. The crashing and breaking of the bottles got his attention.

Next day, all COs and the Chaplain were doing a rug-dance. No fingerprints were taken from the glass fragments and no one confessed to the dastardly deed. The bug-juice machine was still operating the next night and the rum-goodies flowed as if nothing had happened.

Sara was great, and I miss her! – "Mofak"

Ron Knott

CHAPTER FIFTEEN

NEVER GIVE UP

BOB SHUMAKER

It was a dark November night, 1960, when I was flying from the USS *Saratoga* (CVA-60) in the Mediterranean Sea. My job description was "Fighter Pilot," which commanded me to fly the Supersonic F-8 Crusader. I was a dedicated Lieutenant who loved flying the Sader assigned to the Fighter Squadron 32 (VF-32), whose name was the *Sonic Swordsmen*. I really liked flying at night but probably had a change of heart after the events I'm about to describe.

The mission was simple ... just carry out intercepts on the other squadron aircraft which were simulating enemy bombers trying to attack the fleet. The ship's radar crew controlled these practice intercepts. After this mission was completed I was directed to the "marshal" point, which was a holding pattern behind the ship. The planes are directed there and given an approach time to start a decent to the carrier for landing.

This procedure is intended to space out the arriving aircraft so that they arrive for landing at the ship at one-minute intervals. I started my approach on time. When I got about eight miles from the ship I lowered the landing gear, raised the wing (similar to lowering flaps), and placed the tailhook handle in the down position. This is normal operating procedures for landing aboard the ship.

You have a safe indication in the cockpit when the landing gear is down and locked, and when the wing is up. However, there is no clue in the cockpit that the tailhook is down. The pilot assumes that the hook is down when the handle is down. (There is a light in the tailhook handle that indicates that the hook is moving out of the up position, but when the hook gets all of the way down the light goes out.) During day operations your wingman can make a visual inspection to see if, in fact, the hook operated properly. This is not possible at night due to darkness.

I called the "ball" (meatball) with 1400 pounds of remaining fuel (only enough fuel for about thirty minutes of flying time).

Now comes the time for precision flying! Landing a fighter aircraft onto a "postage stamp" in the middle of the ocean in daytime is dangerous to say the least.

Landing at night is a God awful death defying act. During this dangerous phase of carrier operations it is essential the pilot muster his wits and use all his skill to land on that moving object unharmed.

The pilot must wear the aircraft like a glove and precision is the key. You need to constantly monitor three conditions: the meatball, the airspeed, and the lineup. The meatball gives you a visual reference of whether you're high or low, the airspeed indicates whether you're fast or slow, and the lineup is critical to hitting the arresting gear squarely.

If you allow the aircraft to get too low on the glideslope you may get what is called a "ramp strike." That means the airplane hits the back edge of the ship, called the ramp. This type landing is usually not survivable. In fact, not only is the pilot in danger but the many personnel on the flight deck can be killed, or seriously injured as well, by flying fragments

Supersonic Fighter Pilot

from the crash. Therefore, a "ramp strike" can be devastating.

If you are flying too high you will overshoot the landing area, thereby missing all of the arresting cables. This is called a "bolter." It is usually survivable but it makes the pilot look bad. Navy pilots HATE to look bad around the boat. This is one place that you can't lie to defend your approach. All take-offs and landings on the ship are filmed and shown on monitors in many spaces of the ship.

The glideslope (meatball) is programmed to bring the projected landing spot of the aircraft just in front of the # 3 arresting wire. This is called the Target Wire. Every carrier landing is graded, and a "perfect" landing score is "OK 3-wire."

If the tailhook misses all the wires then a bolter occurs. The pilot applies full power, climbs back up to pattern altitude ("go around") for another approach.

The pilot's scan pattern on approach is usually: meatball, lineup, airspeed; meatball, lineup, airspeed; meatball, lineup, airspeed, until touchdown.

Incidentally, there are lights on the nose gear of the airplane that allows the Landing Signal Officer (LSO) to read your angle of attack (speed) during the approach. He can tell if you are fast or slow, or on-speed by these lights.

Now, back to my night landing story on the big boat: I made a perfect pass! Perfect except that the massive tailhook, which purpose it is to catch one of the arresting wires, had not deployed. By all indications in the cockpit the tailhook appeared down, but it was not down. In the old days this would have been disastrous for your aircraft would have plowed into airplanes parked on the carrier's bow.

Fortunately, our carriers have angle decks, which are offset from the ship's keel by about fifteen degrees. So if we miss a wire, we simply add power and try for a second pass. In my case it was three passes before it was determined that my hook had not extended. My tailhook was up so there was no way I was going to catch a wire.

STRIKE ONE!

"This is no sweat," I thought. "I will just head for the beach and land on a nice long runway." It just so happened that the nearest landing field (in Italy) was forty-five minutes away. That option was out because I did not have enough fuel to fly that far.

Again, this is no worry since there is always an airborne tanker overhead the ship for in-flight refueling during flight operations.

Finding the tanker at night is always a challenge though, especially so when your heart is beating extremely fast. But I did manage a quick rendezvous with the tanker aircraft. We made radio contact for the tanker to extend his refueling hose. The end of the hose has a basket-like attachment. The trick is to fly so that your fuel probe goes into the basket; then the tanker can pump precious JP-4 into your tanks. But something went wrong with the tanker. The hose simply would not extend.

STRIKE TWO!

Ah, well, there's always the barricade that I can fly into on the carrier. This thing looks like a giant tennis net twenty feet high and held up on each end by massive poles called stanchions. The stanchions normally retract horizontally into the deck and upon signal, are raised to the vertical position. The airplane usually sustains some minor damage as a result of taking the barricade, but it sure beats losing the entire aircraft and/or pilot.

So here I am, flying up the ship's wake with less than a minute's worth of fuel remaining.

Talk about sweating! Nervous sweat was rolling down my face and into my oxygen mask. When I breathed the bubbling sweat in my mask reminded me of an old time percolator coffee pot.

Would you believe that the stanchions failed to erect to the vertical? This was my last option to land on the ship and it failed as well.

STRIKE THREE!

By this time my Commanding Officer ran to Primary Flight Control to learn the exact extent of my predicament. He made the only logical decision available and that was to order me to eject. At least an ejection might save the pilot.

Now things are getting really serious.

Here I am in a perfectly good airplane, except the darn tailhook will not extend, so I can't make an arrested landing. Then, the in-flight tanker can't transfer any fuel to my aircraft. That means I don't have enough fuel to fly to a big beautiful airport and enjoy a few days of liberty. Now the dumb barricade is broken and I must eject from my place of security before the plane falls out of the sky like a 20,000 pound rock.

Ron Knott

"I should have called in sick before this flight," I thought, but it was much too late for that election. I had to deal with the problem that was thrust upon me.

"Climb and eject!" were my orders.

This is a command that a Navy pilot never wants to hear. But I knew that was my only option to save my life.

"How is this going to affect my career? What are my shipmates going to think? Is there any other possible way to get that tailhook down?" were my thoughts. All possible procedures to correct my dilemma had been exercised, and none of them were able to give me any relief. I must climb and eject!

I almost had to eject a few years back when I was first training in the *Crusader.* My instructor, Doc Townsend, and I were climbing above 50,000 ft. to make a high speed run. The "speed-run," as it was known, was a big event for the student. If he followed proper procedures and successfully completed the speed-run he would be awarded a little gold lapel pin that indicated he had flown faster than 1000 mph. This little pin would give the pilot big bragging rights to his sub-sonic buddies.

In my climb over 50,000 ft. that stormy day, I let my airspeed get too slow as I made a hard turn. That was the wrong thing to do! A hard turn at high altitude with low airspeed, guarantees the airplane will depart and a spin will follow. Spinning an F-8 is a vicious ride. I must assume it is similar to being in a west Texas tornado. You will read a story in this book by Ron Knott, called "Thunderstorm Flight," that indicates how difficult it is to recover from a spinning *Crusader.*

I lost about 25,000 ft., after fourteen whirling revolutions in the spin and finally recovered in a thunderstorm. Thank goodness I did not have to eject that day. I am sorry to say I did not get my 1000 mph pin that day. However, a few days later, I flew well above 1000 mph and was awarded the gold pin.

Back to the problems at hand – that is, I am flying over this dark ocean and must eject from my aircraft.

I started climbing to have as much altitude as possible before the engine ran out of fuel. I only reached four thousand feet when the engine quit with a deafening quietness. It has been said, "An engine failure is the loudest silence a pilot can ever hear."

When the engine quits, so does the hydraulic power to control the aircraft. The cockpit goes very dark very quickly because the generator has no rotation. The air conditioner and/or heater quits. Therefore, the pilot is just along for a terribly uncomfortable ride in an object that is rapidly falling out of the sky.

We're trained on ejecting procedures, thinking all the while, "I will never have to do that." We are instructed to position ourselves squarely in the seat because if you are bent forward, the tremendous explosive impact on your butt can break your back.

The instructors would say, "Position your neck and back in the position you want it to be for the rest of your life before you eject." That is a sobering thought, to say the least.

To initiate the ejection I had to reach overhead and pull the face curtain downward. The face curtain movement is what activates the firing pin and the explosive charge in the seat. The secondary purpose of the face curtain was to protect the pilot's face from the high windblast that will be experienced when departing the aircraft.

When the face curtain is pulled, at almost the same moment, the canopy blows off the aircraft. The seat explosively fires, you are ejected clear of the stricken aircraft, and the parachute opens automatically (provided you're below 10,000 feet).

All of the above is supposed to happen in less than two seconds. Well, that's what they advertise, anyway. We have all heard the old saying, "If your parachute doesn't work just bring it back and we will give you another one."

I blasted out of that sick airplane and felt the furious force of the wind. I counted, "One thousand and one, one thousand and two," (which is the way we're taught to keep up with the passing time), yet after these long two seconds my parachute had not opened.

STRIKE FOUR!

I saw the airplane splash in the water but I didn't feel the comforting tug of my parachute opening. Darn! The thing didn't work! Some days it just doesn't pay to get up.

I later calculated that I fell about two thousand feet, and I've got to admit to muttering a prayer or two. Mostly though, you react to your training which breeds instinctive discipline into your actions.

Although I had only one parachute there was a secondary means to deploy the chute. Just over your heart there is a "D" shaped ring which is supposed to open the chute manually in an emergency. This, I concluded, was indeed an "emergency." The first time I pulled it nothing happened.

Supersonic Fighter Pilot

STRIKE FIVE!

Then I yanked the ring a second time really hard and thank God, the chute opened!

The rest of the emergency was rather unusual, but uneventful. A destroyer picked me up and "high-lined" me to the carrier.

Fighter pilots are a weird lot and they often have a strange sense of humor. Imagine my surprise as I came aboard the *Saratoga* on a "boatswain's chair" to see my roommate standing there dressed in my cherished cowboy boots and Stetson hat. I guess he'd already written me off ... or maybe he was just pulling my leg.

The moral of this story: things are going to go wrong in our lives, and sometimes they go wrong in a chain of events. Life is too precious to succumb to these setbacks. Keep your cool and keep plugging away ... and I pray that your parachute will pop open and save your life just in time, as it did mine.

CHAPTER SIXTEEN

NAVY NORTH ATLANTIC

RON KNOTT

"Launch the duty fighter, enemy aircraft approaching the fleet!"

That ominous command put me in a terribly dangerous situation as you will read below.

We were operating off the USS *Independence* (CVA 62), which was at that time one of the largest carriers in the Navy. There was only one larger, the USS *Enterprise*, and she was the first nuclear powered aircraft carrier. The *Independence* was much larger than other carriers that I had been on so I felt more secure coming aboard her under any conditions (Little did I know!).

We sailed in the North Atlantic above the Arctic Circle for a few weeks. This was not only to test our intelligence but also to test the knowledge of the Russians. They knew we were in the area because a Russian "trawler" followed us around like a hungry seagull during this entire operation. It was humorous to see the Russian trawler answering "darken ship" signals flashed out from our ship, before the other ships in the task force could respond. This was part of the Cold War, the real cold war!

Our primary purpose was to antagonize the Russian bomber fleet of aircraft, namely the Bear, Bison, and Badger. We would intercept these aircraft and fly on their wing

Ron Knott

anytime they crossed an imaginary line 250 miles from the fleet. We knew when they got airborne in Russia but we did not want them to know that we knew. And we did not want them to know that we had the capability of intercepting them beyond 250 miles should a real threat arrive.

Crusader escorting a Russian bomber

In order to play this "cat & rat" game we would have two fighters join them as soon as they stuck their nose across the 250-mile circle and escort them all around the fleet.

All our fighter pilots were issued hand-held cameras and we would take pictures of any and all parts of the Russian planes. We were especially interested in antennas and other objects of curiosity on the Russian aircraft. In order to get good pictures we would fly tight formation on their wing.

Our Navy fighter aircraft would always fly in section (two aircraft) to protect each other in case the enemy got hostile. One fighter would stay aft, in killer position, in case the "Ruskies" tried to shoot down our big Brownie camera.

Our fighters could not stay in position with the long-range bombers for very long. Our maximum flight time was about two hours. To resolve this problem we would be relieved on station by two additional fighters from the ship

Supersonic Fighter Pilot

and this would continue until the enemy exited the 250-mile range.

Not only was this a military plan it was also a plan to save face with the media. If you remember seeing pictures of Russian bombers flying over the fleet you always could see two Navyfighters flying close aboard. The Navy was not about to let anyone think the Russians had slipped up on them as happened years earlier at Pearl Harbor.

In order to be ready for what might happen we would fly CAP (Combat Air Patrol) overhead the fleet during flight operations. However, after flight ops were secured two outfitted armed fighters would be placed on the catapults ready to be launched in seconds, should an enemy target approach the magic 250 mile circle. Pilots ready for action would man these planes.

This was usually a four-hour sitting watch in the cockpit, and was uncomfortable to say the least. We had to be strapped in the ejection seat, wearing full flight gear over our "poopy suits." The poopy suits were actually rubber flight suits that gave the pilot about twenty minutes more survival time in the frigid water. Without this rubber suit one would die of hypothermia in about five minutes. Some of our pilots broke out in a rash due to sweating in this garb with no airflow at all. We teased them about having diaper rash.

Our form fitted rubber flying suits were tested often. The test was to throw the pilots in the water off the fantail of the ship, and a helicopter would swoop down and pick us up by a dangling sling called the horse collar. We would know instantly where any leak was by the cold water rushingin and attacking parts of our warm body.

The other uncomfortable part of this drill was that the chopper would hover overhead at low altitude causing the propeller wash from the chopper blades to throw salt water at your face equal to the pressure of a fire hose. It felt like you were being sand blasted. Then these chopper pilots would sometimes take revenge on the fighter pilots since we called them "rotor heads." They would climb hundreds of feet in the air with us dangling in the sling below the chopper. It seemed like they would take their good time in hoisting us to safety.

I must say, the chopper pilots earned a lot of respect from all of us in recovering downed pilots from the water. They also made many daring rescues in Vietnam.

Being 250 miles from the ship with no rescue helicopters in the area, the rubber suit only prolonged the inevitable of the pilot taking on the form of a "fighter pilot popsicle."

In this far north operating area, way north of the Arctic Circle, it was much too cold to leave the canopy open during our ready catapult assignment. But with a closed canopy the air in the cockpit would get really musty. So we had to open the canopy every few moments just for fresh air. Sleeping in the cockpit was impossible. We could have used our oxygen mask for great breathing but that would deplete the precious oxygen we needed when airborne.

The worst situation was to be launched after about 3.5 hours, strapped in the cockpit, and needing to go to the bathroom. We knew that it would be at least another two hours before any relief was available.

They used to tell us, "Son, you can't buy experience like this in the civilian world."

And we would respond, "And you can't give it away either!" I suppose these were the "good old days."

I was assigned the duty fighter pilot on this particular brutal day. The conditions were considered too rough for the fleet to be flying due to the rough sea. Flight operations were cancelled, but not the duty fighter.

I knew that there was no way they would launch me in such conditions. The conditions were the following: green water was washing over the bow of the ship. That means that water, *not* water spray, somehow elevated itself eighty feet and was occasionally coming over the flight deck.

Another way to evaluate the conditions was to say that the flight deck was diving eighty feet into the North Atlantic. The latter was correct. It seemed I was pulling plus and minus 2 Gs just setting in the cockpit. In addition there was a thin sheet of ice that covered the entire flight deck. This condition made taxiing my aircraft almost impossible. In fact, it took about ten sailors on each side of my aircraft just to get me on the catapult. Each time the ship would roll starboard the airplane would slide right, and each time the ship rolled port we would slide left – this was a helpless feeling. My airplane was secured on the catapult with at least ten heavy chains.

All of a sudden the big bull horn sounded from Pri-Fly (Primary Flight Control) commanding, "LAUNCH THE DUTY FIGHTER!"

I forgot to tell you I was the only fighter pilot on duty that day due to the other catapults being obscured with ice and airplanes.

I thought to myself, "You have got to be kidding."

I had no radio contact with Pri-Fly due to the fact my engine was not running and I had no electrical power for the radio. I noted t the launch crew was swiftly removing the ten chain tie downs that had secured my aircraft. They were moving a portable ground starter toward my plane.

Ron Knott

"This looks for real," I thought. The deck crew gave me the two-finger turn up signal and pointed to my headset. I knew that this was a signal to call Pri-Fly.

Before I could call them they were calling me saying, "We have an unidentified target approaching the 250 mile circle and you must check it out. You will be launched as soon as the ship can turn into the wind."

"My goodness, they are not kidding!" I thought.

President Harry Truman said, "A leader is a man who had the ability to get other people to do what they don't want to do, and like it." I was going to follow orders but I can assure you that I did not like it!

I remembered the lyrics of my favorite song, *"Somewhere, over the rainbow, bluebirds fly. Birds fly over the rainbow. Why then, oh, why can't I?"* There were no dumb bluebirds flying that grim day and there was no rainbow kissing the sea or sky. So why, oh why should I? I told myself, "You wanted to be a fighter pilot, so just do it!" I did.

The waves were so high the Catapult Officer (The Shooter) had to time the frequency of the ships movement, up and down, before he could launch my aircraft.

Frequently the nose of the ship would be buried in a 30-degree dive into the icy North Atlantic Ocean. A launch under those conditions would plant me in the ocean. The next moment it might be climbing on the front of a wave with a 20-degree bow up attitude like a home sick pigeon. That attitude would work well in getting me safely airborne. All the while the ship would be rolling port to starboard 10 to 20 degrees. This was not a good day at sea.

Supersonic Fighter Pilot

I checked all engine instruments, hoping to find a major problem, but had no such luck. I determined that all systems were "go" and I was ready to fly.

It was bred into us pilots to never turn down a mission just because it was not the best one of the day. And besides, that there were 3500 troops on the ship watching this fighter pilot to see if he really was a *real* fighter pilot.

All take offs and landings are recorded and shown on monitors all over the ship. And who knows, this could have been the *real one* attacking our fleet! With all those factors in mind I made a final check of all systems, saluted the Shooter, and set back for the high G catapult shot.

The signal from the pilot to the Catapult Officer that he is ready to be launched is a snappy salute. The Cat Officer then gives the signal to his crew to launch the aircraft. The pilot is usually shot off the ship within a couple of seconds after the salute. At that time the airplane engine is at 100% power, sometimes with the afterburner blazing out a stream of hot air down the flight deck. The hold-back rigging on the bottom of the aircraft will hold the bird at full power until the catapult is fired. When the catapult is fired the hold-back is broken and you and the airplane go screaming down the flight deck.

The mega decibels from the jet engine are not comfortable to those on the flight deck. They want you airborne as soon as possible. My launch was delayed much longer because of the ships attitude. I still had hopes of Pri-Fly canceling the flight. No such luck – when the bow of the ship started up I was airborne in a flash. The catapult is about 250 ft. long. The plane is catapulted by steam power according to its weight and required minimum flying speed. In the F-8 *Crusader* we would get a shot (catapult) that would produce about 160 knots in about two seconds. There was no way you could keep your feet on the rudders with such force. The G forces were fore to aft, therefore, the pilot would not black out as in a vertical G maneuver. We felt like the Roadrunner cartoon as we were shot off the ship and would sometimes key the mike and say, "BEEP – BEEP."

About the time I was recovering from the Cat shot, Combat Control called and gave me vectors to the incoming target nearing the 250 circle.

"Your speed is GATE."

We had three speeds that Combat Control would give us in such missions: Buster, Saunter, or Gate. BUSTER meant full military power. SAUNTER means to conserve fuel. GATE, means wide open with full stereo (afterburner), speed of heat, max power, and the like. The F-8 would accelerate to supersonic speeds in just a few moments, even while climbing at 25,000 feet per minute. In less than ninety seconds I was at 30,000 feet, supersonic, heading for the bad guys.

Supersonic Fighter Pilot

My vector was in the direction of the incoming enemy. I tweaked my radar out to sixty miles (max range) to aid in finding the incoming bandit. In conditions like this the Fleet Commander will place a Destroyer (DD) stationed on the outer edges of the fleet. This DD would be equipped with radar to look even farther out for incoming targets. I was told to contact the DD. I dialed in the radio frequency for his controller, and reported my position.

"Roger, *Silverstep,* we have you in contact," was the reply from the DD.

I said, "Where is the bogie?"

They said, "It appears this was a false target. This is a condition that is sometimes caused by rough seas since our radar is not gyro stabilized."

Wow! I had risked my life for a false target and the most dangerous part was yet to come. I still had to land on the aircraft carrier that was bouncing up and down like a cork.

I thought, "I will not be a war hero; not even a consideration, but could easily die for my effort on this mission." I again had to chalk this mission up as one you can't buy in the civilian world.

In my ten-minute flight back to the boat I knew that my task had just begun. Being shot off the ship was dangerous but the pilot had very little control of that event. You were literally shot into the air. The flying to the target was routine. But I had to land on that same ship that was being beat around like a puppet by Mother Nature. This is no easy task under normal conditions and adding a pitching deck to the approach and landing made it even more stressful.

I was given, "Charlie on Arrival." That means that I could land as soon as I reached the ship. Since I was the only fighter airborne they were nice to me and made sure I had the ship's landing area all to myself.

In general, fighters come back with only enough fuel for about three landing attempts, four at most. This is due to the fact that extra fuel increases the landing weight and could cause the breaking of an arresting cable, or pulling the tailhook off the aircraft. That makes for a really bad day for a naval aviator.

Normally, if a plane needs more fuel due to a crash on deck or a bad landing day, tankers are airborne and available to give them another drink for more flying time by in-flight refueling. We called these tanker pilots, "Texaco Tankers." Since there were no tankers airborne that day I came back with enough fuel for about six landing attempts. Thank goodness I did.

On a normal carrier landing the pilot flies the approach looking at the "meatball." The meatball is a bright light transmitted on a predetermined glide slope. If the pilot follows that glide slope all the way to touch down, the aircraft will land in the middle of the arresting cables, which will result in a great landing.

If the beam of light goes high, this means that you are too high on the approach and if it goes low you are too low on the approach. The beam must be flown precisely in the middle. This meatball is gyro stabilized to keep the beam steady in case the ship is rocking and rolling. However, if the ship is heaving and bucking as it was this day the gyrostabilizer limits are exceeded and the light beam is not accurate. In this situation the Landing Signal Officer (LSO) will control the meatball manually to keep the pilot on a desired glide slope. In other words, he puts the beam where he wants you to fly. In addition, he can judge the frequency

Supersonic Fighter Pilot

of the waves and try to get you on board when the ship is relatively level. In most cases the pilot is not able to see the movement of the ship on his approach. His thoughts are 100% on staying on the correct glide slope. He is saying to himself, "Meatball, Line-up, Airspeed" all the way to an arrested landing.

However, this day I could see the ship's movement clearly and violently. At one moment the ship would be in a 20 degree left roll and the nose high, which is impossible for a landing. That would be like flying into a wall. Next glance, it would be nose low, rolling both left and right. Several times I thought I could actually see the screws (big props) under the fantail of the ship. "Surely not," I thought. I knew that I was going to be in trouble trying to land in such conditions.

The LSOs are wonderfully professional. They are trained for hours just for such conditions as these. The LSO on duty that day was highly qualified. As I recall, his name was Bill Wheat. His soothing voice would calm my tight nerves as he transmitted to me on each landing attempt. He would let me fly in as close as possible, then hit the big red flashing WAVE-OFF lights that meant it was unsafe to land.

I got the WAVE-OFF signal on my first five approaches. And I was doing everything correctly. The LSO would not let me land due to the fact I might destroy more parked airplanes on the ship than a Kamikaze. I only had enough fuel for one more attempt to land on the big boat. If I did not land on this sixth attempt the plane would flame out due to fuel starvation. My only option then would be to eject and make a nylon (parachute) let down into the icy water of the Atlantic Ocean. You can bet I was calling on a Higher Power to help me get this beast on board that big boat. Thank goodness He was watching over me and I was allowed to continue this last approach to a final landing.

I can honestly say that when I felt the tailhook engage I was the happiest man on board the USS *Independence*. There is no doubt when you catch an arresting cable when landing on an aircraft carrier. The aircraft goes from about 160 mph to 0 mph in about two seconds. The landing is just the opposite of the Cat shot when you accelerate to flying speed in less than two seconds – the aircraft decelerates just as fast.

No one had to tell the pilot that he had made an arrested landing. His neck will stretch as his body is thrown forward due to the tremendous deceleration. It feels like some mighty, mystic power is kicking you in the back, trying to push you through the front of the cockpit. And just when you think this is a real possibility the pressure is quickly released. The world will come back into focus again as you taxi across the foul line. You must move from the landing area quickly so another pilot/plane can play the same dangerous game.

Taxiing on the deck of an aircraft carrier can be as dangerous as standing on a high ledge of the Grand Canyon. Space is a most important commodity on the carrier. There are almost eighty aircraft on board. Therefore, each one has to be placed as close to the other and as close to the edge of the ship as possible. The reason carrier aircraft are designed with the capability of folding their wings is to make room for more planes. The pilot must be very careful not to taxi into another plane or to taxi over the side of the ship.

I have seen aircraft taxiing on a slippery flight deck that was soaked with oil, fuel, and rain. The ship would roll to the side due to heavy seas and over the side would go a multi-million dollar machine and pilot. That eighty-foot fall to the water would usually result in death to the pilot.

Even after the pilot has parked the plane and the crew had secured it with many chains his life still could be in danger as he egresses the cockpit. Many times the cockpit will be hanging over open water. Again, the reason for this is space. The Flight Deck Officer would have the planes taxi forward until the nose wheel is at deck edge. The nose wheel on most fighters is well behind the cockpit area. Therefore, when the pilot stepped out of the cockpit there was nothing below him but blue water. He may have to carefully crawl up on top of the aircraft and walk back toward the tail until he has a solid flight deck below him.

A pitching deck gives little comfort during this maneuver. Many pilots and maintenance personnel have fallen overboard and some were lost at sea due to this procedure. One of the maintenance men in my squadron fell overboard at night while working on an airplane. No one saw him fall or heard his scream due to all the noise on the ship. It was several hours before anyone realized that he was missing. A search was conducted but he was never found. That is the sobering reason we have muster frequently, to make sure "All hands are present or accounted for!"

Even though the pilot completes the mission, makes a safe arrested landing, and egresses the cockpit without injury, his worries are still not over. He must walk from the forward part of the flight deck back toward the aft end of the ship to get to his squadron's Ready Room. It has been said, "The area of a flight deck during flight operations is the most dangerous three acres in the world!" There are mules (little tow tractors) dashing all around. Aircraft are landing just a few feet away. If an arresting gear cable should break, it will kill and/or mutilate all within its path. If an airplane crashes on deck this usually results in fire and fragments flying all over the place. So, until the pilot is safe in his Ready Room, he can't afford to relax.

I was a happy camper on board the big boat that rough day in the North Atlantic but my problems were not over yet. I had to taxi out of the landing area. As I stated earlier there was a thin sheet of ice all over the deck. Each time the ship would roll port or starboard, the aircraft would skid in that direction.

Finally, the flight deck crew got enough chains and tie downs on the bird to keep it from taking a salt-water swim along with the pilot. No "church" service this day for one happy pilot.

The ship's Captain came down and congratulated my airmanship. The flight surgeon gave me a few ounces of brandy. Alcohol was forbidden on board except after a night landing or after a hazard experience such as this mission. I headed to my State Room for a little R & R (Rest & Relaxation).

The ship was still bucking and heaving like a wild bronco. Lying in my bunk, it felt like I was pulling plus and minus 2 Gs. The Navy provided us with wide leather straps to secure our bodies to the bunk in such conditions. This keeps us from falling out of our bed onto the steel deck in such violent weather. Again, you can't buy adventure like this in the civilian world.

After my Navy flying I joined the airlines. Many times I was amused at the response of some of my co-pilots complaining about how hard and dangerous airline flying was. Little did they know! I felt like I had retired when first taking the airline job even though I did have many

Supersonic Fighter Pilot

challenges there as well. But nothing compared to landing, day and night, onboard an aircraft carrier.

As we used to say in the Navy, "If you don't scare yourself at least once during a flight you are not doing your best." And so it was on the USS *Independence* (CVA 62).

CHAPTER SEVENTEEN

EJECTION OVER ARIZONA

BOB HOCH

In July 1973 my Reserve Photo Squadron, VFP-306, was scheduled to deploy from NAF Washington, DC to NAS Miramar, CA for our annual two-week active duty training. The rest of Air Wing 30 was completing their annual active duty training at NAS Fallon, NV. These two commands were to make a coordinated attack on one of the targets in the Nellis restricted area just south of Fallon. I was XO of the squadron, a LCDR at the time, and I was to be the advance party, arriving at Miramar the day before the rest of the squadron.

Saturday morning LCDR Bob Norrell and I departed NAF Washington in two RF-8Gs loaded with cameras full of film. En route, we were to take pre-strike photos of the targets and have the photos developed at Miramar in order to have the pictures ready for the target planning.

I led the first leg of the flight to Little Rock Air Force Base. We stopped there for a quick refueling and were on our way. Bob led the flight to Arizona. The weather was clear with only a few buildups over Oklahoma. We had no trouble deviating around the storms at our cruise altitude of 39,000 feet.

Soon we entered a thin cirrus layer of clouds but we started a climb above them. As we climbed through 41,000 I heard a really loud compressor stall (like a backfire) from my engine. Almost immediately my engine flamed-out (shut down). This really got my attention.

I called Bob and reported my flameout. I pulled the throttle to idle and thumbed the igniters and then waited for the re-light. I went through all the emergency procedures for a re-start but the engine would not re-light. My only choice was to extend the Emergency Ram Air Turbine (RAT) for electrical and hydraulic power.

Bob joined on my wing as I went through the re-light procedures. I was able to modulate the fuel flow, which was a good indication that the engine would start. I punched the clock each time I hit the igniters to ensure that I gave the timer the full forty-five to sixty seconds that was required to obtain a re-light. If I recall the handbook correctly, re-lights were not guaranteed above 20,000 feet so I expected that a re-light would certainly occur once I descended below that altitude. However, when I passed 20,000 feet the engine still would not re-start. Apprehension started to build in the cockpit. In the simulator, eventually, the engine would always re-start!

"This was not fair," I thought!

As I passed through 11,000 feet I told Bob that I would try one more attempt to start the engine and if that failed I would eject.

Albuquerque Center, who had been listening to our conversation, told me they had a helicopter heading my way. I had tried to re-light the engine for more than twelve minutes with no luck. So it was time to vacate the airplane.

I ejected at about 9,500 feet. My airspeed was about 220 mph and I thought, "This feels exactly like the ejection seat trainer." I looked down at the aircraft and I could see an empty cockpit where I had been sitting just a few seconds before. That was a strange feeling.

The parachute opened automatically as it was designed to do. As it did my feet flew up to the horizon and then swung back down again. I watched the aircraft descending in a gentle left turn and impact on the side of a hill. "What a waste," I thought. The crash made a big explosion and caused a grass fire in the area. (An old WWII aircraft flew over later and dropped water on the area extinguishing the grass fire.)

The descent was peaceful and quiet and I could see the towns of Miami and Globe, Arizona in the distance. I also noticed some cows grazing in the rocky valley below. I wasn't worried about surviving; I just didn't want to break anything on landing.

I was going to drop my mask when I reached about fifty feet so I could judge the distance to the ground. Suddenly, and I emphasize suddenly, I hit the ground like a sack of concrete with the mask still in my hand. I marveled at how fast I had traversed the last fifty feet to the ground. When I came to rest I checked for broken bones and was thankful I had none. I'd lost an airplane, a set of my uniforms, my civilian clothes, and my briefcase.

I spread the parachute out so it would be visible from the air. Bob was flying overhead my position in a left hand orbit. He could only stay in my area about twenty minutes due to his low fuel quantity. I waited for the rescue team to arrive.

Soon I heard a C-130 coming my way. It flew directly over me. The ramp was open at the rear and a crewmember in a flight suit waved at me and I waved back.

I noticed that this C-130 was equipped with the large U-shaped fork mounted on the nose. They had used these type aircraft to extract downed pilots during the Vietnam War. The way it worked was as follows: they would drop a package containing a harness for the pilot to put on and a large helium balloon with a long steel cable. The downed pilot was to put the harness on, inflate the balloon, and tie the steel cable to the harness.

The C-130 would then fly by and snag the cable hoisting the pilot in the air. They would winch the dangling pilot into the aircraft. I had seen the video of this device and it was horrific. I determined quickly I was not going to be jerked from the ground in such a manner. In fact, I had planned to use my survival knife to poke holes in the balloon if they dropped me one. Thank goodness this was not the case.

The C-130 began orbiting my position.

Then I heard a voice behind me asking, "Can you use some help?"

I turned to see a man and a young boy walking up the hill, hand in hand. They had been out riding trail bikes and saw me floating down in the chute.

I replied, "I could probably use some help. What did you have in mind?"

He responded, "I can give you ride into Globe on the back of my Honda."

We introduced ourselves and shook hands. I told him that a helicopter was allegedly on the way but I would like for them to stay until the chopper arrived.

The C-130 came over again and dropped a small metal box attached to a parachute. It hit the ground about a hundred yards away. It had a PRC-90 two way radio, three pop top cans of emergency drinking water, and three cold cans of Coors beer.

Supersonic Fighter Pilot

Being a naval officer first, I said to Mr. Bell, "Would you care for a beer?"

He said, "Yes, thanks," and we popped the top on two of them. After a sip or two we fired up the radio on guard channel.

When I talked with the C-130 crew they said, "Don't go with the guy on the motorcycle. The helo is only five minutes away. And we need our radio back, and don't tell anybody about the beer."

The Air Force H-34 helicopter appeared in short order. A short, stocky Air Force sergeant ran up to me, asked if I was okay, then grabbed the box and the parachute. I put my helmet back on and mounted the helicopter.

The chopper pilot and copilot were seated above the passenger compartment so all I could see was the back of their legs. They reached down and shook my hand.

After ten minutes or so I retrieved the remaining beer and sat back down. I popped the top and was sitting there holding the can. It was obviously still cold because it was sweating. When the sergeant turned to look at me he did a classic double take. I could tell that he was wondering how I got that beer but he never said a word.

About thirty minutes later we landed at Williams AFB just outside Phoenix, and were greeted by the Base Commander. Bob Norrell and the C-130 crew were there as well. I thanked all of them.

Bob and I rode the ambulance to the dispensary. A flight surgeon took a urine sample and a blood sample and then took about forty x-rays. The x-rays revealed nothing broken but the flight surgeon told me that the urine sample and blood sample showed that I had been drinking. I told him that he hadn't seen anything yet and explained about the beer.

Ron Knott

During the accident investigation the engine was disassembled but no cause for the compressor stall was discovered. The engine had been reworked a few months earlier and it had accumulated only 31.5 hours since that rework. It was never determined why the engine failed or why it would not re-start.

I am very appreciative for the maintenance crews who packed my parachute and maintained the ejection system.

Thanks, you saved my life.

CHAPTER EIGHTEEN

SAYING FARWELL CRUSADER STYLE

GARNETT HAUBELT

This isn't a war story or one of blood and guts, but a vignette where a few *Crusmen* from different locales and times came together to celebrate the end of an era.

It is truly amazing how the 1929 (more or less) *Crusader* Drivers, who flew the F-8 *Crusader,* could experience the same feelings for this trusty old bird ... whether you flew it during the 50s, 60s, 70s or in its retirement years of the 80s and 90s.

In the summer of 1975 CDR Bob Crowl, Executive Officer of NAS Chase Field at Beeville, TX, inquired if there was a possibility to have a static display of a *Crusader,* at Beeville, TX for the retirement ceremony of the Base Commanding Officer, Captain Robert E. Ferguson.

"Fergie," as he was known, flew the *Crusader* with VF-124 (Ops Officer) from 1959 – 1963, VF-51 (XO & CO) from 1965 – 1967 and as CAG 5 in 1967.

It just so happened that Detachment Three of VFP-63, was on a short shore tour at Miramar, and they were elated to provide the request.

Captain Ferguson was transitioning from a fine military career of over thirty-two years of Naval Service to his country to that of civilian life. The decision was made whereby, not only a static display would make a wonderful compliment for such a great career, but a fly-by would be even better. If a fly-by in afterburner was better what would a section fly-by going "Gate" at the same time be like? *Crusader* drivers don't just "do" something unless it's done "right," so the mission was on.

CDR John Peck and I set out to accomplish the mission. Manning our *Crusaders* for our trip from Gunfighter Land to Training Land was the start of a mission that has been firmly burned into my aging brain.

It so happened that the Big Man in the sky was looking favorable that day and provided the best of weather. It was relatively cool (for a southern Texas August day), calm, and not a cloud in the sky. Our planning paid off, big time.

We checked in with Chase Field tower about seventy-five miles out and requested a high speed, low altitude fly-by. CDR Crowl had laid the groundwork for our arrival and the pattern was cleared of all aircraft. Permission was granted for our low-altitude, high-speed fly-by. Chase Tower didn't know what a high-speed, low-altitude fly-by meant in *Crusader* language.

We approached the northwest boundary of the field in super tight formation at 550 knots, and with the oil cooler doors open (this provided mega decibels of an eerie whining sound that would excite the women and kids). Our altitude was somewhere between the ground and the top of the hangar. The hanger doors had been cracked open about fifteen feet (we were later told it was more for audio effect than cooling). We selected "Stereo" (afterburner) as we flew past the hangars. The metal hangars and the folks trembled as our two Chariots of Fire flew by like rockets gone wild.

There is nothing quite like the sound of a *Crusader* going into afterburner at warp speed, particularly when they are at eye level. You can only imagine the effect we had at this event, especially when it all happened at the moment Captain Ferguson's foot stepped on the pavement as he was coming down the gangplank; going from military life to that of a civilian. CDR Crowl surely received the "last mission accomplished" award by making this great fly-by a possibility.

"By the completion of the beautiful, precise, finale I must admit that I was in complete meltdown. The total surprise, exact precision and timing of the fly-by as I departed the ceremony was the final frosting on the cake. I had no idea there would be an F-8 fly-by. It was a complete surprise. It is, to this day, one of my most vivid, treasured memories," were some of his subsequent remarks about the honor we had the pleasure of bestowing upon him.

So much so that by the time we had pulled up and came around for the break doing either a "fan" or "tuck under" break (can't remember which ... if either), landed, taxied to the OPS tarmac and shut down, Fergie's replacement, Captain Red Issacks, who in his own right was a first class LSO and MiG-Master himself, met us with four beers in hand ... one for each of us, even before our feet could hit the TARMAC!

"By orders of the retiring CO," we were told!

Nothing could keep Captain Issacks from whisking us away to the reception as it was his command and the "command" of Fergie to be in attendance in order to receive the proper, "Thank you from the bottom of my heart!"

I can't remember how many hands I shook that afternoon after being introduced as, "These are the Gator Drivers that made my day!" Here it was, his special day, but the Old Salt of a Mig-Master Captain showered us young pup Lieutenants with more congratulations and "attaboys" than we were due. It's stuff like this that warms the heart, at least mine and one retired Navy Captain! F-8s Forever!

CHAPTER NINETEEN

TO KILL A CARRIER

ED "MOFAK" CATHCART

The USS *Shangri-La* CVA 38 was a beautiful sight from 17,000 feet overhead! The huge gray ship was clearly visible against the deep blue Atlantic Ocean. The white numbers '38' stood out boldly between the forward elevator and the bow of the wooden carrier deck. The carrier made a majestic panorama as it was entering a 180 degree turn towards the aircraft recovery heading.

The *Shang* was not nearly as big as the USS *Saratoga*, but my Marine Fighter Squadron welcomed the *Shang* over the *Intrepid* and the slow *Lexington*. It was a very well run ship.

Some folks are surprised that Marine pilots operate from aircraft carriers as well as Navy Pilots. The training for the Marine and Navy pilots is basically the same. Conversely, the Marine pilot's mission is usually for close air support of the ground troops and operates off of land base runways. However, on occasion, a Marine Squadron will be deployed onboard the Navy Carriers along with other Navy Squadrons.

The busy, durable *Shang* had just finished a six-month Mediterranean Sea cruise in mid-August. The sailors had expected to be in their homeport for several months before having to go to sea again. But as you know, the need of the service comes first and for some reason the *Shang* was put to sea again for another short cruise. This did not improve the morale of the Navy crew.

Marine Crusader on the catapult

The date was 22 September 1964. My squadron, the *Warlords* of VMF (AW) 451, was assigned to the carrier for the short cruise in the Caribbean. Most of our squadron pilots had over forty carrier-arrested landings in the *Crusader* and were highly competent when operating from the ship. The *Shang* had a superb reputation and we considered our orders as a great opportunity to excel.

The sixteen *Warlord* F-8s orbited overhead until receiving a Charlie time (landing time). The *Crusaders* then descended in four-plane divisions, moved into the correct flight spacing, and flew up the right side of the ship in tight parade formation. With our tailhooks dangling like wasps stingers, each division of the sleek *Crusaders* passed the island at 500 feet and 350 knots. We were determined to

Supersonic Fighter Pilot

make a good first impression. The breakups and pattern were nearly perfect. Our approach, arrested landing, and deck procedures reflected a high level of experience of my squadron. My pride suffered badly as a hook skip bolter caused me to go around.

It was great to be back to the land of excitement assigned to an aircraft carrier! The screaming, stomach-thrilling, rapid acceleration of the booming catapult was excitement for us all. We eagerly anticipated the hard-jarring, crushing, arrested landing that some had rightfully called a "controlled crash." We were all professionals in carrier operations and wanted all the others on board to take notice. But, we had one junior pilot who was a 2nd LT (gold-bar) that made most of the capable pilots very nervous.

The Skipper had rushed this young pilot through Phase I for his carrier qualification training. The young pilot barely made the flight time requirement. He was dubbed *"the Wedge"* after demonstrating that he was the "world's simplest tool." *Wedge* could be expected to perform in sync with Murphy's Law. Most of us knew that *Wedge* was going to be a problem when landing on the ship.

We flew a heavy schedule right from the start of this cruise. I was division leader (four aircraft) and *Wedge* was in the number four aircraft in my division, as a wingman on the section leader. We were catapulted off the ship individually and had briefed to join up near the ship as soon as the division was airborne. None of us could find *Wedge* after he was catapulted off the ship. He didn't rendezvous with the division, nor did he come up on any radio frequency. We were not aware that he had a radio failure until after he landed. Frantically, we tried to find *Wedge*.

An airplane from another squadron reported observing a *Crusader* chasing flying fish about twenty miles from the ship – that was *Wedge*. *Wedge* finally showed up at the ship after every one had landed. His first two attempts to land were unsafe and he was waved off by the LSO. Finally, he made an arrested landing on the third pass. *Wedge* mentioned that he had only 200 lbs of fuel after he landed. This meant that his aircraft would have flamed out due to fuel starvation in just a few minutes had he not landed on that pass. He broke all of the rules of flying around the ship that day.

After his unsatisfactory performance I told the Ops Officer to never schedule *Wedge* to fly with me again. *Quaker* Rice, our young and talented LSO, asked the Skipper to ground *Wedge*. The Skipper chewed on *Quaker* while stabbing his index finger inches into *Quakers* chest. The Skipper said that *Wedge* had wings therefore he must be qualified for the carrier.

The next afternoon *Wedge* was launched from the ship again. This time he kept his radio procedures and his flight fairly routine. That is, until recovery aboard the ship.

He called, "*Sader* ball, three point one, manual."

The LSO acknowledged by saying, "Roger, keep it coming." A few seconds later the LSO called, "Power! Power!" (This is usually the first indication that the pilot is getting himself in deep, serious trouble.)

Then the LSO screamed, "POWER! POWER! WAVE-OFF! WAVE-OFF!" This frantic call from the LSO was necessary because *Wedge* was about to kill himself and others, by flying into the back of the ship. He had gotten much too low on the approach. W*edge's* airplane did hit the round down (back of the ship) just aft of the main landing gear. The left gear collapsed and the tail section burst into

Supersonic Fighter Pilot

flames. The F-8 bounded up the angle deck looking like an ignited napalm canister. Fire and wreckage covered the flight deck.

The doomed *Crusader's* hook snagged the last wire. *Wedge* hit the afterburner (full power) during deceleration. This caused the plane to pull out an excessive amount of the arresting cable. In fact his airplane hung over the port side of the ship and came to rest in a 90 degree bank angle. The bottom of his airplane was pressed against the side of the ship. The aircraft's nose was pointing toward the bow of the boat while the windswept burning fuselage and the afterburner roared into the ship's ventilation system.

Crusader hitting the ramp

The LSOs on the platform were being barbecued by the big fire and had to quickly evacuate their duty station for obvious safety reasons. Bob Lawrence remembered the afterburner plume and the blazing fire fanned by the wind across the deck hitting directly on the Fresnel Lens (it was completely melted before the fire was extinguished).

The crash crew personnel pulled *Wedge* from the cockpit. Typical *Wedge*, he was quickly yanked back toward the fire by his oxygen hose which he had forgotten to disconnect from the seat pan. After what seemed an eternity, the deck crew finally shut off the engine thereby securing a lot of the hot gases going into the ventilation systems of the *Shang*.

The fresh air intake for the ship's ventilation system was just aft of the crash site on the port side. The smoke and debris from the burning tires, fuselage, jet fuel, hydraulic fluid, and other materials were carried throughout the ship's interior via the ventilation ducts.

The inside of the carrier was virtually a fecal sandwich. The soot and black tar substance from burning debris that entered the air ducts was even inside our safes. The staterooms were virtually unlivable.

The other two pilots who were flying high above the *Shang* observed the inferno on deck and knew that there was no way they could land on the burning ship.

They said, "We are out of here and en route to our land base runway at Marine Beaufort."

The aircraft that were still on board were catapulted ashore the following morning. *Wedge* had the distinction of almost single handedly destroying a fine sailing ship of the US Navy. The ship had to go into dry dock for extensive repairs for many months after this accident. Although his squadron mates looked down on *Wedge* he was somewhat of a hero to the sailors on the ship. Many of the ship's crew came to visit us that last night at sea and toasted our squadron for terminating the cruise early. Their shore period had been much too short anyway. "Request permission to go ashore, Sir!" Marines – 1. Navy – 0.

Supersonic Fighter Pilot

Wedge had the proud distinction of being the last Naval Aviator to land on the wooden deck of the *Shang*. I was told the old wooden deck was replaced by steel during the post accident dry dock. *Wedge* lost his wings a few weeks later by a Pilot Disposition Board.

The next chapter indicates how *Wedge* looked from the LSO platform.

CHAPTER TWENTY

FROM THE PLATFORM

BILL RICE

Mofak was, and still is a Fighter Pilot's fighter pilot. I would like to offer a few editorial comments that might be helpful in filling in some of the little known facts about the *Wedge*.

The *Wedge* was fairly good in the aircraft with his "hands and feet." However, he demonstrated little or no headwork in support of his hands and feet. You never knew what he might be thinking or even if he was thinking. There was absolutely no telling what the *Wedge* might do in any given moment in any situation.

The *Wedge* had absolutely no business being anywhere near an aircraft carrier, let alone a carrier conducting fleet operations. The Skipper had decided that the *Wedge* would be on the squadron roster for the upcoming Springboard cruise on board the USS *Shangri-La* (CVA-38).

The *Wedge* flew night and day to get through the tactical qualification syllabus and the FCLP requirements. After three weeks of FCLP practice bounces, I informed the Skipper that the *Wedge* would not be ready to make the upcoming cruise.

Whereupon, I was ordered, "YOU WILL HAVE HIM READY."

No, the Skipper was not happy. After the final work up session and prior to going aboard the ship, I informed the

Ron Knott

Skipper that I would not certify the *Wedge* for shipboard operations.

The Skipper hit the roof and quickly informed me that he, as Squadron Commander, did not need my certification to decide whom he would have on the squadron pilot roster for the cruise. Indeed he could, and did exactly that, in spite of my written recommendation against such action.

I was working the platform (LSO) during the recovery cycle of VMF (AW) 451. The CAG LSO, a Commander, arrived on the platform as an observer. He asked if he could work the last *Crusaders* just for practice. I recommended against working this *Crusader* since the pilot was low time, and very unpredictable.

The CAG LSO, somewhat arrogantly (probably because he was talking to a Marine), said that the pilot's lack of experience or unpredictability would present no serious problem for him. So like a good Junior Officer, I stepped aside and the CAG LSO assumed control of the LSO platform.

I recommended to the CAG LSO not to accept anything other than a perfect approach and by all means do not attempt to "work" *Wedge* to the deck.

That is precisely what the LSO did. As the *Wedge* entered the stack burble there was a slight reduction of power, the nose dipped slightly, and the CAG LSO gave the typical call, "Power – don't settle – fly the ball" – instead of hitting the wave off lights.

I immediately called "POWER, POWER, WAVE OFF, BURNER, BURNER!" using the override phone. But it was already too late.

The burner kicked in but the *Wedge* was already too low and headed for the ramp. The observers on the platform were heading quickly for the escape net. The aircraft trajectory had started to climb – but the aft empennage of the aircraft hit the ramp just forward of the ventral fins, and exploded in a large ball of fire.

I pushed my writer off the platform and immediately followed right behind him into the escape net, amid a cloud of burning magnesium and F-8 bits and pieces.

On the second bounce the aircraft engaged the # 4 wire and was now hanging suspended over the port side deck edge, supported only by the tailhook and right main landing gear. The aircraft was still in afterburner and was torching the Fresnel Lens, and the crewman assigned to monitor the lens and light systems.

The boys in the asbestos suits opened the canopy, reached in and shut off the engine master switch, released the seat fittings and lifted the *Wedge* onto the flight deck. He was not injured. Those two firefighters were real heroes that day and probably received little or no recognition for their outstanding service.

The *Wedge* was clearly in a state of shock and totally oblivious to what had just happened. He was seemingly unaware that those two sailors, by their selfless quick action, had just saved his life.

Skipping over a lot of details related to the smoke, collision alarms, discharge of the hangar deck fire extinguisher system, and general confusion in the aftermath of the ramp strike, there was a very clear call coming over the sound system.

"LSOs report to the bridge."

When I reached the O7 level, the Skipper met me. He told me that the incident was entirely his responsibility and that in the meeting with CAG and the Captain of the ship I was to speak only if spoken to or asked a direct question.

There we were, the 451 Squadron Skipper, the CAG LSO, and yours truly "standing tall" on the green carpet in front of CAG and Captain of the ship. We were waiting for the roof to fall on us.

The CAG LSO volunteered that he was the LSO working the aircraft. The Squadron Skipper, man that he was, stepped up and attempted to take full responsibility for the entire incident.

The one sided verbal tirade from the other side of the table was something to behold. I would never want to experience that kind of tongue lashing ever again. Most of the incoming verbal bombardment was directed toward the CAG LSO and Squadron Skipper.

And that, as they say, was the end of that story. Well, almost the end. There were some fairly serious repercussions that resulted from this accident.

1). There were serious burns to the sailor working the Fresnel Lens. 2) The aircraft carrier had to return to the port for repairs. 3). A beautiful F-8D *Crusader* was lost. 4). The Squadron Skipper, who set the entire incident into motion that day, reached his "terminal velocity" in the rank structure. 5). The *Wedge* lost his wings!

In any event the planned *Springboard* cruise ended just two weeks after it started. The Marines received a standing ovation from the Navy crew because the ship had to go into port for repairs. Arrogance will do it to you every time!

[Authors Note: The remarkable Pete Shepherd of the British Navy's Historical flight said the following, "Prince Charles was on a visit aboard Ark Royal. Pete, as LSO, was

Supersonic Fighter Pilot

given the job of showing him around but *His Royal Highness* made it clear that he would like to visit the flight deck during land ons. Pete explained as much as he should, but further told *HRH* that it was a dangerous place to be and particularly pointed to an escape chute that went down a deck or two in the event of a nasty."

Pete went on to say, "Sir, this chute should be used as an emergency exit for both of us on my say so. That is to say that if an aeroplane, or a wire breaks, that is the way we go. Sir, one other thing, your Mummy has no doubt told you that you are first in line of descent, but I am here to tell you that should there be an emergency you will follow ME in the descent."] ☺

CHAPTER TWENTY-ONE

NIGHT PHOTO MISSION

CHUCK ANDERSON

"Bong – Bong – Bong! General Quarters! General Quarters! This is no drill! This is no drill!"

From a sound sleep in my stateroom at 0200 in the morning, I flew out of my rack and put on my stinky flight suit in seconds. Then, I ran to the Ready Room to see what the emergency was all about.

This was in the spring of 1965 aboard the aircraft carrier, the USS *Ranger* (CVA 61), which was located about one hundred miles east of Da Nang, Vietnam. The Vietnam War was hot and heavy during this time and we never knew from one day to the next what might happen, or what mission we might be assigned.

I was trained and assigned to fly the RF-8 (photo version of the F-8 *Crusader*). Instead of having guns and missiles it was equipped with cameras for intelligence collection. This is the same model airplane that took pictures of the Soviet missiles during the Cuban Crisis. It was used to take pictures of suspected enemy targets for bomb damage assessment (BDA) and the like. They nicknamed the aircraft as *The Eyes of the Fleet.*

This fast machine could take pictures from all altitudes, day or night. For night photography the RF-8 was armed with flares that the pilot could detonate when needed. These flares (flash bombs) produced 1.5 million candlepower of light. That is almost like looking into the bright sun.

When I arrived at the Ready Room I was told to put on my flight gear and hurry to my airplane that was waiting for me on the flight deck. The authorities told me that I would be catapulted off the ship and would be given my orders by radio, after getting airborne.

When I arrived on the flight deck it was very, very dark. There is nothing darker than being in the middle of the ocean at night with a heavy overcast sky. That night there were intense clouds in every direction. It has been said, "Darkness on the ship at night is as black as black can be." However, I manned my aircraft like a pony express rider heading for the next relay.

My aircraft was parked on the stern of the ship. The catapults they were using this gloomy night were on the bow of the big boat. That means that I had to taxi almost the full length of the ship, about 800 feet, to get to the catapult.

Taxiing on board an aircraft carrier is tedious in the daytime. At night it is terrifying, to say the least. These are just some of the circumstances the pilot must deal with when taxiing for a night launch. The deck is dark (no taxi light is allowed because this would blind the deck crew). The ship is rolling, rocking, and vibrating; the taxi director is giving you signals with bright baton looking objects; you feel movement, but you don't know if it is the ship that is moving or if your aircraft is moving; you have no references of speed; you may even get vertigo before reaching the catapult.

Then they shoot you off in the dark night and expect all your reckoning to be precise. You have this "tiger by the tail" that went from zero airspeed to almost 170 mph in about two seconds. You better be flying this beast within these two

Supersonic Fighter Pilot

seconds or it will be "church" for you at the next memorial service. Therefore, rapid recuperation of your senses is essential if you plan to stay among the living.

They shot me off that big boat and then transmitted for me to join up with an F-4 *Phantom* who would act as my fighter escort to the target. Fighter escorts were necessary because the photo mission had to be flown precisely, in order to get the needed intelligence. Therefore, the escort duty was to protect me from any enemy aircraft attack while I was making the pictures in my fast flying "Brownie camera."

I climbed up through the lower overcast, which was at 300 feet. That first overcast now became an under cast as I found myself sandwiched in between it and another overcast layer that was at an altitude of 3,000 feet. I climbed above the 3,000 foot deck to be on top of all the clouds. When I got there I found that there was no moon and no stars, due to another cloud layer at 15,000 feet. It was dark, but I found the F-4 in this black sky. We made radio contact and headed for the target area. My call sign was *Papa 302* and the escort's call sign was *Papa 303*.

I was then instructed that our mission was to photograph a large number of high-speed watercraft that had been detected by Da Nang radar. Intelligence thought these small boats might be North Vietnamese torpedo boats. We had to make a positive identification before we could take action against them. They could have been "friendly boats" as well. It was my job to take their picture this dark night, bring the film back to the carrier, and the intelligence folks would determine if they were friend or foe.

When we arrived at the target area I told my escort, *Papa 303*, to orbit overhead while I went down through the under-cast to see what was down there. I broke out below the under-cast at about 300 feet and was shocked at what I found. There were about 50-75 white lights spread out on the water below me.

I dropped down to one hundred feet altitude to fly over a couple of the lights. They all looked like small sampan fishing boats from my position. I lined up to pass over three of them that were almost in a row. As I flew over them I set off a series of the 1.5 million candlepower photo flash bombs to take their pictures; this lit up the entire area. The photo flares were like big lightning flashes that penetrate many layers of clouds.

Instantly *Papa 303* radioed in a loud scream, "*Papa 302, pull up!* They are firing at you!"

I pulled the *Crusader* almost straight up, applied full power and got out of there. *Papa 303* said I came through the clouds like a Roman candle.

In his most excited voice, *Papa 303* told me, "There were great gun flashes near your position."

It was at this point that I realized that my escort, *Papa 303*, had never seen a photo flash flare explode producing a 1.5 million candlepower flash. What he actually observed was my photo flares going off and thought I was being shot at. No one had been shooting at me. Oh well, at least I had a picture of three small boats to take to the intelligence group on the carrier. And I am sure that the folks in the little fishing boats thought that they had met their Maker that black night.

Papa 303 and I joined up and started back to the ship when I noticed that my hydraulic warning light came on. When I checked the hydraulic gauge it also indicated a complete hydraulic failure. I learned later that this failure was not caused by a hit from the enemy, but from a failed line in the hydraulic system.

Supersonic Fighter Pilot

I radioed the ship and told them about my hydraulic failure.

The Air Boss said, "Do not return to the ship in this predicament."

They ordered both of us to go directly to Da Nang Air Force base and land. Consequently, *Papa 303* and I headed for Da Nang.

Although the hydraulic pressure was gone I could still safely configure the airplane for landing, by using the emergency air bottles that would blow the gear down and the wing up. When we arrived at Da Nang the tower told me to make a high steep approach as the Viet Cong were shooting at airplanes on the landing path.

With no hydraulic pressure I had no hydraulic brakes as well. This is a no brainer for a Navy pilot since all their carrier type airplanes have a tailhook and can make an arrested landing. Consequently, upon landing I put the tailhook down to catch the safety wire on the overrun end of the runway to stop my aircraft.

As I touched down the tower operator said, "*Papa 302* you are on FIRE!"

I stopped the bird as quickly as I could and jumped to the ground to get away from the reported fire. As I was running to the edge of the runway I looked back to see my burning aircraft. There was no fire. All this confusion was caused because the Air Force tower operator had never seen a Navy plane land with its tailhook extended. When the steel pointed tailhook drags across the runway a lot of sparks are created that can easily be confused for a fire, especially at night. This was the second false alarm for me in one night.

Papa 303 landed and I gave him the precious film to take back to the ship. There I was with a broken airplane, at the Da Nang airport, and it was 3:30 in the morning. I walked over to the maintenance shack and met a tall, slim Vietnamese pilot, in a tailored flight suit, with a purple scarf around his neck. This just happened to be Major Kee, the Squadron Commander. (He later became president of South Vietnam and ended up in California after the war.)

I only had my dirty stinky flight suit and I was tired and needed a place to sleep. The sergeant on duty told me that the Officers Club was open 24 hrs a day and they would know where I could bunk down. They directed me to a barracks with an extra cot. I finally went to sleep about 4:30 AM.

The next morning I met some Aussie *Caribou* pilots. They had just landed after taking a few 12.5mm rounds through the cockpit. (Thank goodness no one was hit.) I apologized for my stinky flight suit and told them my story of how I arrived at this airport. They were very friendly chaps. We enjoyed exchanging war stories for the next few hours.

Finally, the next day, the necessary parts arrived to repair my airplane. After the repairs were completed I flew back to the USS *Ranger*. And that was just another day/night in naval aviation.

BACK IN 1964

I had a similar experience during the 1964 cruise on *Ranger* (CVA 61). I was assigned the duty of flying the photo *Crusader* with VFP-63 on that cruise. One dark morning at 2 AM I was launched off the ship along with four A-4 *Skyhawks* and a tanker aircraft. My mission was to make photo bomb damage assessment (BDA) on a truck farm in the middle of the jungle after the A-4s had dropped their bombs. The A-4s spent an hour dropping flares looking for the truck farm but never found their target.

This left me with a lot of fuel in my tanks and forty 1.5 million candlepower photo flash flares. It was standard operating procedures not to land on the carrier with these photo flares due to safety reasons. I could have just dumped these flares in the ocean but that was no challenge – I had a better plan. We were near Route One on the west side of Vietnam. This was one of the main roads the enemy used to transport their supplies to the south. There was a full moon that night so Route One was really easy to see.

I started to descend down to treetop level and headed straight down Route One traveling above the speed of sound. As I approached the large intersection of the road I released the forty – 1.5 million candlepower photo flash flares directly on top of the enemy, and got out of there as fast as I could.

My flight was a two-fold harassment on the enemy. The shock wave (sonic boom) produced by the supersonic fly-over is enough to knock a man down and break windows on the ground. Then add the exploding forty flares at treetop level for the fireworks, and you have disrupted any sense of security for hours. To this day I bet there are some Viet Cong who are still going around blinking their eyes in wonder. This was my only shot in anger!

IN FLIGHT REFUELING

Another interesting night occurred in August of 1964, while flying off the USS *Ranger.* That dark night over North

Vietnam I had a generator failure. I lost all of my navigational aids, plus I started having radio problems, so I headed for Da Nang AFB. By the time I got to Da Nang I was low on fuel and needed to land; however, there had been a crash on the runway and the field was closed. I asked the tower if I could land on the taxiway. They said it would take ten minutes to clear the area.

I circled at 15,000 feet and watched the fuel gauge go lower and lower. All of a sudden one of our A-3 tankers appeared (he had overheard my fuel problem and had come to my rescue). He gave me the "take fuel" signal and I gave him thumbs up. He then headed out to sea toward the carrier and deployed the hose and drogue. I flew up along side of him and shook my head and gave him an "orbit" signal as I didn't want to get too far away from Da Nang if I could not plug in.

The tanker started to orbit to the left and I made my approach but being in a turn caused the drogue to drift out to the right every time I got close. I over shot once and slid under the drogue and it bounced off the canopy and banged a complete circle around the cockpit before I could back out. By this time my fuel was really low. I had to get plugged in to that tanker or swim. Just as I got close to the drogue it started to slide out to the right again so I pushed in right rudder and goosed the throttle and bang, I connected! By using my considerable skill I managed to ease the plane back into position and started to take on fuel. It sure was a great feeling watching that fuel gauge increase. We then flew back to the ship and I landed A-OK. This was just another exciting night of carrier aviation.

CHAPTER TWENTY-TWO

MY MiG – ALMOST

HENRY LIVINGSTON

I was assigned to Fighter Squadron VF-211 as a first-tour aviator during a hectic phase of the Vietnam War. I joined the *Checkmates* in April 1971 and remained with that squadron until December 1973.

On 20 June 1972, CDR Jimmy Davis, VF-211's Skipper, was shot down over Mu Gia Pass, which was one of three major exit routes from North Vietnam into Cambodia and Laos. He spent two awful days and one night on the ground before he was rescued.

He had made a strafing run on an area he had just bombed, violating one rule literally written in blood: "Never fly over the same ground twice." The 23mm flak sounded like someone knocking on his door. His F-8's hydraulic system came up red and the stick froze. He ejected in a flat spin. When his chute opened the shock was so strong it paralyzed one half of his body.

Fortunately, the jungle was deep but the Karst Ridges were also very steep. We kept an airborne vigil with A-4s in orbit and an occasional F-8 working with the on-scene commander to sanitize the area.

The *Sandys* – the Air Force A-1 *Skyraiders* from Thailand, finally arrived. I was on my way to the scene when one of the *Sandys* called, "I'm hit and I'm losing it!" He bailed out. Now there were two pilots on the ground in enemy territory.

The *Jolly Green Giants*, the Air Force rescue choppers, came in and rescued the *Sandy* pilot, but they could not retrieve CDR Davis because the enemy was too close to him.

The following day the *Jolly Green* started his run down the valley to make another attempt to rescue CDR Davis. CDR Davis was flashing his signal mirror and in accordance with Murphy's Law the sun went behind a cloud, which made the signal mirror ineffective. The helicopter pilot could not see him and turned the wrong way. However, there was an alert A-4 pilot overhead that noticed the problem and directed the helicopter pilot over to CDR Davis. CDR Davis caught the jungle penetrator hoist and was returned to the *Hancock*. He was a bit too stiff to fly for a while but at least he was not a POW.

Shortly after CDR Davis returned to the aircraft carrier an Army General named Hollingsworth, bedecked with pearl-handled pistols and a big brass belt (we thought he was surely the son of George Patton), came aboard and strode into our Ready Room.

He demanded, "Who is the son of a gun that diverted air strikes from my Military Zone III Corps in South Vietnam?"

We all were standing at attention except for CDR Davis, who had remained seated due to his wounds. He simply answered the irate General by saying, "I did, Sir!"

The general looked at him for a moment in total silence. Then he said, "I'm darn glad to have you back but next time don't cost me so many air strikes!"

He then began to describe what an incredible job the F-8s had completed when bombing the town of An Loc, north

Supersonic Fighter Pilot

of Saigon near the Cambodian border. He continued to tell us that although they were surrounded by three North Vietnamese regiments with 100mm guns and tanks. The South Vietnamese had held the town for more than sixty days. It was the first battle where the communists used tanks. Every tactical Navy aircraft, including *Crusaders*, had been stacked up three or four flights high as they waited their turn for the Forward Air Controllers (FAC) to bring them down to bomb the town's perimeter.

I had been in that circus over An Loc. Brian Foye and I were a section of F-8Js loaded with MK-83 bombs and 20mm cannons. We checked in with the *Pave Nail* the OV-10 FAC and he directed us around the southern perimeter. The wind was about two knots from the southwest.

FAC said, "I can't work you down unless you can give me precision bombing." He was trying to lay down ordnance on a column of tanks approaching the town wall on the eastern side. The lead tank had come out of the jungle and started toward the wall.

Brian had the lead when the FAC called us down on that lead tank. Brian rolled in, diving down between columns of white clouds and I watched him until he went out of sight below one of the clouds.

I arced around to the roll-in point at 12,500 feet, 220 knots, and could see the concentric shockwave of an MK-83 bomb that detonated near the tank. I watched the tank moving sluggishly into a crater that was filled with water. I lined up my sight and adjusted the sight to 107 mills. A quick glance showed that I was in a 65-degree dive, which feels like you are going straight down.

My airspeed increased toward 400 knots and my altimeter staggered around the dial, plunging toward the

6500-foot release point. When all the necessary numbers looked good for a bull's-eye, I released the bomb. Suddenly, the F-8 gave its characteristic wing flex as the half-ton bomb released from my wing. After a slight pause, the Gs began to increase as I began to pull my nose up when I came across the target. I could see the broken trees, craters, and a smashed tank. The air was dark under the clouds but the smoke was thick. I thought I was going through the gates of hell.

I pulled the nose up hard to recover from the steep dive. I knew that I had stayed too long over the target and had a classic case of target fixation. Target fixation has killed many pilots when they spend too much time looking at the target and go below the minimum safe altitude for recovery.

I did not know at this time that the tank commander had abandoned his tank. In fact he ran toward the jungle to get out of the target area. But his crew had been chained to their positions. Brian's bomb had exploded so close to the tank it got the commander's attention. And he knew that another bomb would hit this same area within thirty seconds. About thirty seconds later my bomb did in fact, detonate on target. It upended the tank and blew the escaping commander away as well.

General Hollingsworth handed out pictures that were enlarged to 3' x 2' of the tank. I am proud to say that was our target and it really took a beating. The tank was captured and eventually set upon a cement block in Saigon as a memorial to the Battle of An Loc.

Both fighter squadrons, VF-24 and VF-211, were used as bombers in 1972, but only in South Vietnam. In North Vietnam we did not bomb, but were fighters doing escort of BARCAP, TARCAP, MIGCAP, photo escort, or *Iron Hand*

Supersonic Fighter Pilot

SAM suppression missions. We were also assigned as flak suppressors, going in ahead of the strike force to protect the A-4 *Skyhawks* as they maneuvered into position to bomb their targets.

Route One north of Vinh usually had something interesting going on. It was a visible landmark although the AAA and SAMs were always present along that road. This made for vulnerability, to say the least. As we flew through layers of clouds over the rain soaked rice paddies and hamlets below, we could hear radio chatter that one flight had found a new target. It reminded me of a bunch of young hunters noisily scrambling into the woods after their quarry.

Suddenly there was a *Mayday* call. Repsher and I were jinking in tight combat spread, less than three-quarter mile abeam. We were loaded with two *Sidewinders* each and had 20mm as well. (Repsher and I were roommates as well as assigned wingmen.)

The *Mayday* call came because LCDR Tom Latendresse had ejected in a wild spiraling ride from his damaged A-4. He was in the number two aircraft on the flak site. He had taken a direct hit and had to eject from his wounded aircraft. When he hit the ground his right arm was wrapped behind his back and his right hand over his left shoulder. He was laying on the ground near his parachute in the muck of a green rice paddy. His chest was heaving from shock and one of his legs had almost been severed at the knee. He managed to push out his PRC 90 (the small personal survival radio each air crewman carried) and began a labored transmission for help. After initial difficulty in making a clear call, he finally came through loud and clear.

"I'm surrounded ... send some ordnance down!"

Repsher and I were first on the scene and by coincidence were already in a 10 degree strafing perch. *Sheepdog* called in hot, as he was entering a firing position. I began to set up the Search and Rescue (SAR) effort.

Finally, Repsher and I rolled in side by side at only 800 feet above the ground. Looking through my gun sight I adjusted my hits with the rudders to avoid hitting the downed pilot and his chute. I tried to walk a burst of 20mm cannon fire at the approaching black *pajama clad Viet Cong* troops that I saw approaching his position. We watched the enemy closing in on Tom through the tall grass and Repsher and I heard Tom's last transmission.

He transmitted, *"I'm surrounded. Don't shoot. Tell my wife I love her!"*

Then it was quiet.

All of our military aviators had the idea that if nothing else made sense we were sure going to do our best to rescue our downed pilots. So many lives were wasted by the political leadership – the only morals left were our own. In other words, instead of Washington assigning targets of bridges and suspected truck parks from photos, the leaders should have gotten a fix on winning the war and not with a half-and-half military-political response. Great news! LCDR Latendresse was eventually released in 1973 after becoming one of the last POWs of the war.

The *Chicago* controller immediately turned us south toward a "bogey" and asked us to come up on secure voice radio frequency. As we were checking in we were advised that a *Red Bandit* was headed towards us from the Haoi/Haiphong area. (*Red Bandits* were MiG-17s; *Blue Bandits* were MiG-21s.)

Supersonic Fighter Pilot

I asked my flight lead, Ed Schrump, if he didn't smell a rat because the North Vietnamese never sent a solo MiG-17 out over the water.

The *Chicago* came right back with, "Oh, yeah, there are six *Blue Bandits* in trail."

Ed and I thought it sounded like a fair fight. Since my radar was the only one working in the flight he passed the lead to me, at which point I went under the hood (radar), and back to our clear combat frequency.

As our two heavy F-8s, armed with *Sidewinders* and cannons blasted head-on toward the MiG gaggle, the MiG-17 began to make a slow left turn, effectively crossing our bow. That gave us a perfect rear aspect intercept, except we were still forty miles away from the MiGs. We were really closing in on the bandits. A MiG-17 was dead ahead of me but going faster than I was. At seven miles we were still not getting good visual identification on the aircraft. At five miles the *Chicago* ordered us to break it off because we were crossing the magic no-go line. We continued after them a few seconds more. Finally, we had to break away about 2½ miles from the MiGs which was just out of *Sidewinder* range.

I almost got a shot at a MiG, but it was not to be.

CHAPTER TWENTY-THREE

COLD CAT MIDWAY

HANK SMITH

Here is the account of my "F-8 Cold Cat" incident. I have used this accident in many ways and to different audiences to underline the importance of knowing your emergency procedures, without having to refer to your procedural manuals. This story was really useful when I taught Human Factors topics in the School of Aviation Safety at the Naval Postgraduate School in Monterey, California.

I was told at the time I was the first pilot ever to get out of an F-8 alive after experiencing a "cold cat shot." The date was 28 July 1959 aboard the USS *Midway*, off the coast of California during a missile shoot exercise.

I thought the F-8 was a fine, fine airplane and I was really happy to be flying it. It commanded a tremendous amount of respect and I always treated it that way. As a junior officer with time to spare I frequently went over my emergency ditching procedures and demonstrated that I knew them cold. I tried to abbreviate them as much as possible. But I always left out the last part of the procedure, which was to inflate my Mae West. "That was a no brainier," I thought, "Any fool in the water will remember this simple procedure." I just concentrated on the things I really needed to remember.

Ron Knott

In conversations with my roommate, Pat Crahan, after our CAP (Combat Air Patrol) missions, he would mention how boring he thought these flights were because all we did was fly in a race track pattern about 200 miles from the carrier. I told him that I thought they were exciting because the pilot requirements were light enough that I could practice my emergency procedures and they got me all juiced up. He said something to the effect that I must be some kind of masochist.

On this July day, I was assigned to fly F-8A Bureau No. 145390. I arrived five minutes early to man my airplane. Harry Sarajian, a squadron mate, was in the airplane that I was assigned to fly. In fact, I had to climb up on the side of the airplane and bang on the canopy to get Harry out of my bird. He did not want to get out because we all wanted as much flight time as we could get. In fact we all wanted more flight time. Reluctantly, Harry slowly got out of my *Crusader*. He did not know it at the time but getting out of my aircraft was a very smart move on his part that day.

Shortly after I strapped in the cockpit I received orders to launch. I taxied to the single catapult on the angle deck. The deck crew hooked my aircraft to the catapult. I checked that all systems were ready to go, selected afterburner, and gave the cat officer the customary salute, indicating that I was ready to be shot off the ship.

The *Shooter* dropped his arm, which was the signal to the catapult crew to launch my jet. Immediately, my aircraft started down the catapult tract. At first, everything seemed normal and I was thinking, "I have another exciting cat shot."

However, about halfway down the catapult track I heard a loud explosion under the nose of the aircraft. It sounded like a 20mm cannon going off. Instantly, my head came

Supersonic Fighter Pilot

forward and my body slammed into my shoulder straps from the rapid change in acceleration. I made a quick peek at the airspeed indicator, and it told me that my speed was only about 110 knots. The airplane needed at least 150 knots to fly! I knew that I had to do something and I had to do it quick.

F-8 getting ready for cat shot

I immediately pulled back the power to idle and got on the brakes as hard as I could. I tried to steer the airplane up the straight deck with nose gear steering. The area up the straight deck was clear. I was hoping that I could get the airplane stopped before I went over the side of the ship and into the ocean. But I quickly discovered that was not an option because when the catapult pennant blew out from underneath the airplane it broke my hydraulic lines and thus made my nose gear steering inoperable. In addition, it was clear to me that my braking was ineffective on the steel deck. (Later I was shown pictures of smoke streaming from my tires as I was trying to stop.)

Many friends asked me why I didn't just eject and get out of the airplane. The answer is that I was out of the envelope for ejecting. The ejection system in these early *Crusaders* required that you had to have at least 200 feet altitude and 90 knots of airspeed for the seat to function properly. I had the airspeed but the deck was only sixty-three feet from the water. I didn't have the altitude I needed so I stayed put in the airplane.

When I determined that the aircraft could not stop I jammed the throttle back to full power. I had hoped to get into afterburner and become airborne with what little deck I had left. Hope springs eternal, doesn't it?! As I glanced down at the engine rpm gauge it was obvious I was not going to get the extra power needed and I was going to get wet!

After going over my emergency ditching procedures in my mind, I still had about twenty-five feet of deck left before making the high-dive. At that point I remember relaxing somewhat, because there was nothing more that I could do until I hit the water. And when the bubbles stopped I would get out of the aircraft.

Our water ditching training was adamant about waiting until the aircraft stopped moving before trying to unbuckle and get out of the seat. As I left the edge of the deck, I had enough elevator control to keep the nose of the aircraft about 30 degrees nose down. I didn't want to go straight in because the plane would go deep. I didn't want to hit the water at a flat angle because I was afraid the impact might break my back. I remember the ride from the deck to the water as being very pleasant and quiet. The guys in the catwalk had a strange look on their faces as I went by them.

Supersonic Fighter Pilot

When I hit the water all hell broke loose. The airplane literally exploded! The wings came off, the engine blew turbine blades up onto the flight deck, and the front of the canopy broke. All I remember seeing at that point was pure white water coming into my cockpit so forcefully that it pulled my oxygen mask to one side. Water was forced down my throat even though the mask was still fastened to my helmet. I reached up and pulled the mask back into place with both of my hands so it would act as a barrier to the tremendous water pressure. The water pressure was so great it felt like a fire hose was being directed right into my face.

The cockpit filled with water rapidly. The airplane seemed to be rolling around and around. I waited for what seemed like a long time for the bubbles to stop. It was getting dark fast. I knew that I was sinking fast and I was afraid that I would not be able to make it to the surface. I decided to pull the ejection seat face curtain to shoot me out of the cockpit. I pulled it three times and nothing happened. Then I realized that I was going to have to get out of the airplane manually. I pulled the "T" handle near the sunscreen which sheared the rear canopy hinges. This also activated a 2600 psi bottle of nitrogen that blew the canopy up about six inches. I pulled my umbilical cords (oxygen, g-suit and radio cords) with my left hand, squeezed the ditching handle with my right hand, and chinned myself with both hands on the canopy bow to free myself from the airplane.

I did the breaststroke to get to the surface. As I reached the surface I noted that the carrier was now about one and a half miles away from me. I was gasping for air. I was carrying so much weight in addition to my body weight. A pilot normally has about fifty lbs of survival gear attached to his body when he leaves the cockpit. One should get rid of the unnecessary items as soon as possible. That day I had my backpack, parachute, seat pack with raft and other supplies, boots, torso harness, g-suit, helmet, oxygen regulator, mask, .38 pistol in holster, belt of .38 ammunition, flight suit, survival vest with an additional ten pounds of equipment, and my un-inflated Mae West. Every wave that came by engulfed me because my mass was so great that I could not ride up with the swells.

Significantly, I never remembered to inflate my Mae West. Every time I went over my emergency ditching procedures, I always left that part out. I figured any dip$#@& who was in the water would naturally think of inflating his Mae West! But I was in cognitive overload. It was all I could do to keep my head above the water as each wave went by.

Fortunately, it was not necessary to attract the plane guard helicopter. In a very short time it appeared overhead. The crew lowered the horse-collar slowly for me to place around my body. I had to hold my head under water to maintain a position suitable for hoisting. Man, was that ever a chore! I was gasping for air whenever I could and holding my head underwater while they took the slack out of the cable to hoist me up. When I finally got inside the door of the helo the crewman couldn't believe all the gear I had on.

He kept saying, "Jesus Christ, you're a strong swimmer!"

Finally, I said, "You'd swim, too!!"

After the traditional shot of brandy I hiked back to the Ready Room still soaking wet. I went over to Harry Sarajian and said, "Harry, I'll never take your airplane again!"

Larry Renner, our schedules officer, said, "I told him I heard the screws of the ship go by as I sank with the airplane."

Supersonic Fighter Pilot

Two days later they shot me off again and this time, it worked as advertised. But just to emphasize what a tremendous effect this cold cat shot had on me, every time after that when I saluted the cat officer my whole body was shaking in convulsions all the way down to my feet on the rudder pedals! The only way I could calm myself down before the shot, was to tell myself that it was going to happen again on this shot and to get ready. "You did it before and you can do it again," I thought.

Part of the reason for all my concern was that the problem with the catapults was not fixed. It was the result of a manufacturing defect in the swegged claw of the catapult pennant. After my accident they reduced the number of uses of the pennant from unlimited to one hundred shots. About two months later another F-8 on the USS *Hancock* had the same thing happen and they reduced the number of uses to fifty shots. Then two months after that another *Crusader* on the *Hancock* had a 'cold cat' caused by a bad pennant and it reduced maximum allowable uses to ten shots!

I guess it's understandable why my body turned into a shaking blob on every cat shot for the rest of our 8 1/2-month cruise. I can say *there was a lot of shaking going on*. But I did not quit flying. In fact I loved it.

CHAPTER TWENTY-FOUR

THE GUNFIGHTER

ROBERT KIRKWOOD

All the fighter pilots in my squadron wanted to shoot down a MiG – that is what we had trained for. Getting a MiG was the ultimate prize of a fighter pilot. Pilots would actually try to talk you out of your mission if they thought you might meet MiGs in the air! Both of the F-8 squadrons on board our ship wanted to shoot down MiGs in the worst way.

The Vietnam War was escalating and the Navy needed pilots badly. They were so short of pilots they were assigning Lieutenant Commanders to jobs normally occupied by junior officers. I received orders to the F-8 RAG (Replacement Air Group). After completion of the training I was sent to Fighter Squadron 24 (VF-24) on board USS *Bonhomme Richard.*

The North Vietnamese Air Force normally didn't fly while we were airborne. However, on the afternoon of July 21, 1967, I was about to get a good look at some MiGs.

That day four of our fighters were assigned to escort a strike force composed of eight A-4 attack aircraft, to their target. We didn't expect to see MiGs on that mission. It was a beautiful day for flying. Our squadron XO (Executive Officer), Red Isaacs, and his wingman, Don McKillip, flew below and right of the formation while my wingman, Phil Dempewolf, and I joined on the left side.

I saw some MiGs as we were flying toward the target. I had never seen an enemy fighter in the sky before and I was amazed! But there they were, big as life. Four shiny MiG-17s were at our 12 o'clock position in level flight. They appeared to be about 500 feet above the A-4 *Skyhawk* aircraft that we were escorting. It was incredible!

I did not believe my eyes and I had to check with everyone else to make sure I was really seeing what I was seeing. "They must've completely screwed up their intercept," so I thought.

Quickly everyone realized that this was for real and we started after them. Just as we did I heard "Whoooom" and several big white tracks came screaming by my canopy. I first thought that the fired missiles were from my wingman. They were very close!

No, a MiG was *firing* at me! I selected full power and went after me a MiG. But I got "buck fever." I was so excited! I couldn't get a missile tone but I fired the missile (*Sidewinder*) anyway. It went "stupid" and missed my target.

My error settled me down a bit. I again placed my nose on another MiG. This time I got a good solid missile tone. I fired and watched the missile accelerate towards the MiG.

Just before my missile hit the target the MiG blew up in a big fireball. I thought, "What is going on?" Apparently Red Isaacs had fired a missile at the same MiG just a few seconds earlier. His *Sidewinder* had gotten there first. Anyhow, one MiG was knocked out of the air.

Everything was happening very fast. We were all excited. Unfortunately, we broke one of the basic elementary rules of air combat. None of us were watching our tails for enemy aircraft.

Supersonic Fighter Pilot

Four MiGs had slipped in behind us. All of our attention had been focused on the MiGs in front. We had to switch from offense to defense very quickly.

I saw Red Isaacs execute a hard defensive break. He was the first to notice the other MiGs. A volley of tracers went by his right ear from behind his aircraft. His first reaction was to chastise his wingman for firing too close to him. But when he turned around to look at his rear he was surprised to find a MiG-17 firing at him! The MiG scored a few hits on his right wing. This caused a hydraulic fire on Red's aircraft. Red was an outstanding pilot. He made a maximum turn to the left and for some reason the MiG departed the fight.

General George Patton said, *"If you are doing your job right you are going to be shot at."*

At the same time I was after another MiG. The MiG pilot must have been inexperienced. It was very easy to stay behind him.

At that time I wasn't aware that my airplane had suffered damage as well. The missile that came by me had shot off most of my horizontal stabilizer. This reduced my turning ability considerably.

I aggressively continued my attack. I followed the MiG through a gentle 180 degree turn. I acquired a good missile lock-on and fired another sidewinder. The missile went directly to the target and detonated but the MiG continued to fly undamaged! He was lucky but his luck was about to run out. Then he reversed his turn, not abruptly or violently, just a gentle turn back to the right. I went into burner and closed on him. I was well within range to shoot him down with my guns but I wanted to be as close as I could be before firing for the following reasons: the four 20mm cannons had

217

tremendous barrel whip. This caused the bullets to be scattered all over the sky. The guns also jammed at the slightest provocation. The ammo feed mechanisms would break easily if the guns were fired while pulling high Gs. The guns were pneumatic operated and tended to leak air once they were charged. So our procedure was, don't turn the armament switches on until you are ready to fire! Also, the *Sidewinder* missiles were somewhat unreliable. Thank goodness the Navy resolved these problems later in the war.

With all of this in mind I kept closing on the MiG and didn't charge my guns until I was almost in range. I resisted the temptation to pull the trigger until I was about 600 feet from the MiG. I continued to fire until I was only 300 feet behind him. I could see patches of skin coming from his aircraft. There was also bright white fire leaking out through the skin of the MiG. My 20mm cannons were making contact with the enemy. I had to make a quick left turn to avoid a mid-air collision with this crippled bird. I turned back toward him and saw the pilot eject. His parachute opened as he floated down.

As I was pressing my gun attack on the MiG I heard *Pageboy Two* (Red Isaacs) call that he'd been hit and was heading out of the fight. I found Red and escorted him back toward the ship. The other two pilots remained in the area looking for more MiGs. The A-4s continued on to the target as they were supposed to do while we were fighting the MiGs.

After joining on Red's aircraft I noticed a small fire and extensive damage to his right wing. The fire went out quickly.

He looked my aircraft over and reported, "*Pageboy Two*, you have damage to your starboard UHT."

Supersonic Fighter Pilot

My adrenaline must have been pumping pretty hard during the fight because I hadn't noticed any problem. The missile should have gone right up my tailpipe but it missed by a couple of inches. It sliced most of my starboard horizontal stabilizer off and left scrape marks up the right side of my fuselage. It even knocked one of my missiles off its launcher! I was not aware that the missile had hit my aircraft.

We flew back to the ship with no problem. I knew there could possibly be serious problems in controlling my aircraft when I slowed for landing. On my first landing attempt I noticed that I had to hold excessive backpressure on the control stick to maintain my desired speed. Phil Wood, the LSO, waved me off because of a fouled deck.

Phil apologized to me later; he said, "If I had known that you had a problem I wouldn't have waved you off." I landed on the next pass without any difficulties.

Red had shot down one MiG. I shot down another. Tim Hubbard, the *Ironhand* escort, had downed another one with missiles and guns. That made three confirmed kills and Phil Dempewolf claimed a probable kill. This was a great day for the Air Group!

Apparently, before we returned to the ship the word got out about the kills. Everybody on the ship was excited. My gun ports were all blackened from shooting the 20mm; the ordinance crew was thrilled their labor had paid off! They had worked hard for years loading ammo without seeing any results. So this was a great day and a morale booster for them as well.

In retrospect, I was one lucky pilot. They almost got me but I got one of them instead, in my trusty F-8. The *Crusader* was the greatest airplane that I have ever flown.

Brigadier General Robin Olds, USAF said, "A fighter without a gun … is like an airplane without a wing."

CHAPTER TWENTY-FIVE

CUBAN MISSILE CRISIS

RON KNOTT

The movie, *Thirteen Days,* explains just how threatened the United States was with nuclear war during the fall of 1962. Most Americans know very little about this impending danger that could have destroyed a major portion of our population. The movie explains the political predicament very well but only skims over the military function that I and many others endured not only for thirteen days, but also for more than thirteen months. As indicated in the movie, the powers that be in Washington almost lost control of the situation several times during those thirteen days. Thank God a peaceful agreement was achieved.

Retired Admiral Paul Gillcrist represented the Navy and the pilots very well as the military adviser for the movie, *Thirteen Days.* He was my boss in Fighter Squadron 62. We flew many missions together in and around Cuba during those uncertain days. There were also several aircraft lost and pilots killed during this operation that was not contributed to hostile activity. The movie only noted the loss of one aircraft and one pilot who was brought down by a Surface to Air Missile (SAM).

Our Air Group was placed on alert during the first week of October 1962. We were briefed about the missile build up and to be ready to strike our assigned targets in Cuba at a moment's notice. The entire Air Group (about eighty aircraft) would hit selected targets and destroy the SAM sites when the orders were given.

All pilots were restricted to the base at Naval Air Station Cecil Field, FL and could not tell family members when they would be home or why they were being retained on base. We could only view pictures of our assigned target in a dark room with our Top Secret clearance in hand. It was interesting to note that these same pictures were published in *Time* and *Newsweek* magazines the following week.

After a few days into the missile crisis we were deployed to Key West Naval Air Station, FL with our F-8 *Crusaders* fighter aircraft for alert duty. This placed us only ninety miles from the island of Cuba. That was only about nine minutes away in the supersonic *Crusader*. We were scrambled many times when MiGs got airborne in the little island to the south. The Ground Control Intercept (GCI) site was very good at supplying our pilots with the MiG's heading, altitude, and speed. If the MiG headed north or toward an American surveillance aircraft, we would be vectored in for the intercept at the "speed of heat." Somehow the MiG pilots knew when we were in hot pursuit of them and they headed back to Cuba as fast as possible.

We never got a shot at a MiG although we chased many away from the fleet. We were like a big brother coming to the aid of the surveillance aircraft. If some MiG harassed them we took over the fight since they had no weapons to defend themselves. Many times we would be skirting the three-mile limit off the cost of Cuba. That limit was later changed to twelve miles from the shoreline.

Our signal to scramble was when the *Red Alert Phone* rang in our Ready Room. The two duty fighter pilots in full

Supersonic Fighter Pilot

flight gear would run fast as they could to the flight line. We were on the second deck of a big hangar, which was about one hundred yards from the armed airplanes. At the first tingle of the *Red Alert Phone* we were off and running to the flight line. At the same time the line personnel were notified of the alert; the plane captain would have the airplane engine started by the time the pilot arrived. We only took time to fasten the two upper fittings on the torso harness, close the canopy, and head for the runway. Unfortunately, many pieces of support gear were blown over by jet blasts from our high power settings while taxiing.

The tower would clear us for take-off with a green light. By the time we got airborne our radios were warmed up and we could hear the vector commands coming from the GCI site. Because we were breathing so hard from the hundred-yard dash our initial communications were sometimes garbled.

A humorous event took place during one alert when LCDR Paul Gillcrist and I were scrambled. When the *Red Alert Phone* rang Paul had just taken a bite out of a big donut, which was covered with white powdered sugar. Paul ran out the Ready Room with the donut in his mouth. He was about two paces in front of me and was unaware that an Admiral was about to turn the corner in the passageway. He and the Admiral hit head-on.

As I passed the bodies tumbling on the floor I noticed the white powder coming out of Paul's mouth. I thought of "Puff the Magic Dragon" as I ran by.

I ran to the airplane, got airborne, and was laughing so hard I could hardly talk to the controllers. Sure enough, there was a pair of MiG-17s making passes on an Air Force C-121 (AWEPS) aircraft just off the coast of Cuba. The MiGs departed just before my arrival. The Air Force brothers were sure glad to see me on their wing.

If I recall correctly the record time for getting airborne after the *Red Alert Phone* rang, was less than three minutes. An Air Force fighter squadron was stationed in portable buildings next to the flight line and we would easily beat them in the air.

Jim Brady, who was one of our outstanding pilots, wrote the following report. His statement indicates how critical the situation was in those days.

LT Howie (Kickstand) Bullman and LTJG Jim (Diamond) Brady of Fighter Squadron 62 were on minute alert duty at Boca Chica NAS in Key West, Florida. The purpose of this "hot" alert was to provide cover and protection for our surveillance aircraft that were photographing Russian ships bringing medium and short-range nuclear tipped missiles into Cuba.

On the day in question, LT Bullman and LTJG Brady were scrambled to intercept two MiG-17s that were making gun passes on several P-2Vs and P-3Vs that were patrolling the Florida Straits. These Navy aircraft were taking low altitude photos of the decks of Russian ships carrying numerous missiles into Cuban ports for placement all over Cuba.

LT Bullman and LTJG Brady were airborne in two and one half minutes from the sounding of the alarm claxon (*Red Alert Phone*). They made a section takeoff in afterburner, and accelerated and climbed rapidly to 25,000 ft., where they continued to accelerate to supersonic speed while taking vectors from BrownStone, the ground control radar station which was charged with the task of guiding such intercepts over the Florida Straits.

Supersonic Fighter Pilot

The Cuban Missile Crisis was without a doubt, the seminal point of the Cold War, in that there was never a time when the two nuclear powers stood more sternly, eye to eye with the potential for nuclear war as the result. The movie, *Thirteen Days,* in recent years clearly depicted the level of tension that existed between the antagonists during this period.

***Crusaders* chasing MiG-17s near Cuba**

About 63 miles from Key West and perhaps six minutes from take off, both LT Bullman and Brady contacted the two MiG-17s via their APG-94 radar systems. BrownStone confirmed the targets and LT Bullman acknowledged taking over the intercept by calling "Judy" which was the code word for assuming control over the intercept in the cockpit.

The MiG-17s never saw LT Bullman or LTJG Brady as they slid in behind and slightly below the rapidly departing MiGs that were heading south toward Santa Clara, Cuba. With their Sidewinders growling in their headsets, indicating

Ron Knott

an infrared lock on the tail pipes of the MiGs, LT Bullman requested permission to attack by firing their missiles. There was what seemed like an interminable silence from BrownStone. Actually, the delay in responding was probably less than twenty seconds.

There command was to, "Break off the intercept and return to base."

LT Bullman acknowledged the command and the section of F-8s headed back to Key West. Many hours were spent in debriefing the pilots by a host of military and civilian officials.

Post Script: it was many years before both pilots came to understand why the attack had been called off. Negotiations between the White House and the Kremlin had reached a critical stage and the destruction of two Russian built, and probably Russian flown aircraft, would have perhaps, led to the outbreak of hostilities between the nations. No one can ever know for sure what would have happened had LT Bullman not requested, or had these two F-8 pilots been allowed to fire, on any aircraft engaged in a hostile or threatening act against any elements of the Armed Forces of the United States. LT Bullman, through his cool-headed handling of the situation may have prevented a chain of events from unfolding that could have been extremely unfortunate for both nations as well as the entire world.

After many weeks at Key West our squadron deployed on board the USS *Lexington* (CVA 16) for Combat Air Patrol near Cuba. Our primary mission at the time was for air superiority in case a MiG harassed the Photo aircraft taking *Brownie* pictures of Cuba. These Photo Birds continued the surveillance flights for months after the so-called "thirteen days" had passed.

Supersonic Fighter Pilot

My squadron also flew CAP (Combat Air Patrol) from the airport at Guantanamo Bay, Cuba (*Gitmo*) for many weeks. Again our mission was to be on station, usually above 40,000 feet, orbiting just off the south coast of Cuba. We were there ready for action should a MiG make a run on one of our surveillance aircraft that was flying across Cuba.

There were two air fields at *Gitmo* at that time, Leeward Point, which was 8000 ft. long and McCalla Field, east of the bay, which was only 4000 ft. long.

The "powers that be" decided that the long runway at Leeward Point needed to be resurfaced during this time of threat. This left McCalla Field as the only operating airport at *Gitmo*. This 4000 foot runway was the only one available for take offs and landings.

A fully loaded F-8 in afterburner could get airborne in less than 3,000 ft., even on a hot day. But the same airplane required almost 8000 ft. to stop on a dry runway. Installing arresting gear midway down the runway to trap our fast flying fighters on landing solved this problem. The same tailhook that caught the cable for shipboard landing was used to arrest the airplane on the short field. It worked and was fun. But if you got a hook skip or missed the wire, you had to immediately go to full power in order to keep from becoming a big jet ski off the end of the runway.

Normally there were two aircraft returning from each mission. Both planes had to make an arrested landing. It took about ninety seconds to reset the arresting gear after the first fighter landed, before the second fighter could land. We had to somehow delay the second plane from landing by at least ninety seconds. We could not fly but a few hundred yards north of the airport because of the border between the good guys and the bad guys. The bad guys had anti-aircraft

227

weapons trained in our direction and we did not want to give them an excuse to use them.

We could have separated prior to reaching the field and delayed the second fighter from entering that sacred airspace for a couple of minutes. But this is not the way a fighter pilot thinks. He wants to be joined on his leader's wing in tight formation at the speed of heat all the way to break.

The problem was simple to solve with fighter pilot logic. As the first fighter pitched out for landing, the second airplane would automatically pull up into a vertical loop. That stopped his forward motion and gave the ground crew the extra time needed for the arresting gear to be re-set. More importantly, it allowed the pilot to demonstrate his real "tiger" spirit. His overhead loop should end where it started if executed properly, and he would then pitch-out for landing.

We got by with this procedure by telling the "many-motor" pilots in charge of base flight operations that was our only option. Those were the days when we thought, "Having multi-engine time in your log book would be worse than having 'VD' in your health record." The many-motor, station safety officer thought we were a wild bunch, to say the least. When we first arrived at McCalla Field the station Commanding Officer welcomed our squadron on board. He asked us to make low passes over the base housing area when taking off so the dependents would know that the fighters have arrived.

"During this tense time your presence would give the civilians an added awareness of security," he said.

That was authorization a fighter pilot loved to hear. We obeyed his worthy request by making a hard right turn on take-off heading for the dependent quarters. We were so low that I am sure some of the shingles were blown off their roofs. And with an F-8 afterburner blazing they were pounded with mega decibels. These stunts had to be frightening to say the least. Our fun only lasted one day.

The Commanding Officer came back the next day and said, "They know you are here! You guys are shocking them more than the Cuban threat. Knock it off!" We did!

At the end of this 4,000 foot runway was a steep drop off. It was about fifty feet straight down to the bay where a squadron of P-5Ms and other Navy float planes were moored. They had this little secluded cove all to themselves like a flock of contented ducks along the sandy beach. We had to get their attention: on take-off we would suck up the landing gear, drop down to their altitude, and rake their place of tranquility with the deafening noise of the F-8. In just a couple of days they moved all aircraft far away from our area. As the old saying goes, "Here comes the fighter pilots; lock up the women and kids." We tried our best to live up to our reputation.

Other interesting aspects of flying out of *Gitmo* were the danger the pilots faced in case they had to eject near the runway. Hundreds of sharks could be seen swimming in the bay at both ends of the runway where the natives dumped garbage. Therefore, a water landing was not a good decision. The Marines had land mines placed all around the perimeter of the base and stationed their big K-9 watch dogs throughout the property. Landing on an explosive mine or in the mouth of a German Shepherd was not the leisurely place one would expect in the picturesque Caribbean. Perchance, had the pilot landed across the fence in mainland Cuba just a few hundred yards from the end of the runway; he would become a prisoner of Cuba. Our resolve was not to eject in this area. If all else failed we would go out to sea and to make a nylon descent (parachute).

The *Red Alert Phone* rang. I was duty fighter pilot. I ran to my airplane and mounted up like a professional fighter pilot heading out to war, or so I thought. In my excitement I turned the corner too quickly and this caused the right main tire to blow out. The airplane was flopping down the runway like driving over a plowed field. A blown tire was not about to stop me. I had to go. The *Red Alert Phone* was not to be ignored.

The airplane had enough thrust to get airborne with a blown tire. But my directional control was out of hand. She was heading for the ditch on the right side of the runway as I was quickly accelerating.

Going off the runway could have ruined my whole day. So in order to have symmetrical control of the airplane and to correct the extreme right drift, I just locked the left brake and blew that tire as well. My directional problem was solved but the ride was terrible. In a few seconds I was airborne looking for my bogie. Flat tires were the least of my concerns. I learned long ago that an airplane is no good on earth.

The tower was screaming, "*Silverstep* 209 you blew a tire on take-off!"

I said, "No, I blew two tires on take-off and I am switching frequencies to Combat Control."

When I called the controller I said, "This is *Silverstep* 209, where is my target?"

They said, "Your target is flying around the east end of the island at 2000 ft. at 160 knots, vector 095 degrees for join-up."

Supersonic Fighter Pilot

I thought, "Did I hear join up at 2000 feet and 160 knots?" I said, "Say again," with a lot of uncertainty in my voice.

The controller repeated what he had said but added a little more information during this transmission.

He said, "Your target is a Navy R4D (DC-6) carrying a group of Congressmen from Washington. They want to take pictures of a fighter flying wing on them in this hostile area."

I said to myself, "What?" Here I almost destroyed a beautiful fighter and possibly myself, just so a group of Congressmen could go back to Washington with pictures of a Navy fighter flying escort on them!

I made sure they got some good close-ups as I almost put my wing tip in their face. The R-4D pilot was a little nervous to say the least.

Here I was airborne, armed for a kill with two live *Sidewinder* missiles and 550 rounds of hot 20mm ammunition on board, and my mission was no more than a photo op. Dumb!

I flew with the politicians for a few minutes then headed back to McCalla Field for landing.

When I called the tower for landing instructions the tower operator said, "*Silverstep* 209, stand-by one!"

In a moment a very stern and authoritative voice from the tower radio penetrated my helmet with the following.

"*Silverstep* 209, this is the Safety Officer speaking. You will not be allowed to land at this airport because you have a blown tire."

I said, "McCalla Tower, I have two blown tires. I can easily make an arrested landing with no danger to me or my airplane."

231

He said, "*Silverstep* 209, your airplane is fully armed and could blow up on landing."

I thought to myself, "I know why this senseless pilot is stationed at this remote place. He is out of touch with reality."

He said, "The USS *Lexington* is just a few miles south. You will have to fly there and make an arrested landing on that carrier. You will not be allowed to land on my airport with blown tires and live ammo."

I switched over to the USS *Lexington's* radio frequency, told them of my problems and requested permission to land on their ship. I had flown on and off that boat many times and was well qualified to land there on.

The Air Boss of the ship said, *"Silverstep* 209, stand-by one!"

I thought, "Here we go again!"

In a moment the Air Boss called and asked me if my plane had made an arrested landing at McCalla Field in the past few days.

Of course, it had and I said, "Yes, Sir."

He said, "In that case, *Silverstep* 209, you will not be allowed to land on this carrier."

I said, "Why not?"

He replied, "There is a regulation that requires the tailhook to be inspected after landing on a concrete runway before it can make an arrested landing on a ship." He continued to say, "It is possible that the tailhook point may be hardened after such a landing on concrete and could possibly break upon landing on his ship."

I said, "Sir, they won't let me land at the airbase and you won't let me land on the ship. I am too low on fuel to go to another airport. What do you recommend?"

He said, "*Silverstep* 209, stand-by one!"

By then my oxygen mask was percolating with cold sweat like a cheap coffee pot boiling over.

Finally, he came back on the air and said, "*Silverstep* 209, this is the Air Boss speaking."

I said, "Yes sir, go ahead. I hear you loud and clear."

He said, "I have worked out an agreement with the tower controller at McCalla Field. You can make an arrested landing there, but first you must expend all ammunition and dump fuel down to the absolute minimum."

I said, "WILCO, SIR," which means I understand and will comply with his command. "Piece of cake," I thought, "Now I have a place to roost this crippled bird."

LT John "*Pirate*" Nichols was returning to McCalla Field from CAP station and heard our conversation. He joined on my wing and flew safety observer while I fired 500 rounds of 20mm ammunition and two live *Sidewinder* missiles into the ocean. I then dumped fuel down to the minimum and headed for the airport. John checked my landing gear to make sure the blown tires had not damaged other systems in the wheel wells. He landed ahead of me in case my landing might cause the field to be closed for a while if things went wrong. My landing was a normal Navy arrested landing that stopped my plane in just a few hundred feet.

After stopping, I noticed hundreds of people lined up on both sides of the runway to see this pilot and airplane go up in flames. I thought, "They must have sold tickets for this event." Well, I disappointed them and lived happily ever after, most of the time.

A few days later LT Dick Oliver and I were flying CAP at 45,000 ft. when two additional fighters relieved us on station. After flying the race tract pattern for almost two hours we

233

were ready for a little rest and relaxation. We started descending rapidly and accelerated beyond the speed of sound in a very short time as we were heading for McCalla Field. It was always fun to let the *Crusader* do what it was designed to do and that was to fly extremely fast. In fact, the *Crusader* was the first US production aircraft that was able to exceed 1000 mph.

We were smoking through the air at the speed of heat when all of a sudden LT Oliver's aircraft slowed down quickly. I was not expecting his rapid deceleration and slid past him. LT Oliver was a smooth pilot and would never try to throw his wingman out of position like that. Something had to be wrong with his airplane.

I heard a muffled transmission but could not determine what it was or where it was coming from. I pulled almost straight up to stop my forward motion in order to get back in position on my leaders wing. I rolled inverted and observed him several thousand feet below flying very slow. In fact he had his airplane configured for landing, with gear down, wing up, and we were still about seventy-five miles from the airport.

I had to perform all kind of "S" turns to get back in position. All the while I was calling him on my radio but was only getting garble transmissions in return. As I was joining on his starboard wing I noticed that his canopy was gone. Wow! That explained his rapid deceleration and the muffled transmissions I had heard.

Losing a canopy at any altitude and airspeed can be a frightening experience. A canopy loss at 35,000 ft. and at 1.2 Mach is dangerous for many reasons. It is highly likely that the pilot can be ejected from the airplane without notice. This is due to the fact that the Martin Baker ejection seat is designed to fire, or eject when the face curtain is pulled out of its holder. The purpose of the face curtain is two-fold. It is attached to the armed ejection pin by a cable and is actually the trigger that fires the seat. It also helps protect the pilot's face from the sudden windblast during ejection.

As I looked at LT Oliver's airplane I noticed that his face curtain was flapping in the wind. That meant his ejection seat could fire at any moment. All that was needed was another half-inch of travel and he would have been shot out of the airplane.

After we slowed down, our transmissions were easier to understand. I told him what I observed and the possibility of an unexpected ejection. We had no choice but to continue to the airport, not knowing what might happen.

The other major consideration was the fact that he would have to make an arrested landing at the short field as noted above. In an arrested landing the airplane decelerates rapidly. If we made it to the airport without the seat firing there was a good possibility that the seat may fire during the sudden stop when catching the arresting cable.

These older F-8s did not have ground level and zero airspeed capability of saving a pilot. As I recall, we had to have at least flying speed for the parachute to completely deploy. Our concern was, if the seat fired at the time of the arrested landing the pilot probably would not survive. To say the least, the remainder of that flight was very tense. It sure would have been nice to have an 8000 ft. runway nearby.

We carefully continued on to McCalla Field for landing. The tower was notified and all the emergency equipment was standing by for our arrival. In fact the tower wanted me to land first in case the seat did fire causing the airport to be closed. After I made my arrested landing and was taxiing to the flight line I observed LT Oliver catching the wire, coming to a rapid stop, and climbing out of his airplane as quick as possible.

We noticed after landing that this canopy had not separated from the airplane as we thought. The canopy frame was still locked and attached. The problem was the glass in the canopy had broken, but the results were the same. They could not fault the pilot for not properly locking his canopy.

These are just a few of the good, the bad, and the ugly times we experienced during the Cuban Missile Crisis. Such events were not out of the ordinary when operating high performance aircraft from land or sea. There are many similar stories from those who flew missions in all branches of the military in all types of airplanes or helicopters. When you're operating on the EDGE, the normal can become abnormal instantly. We all required a lot of professional attention and help from the Almighty to survive.

I can honestly say that my military comrades are some of the most respected folks that I have ever had dealings with. We worked together as a team no matter the rank or rate. We had a mission to perform and we did it. I honor those who gave all for their country no matter where or when.

I recorded these accounts for my children and my children's children. I would encourage all to take the time to jot down some events of your past that can be passed on to others. I have noted in my "remembering" that a part of me is awakened and the review is a tonic for my soul. We were there. We did it. Record it.

Supersonic Fighter Pilot

[Author's Note: Just a little review of why and how the military can use Guantanamo Bay, Cuba (Gitmo) for their operations. It was leased by the US Government in 1903, during the administration of President Teddy Roosevelt. The original agreement was reaffirmed by a treaty signed in 1934 by President Franklin Roosevelt. The treaty, still in effect today, gives the US perpetual lease on the land. Cuba has tried to break the lease many times but the US would not cancel the contract with them. One strange situation, especially during the Cuban Crisis, was the fact that native Cubans worked on the Naval Base as employees of the US government. They come in from mainland Cuba each morning and go back through the security gate each evening. We always questioned the security of such an operation. Gitmo is the oldest overseas Naval Base and the only one on communist soil.]

CHAPTER TWENTY-SIX

"ROCKY" THE FLYING PHOTO SQUIRREL

LEN JOHNSON

INTO HARM'S WAY OVER NORTH VIETNAM

In the spring of 1963 LT Wright showed up on the Bowdoin College campus-recruiting seniors for Naval Flight Training. This seemed like a good idea at the time. Three years later, getting shot at over NVN (North Vietnam), I wasn't so sure.

I reported to my first fleet squadron in September 1965. The Naval Aviator *Wings of Gold* on my blouse were bright and new. VFP-63 provided photo reconnaissance capability to the Pacific Fleet 27-C class carriers (the old WWII boats retrofitted with an angle deck and catapults). A carrier detachment consisted of three RF-8G *Crusader* aircraft, thirty maintenance personnel, four pilots, and two photo interpreters. The RF-8G was a single engine, single pilot supersonic fighter equipped with internal cameras. The aircraft was fast and maneuverable. On missions over NVN a fighter escort accompanied us. The photography was done below 5000 feet because film resolution was not too good above that altitude. At these low altitudes the aircraft were vulnerable to anti-aircraft fire (AAA) and surface-to-air missiles (SAM).

I have been told that our unit suffered the highest loss rate of any group. I don't know if that is true, but I remember the reaction of fellow aviators when I told them my squadron was VFP-63.

They said, "You poor sob!" It was kind of like you told them you had cancer. In 1966 my squadron started placing a plaque and planting a pine tree at the 18th tee at NAS Miramar golf course, for each pilot that was lost. There is now a beautiful stand of pines surrounding that particular tee. The plaques have been removed, and I wonder if any of the golfers wonder at the incongruity of those pines on that desert course?

Photo *Crusaders* overhead the USS *Hancock*

Detachment (Det) LIMA on the USS *Hancock* lost its first pilot in January 1966. Tom Walts was hit over Vinh. The damage sustained precluded a safe landing, so it was decided that he would make a controlled ejection off the coast of South Vietnam.

For some reason Tom's flotation gear did not inflate and he was dragged below the surface by the parachute. The

Supersonic Fighter Pilot

rescue diver jumped into the water, grabbed a piece of Tom's chute, and hung on to it as long as he could. Finally he had to let go as he too was being dragged below the surface. The weight of Tom's equipment and the sinking chute ended his life.

After this the first two pilots who were assigned as replacements turned their wings in and quit flying. The third pilot developed stomach pains and started canceling training flights. He too eventually decided on another line of work.

Without giving it much thought or consulting with my wife, I walked into the Skipper's office and volunteered for duty flying over North Vietnam. I had not completed my training, had very little flying time, and no combat experience. I was a disaster waiting to happen. The Commanding Officer (CO) didn't give it much thought either. He accepted my offer on the spot! Obviously, I had solved a problem for him. It was a really dumb thing for me to do. I wasn't at all ready for what awaited me.

The following two weeks was a whirlwind of activity. I had to relocate my wife and month old son to another state. And I needed to complete night carrier qualifications. A few priority messages were sent, and one night I got exclusive use of an aircraft carrier deck. I think it was the USS *Ticonderoga*.

The F-8 is not an easy aircraft to bring aboard a 27-C (small deck) at night. Completing night carrier qualifications in the *Crusader* is normally a source of pride and time for celebration but I had no time for either. It was another box to be checked before heading west. I flew out and back to the *Ticonderoga* as a solo flight on a black silent night. I felt very much alone. There were to be no happy faces and back slaps at the O'Club.

Ron Knott

The time interval between walking into the Skipper's office and landing on the USS *Hancock* two weeks later is a blur. I had boarded an express train to my destiny. My fate was no longer mine to influence. It certainly was not going to be my skill that would get me home. I learned early in life to feed my faith and my fears would starve to death.

My first impression of *Hancock* was the heat. I had never experienced sleeping spaces so hot. Only a few spaces on the ship had air-conditioning. My Stateroom was four decks down and had a big steam pipe running through it up to the flight deck to power the catapults. No surprise that there was an empty bunk in that hot house. That first night I lay there naked and completely soaked the sheet with my sweat.

Assignment to photo F-8 flying during wartime, although dangerous, was a great opportunity for a new pilot. Instead of flying on a senior pilot's wing for a year, the nugget RF-8 pilot was completely on his own. I planned and led one hundred flights into NVN. I flew very fast and very low. What young kid doesn't dream about that?

The basic rules of survival were don't fly below 3000 feet (anyone with a pea shooter can hit you down there), go very fast (600 knots plus), and keep the airplane constantly moving around the sky.

Unfortunately, to take photos it was often necessary to fly straight and level at 3000 feet over a fixed point. This greatly simplified the shooting geometry for the guys on the ground. Often the gunners didn't bother with geometry. They could see the patch of sky we intended to penetrate. Their gunnery solution consisted of merely filling that patch with lead and letting the "recce" (reconnaissance aircraft) fly through it. I learned early on that tracers have the right of way.

Supersonic Fighter Pilot

Four weeks after I reported aboard detachment LIMA, John Heilig, our ops officer, was shot down. He was taken prisoner and thank goodness he survived the war. Len Eastman, his replacement, was with us for only two weeks before he met the same fate. He too was taken prisoner and eventually returned home. The squadron did not send us any more replacements.

Detachment LIMA for most of the cruise had only three pilots instead of the allotted four. In all, nine Naval Aviators were assigned to detachment LIMA during the *Hancock's* 1965-66 Westpac cruise. Three refused to go. Three were brought down by enemy fire. Only three of us went and came back at the end of the cruise. Unfortunately, one died.

Flying off the *Hancock* in 1966 and 1967 was the most exciting and challenging events of my career. Although it was exciting, it was not enjoyable because of the strong possibility that I might not come home. There were certainly plenty of thrills and we did have fun, but it was always tempered by the reality of the situation.

HOW I GOT THE NICKNAME ROCKY

My mission was a road "recce" in the Thanh Hoa area. Dennis Duffy was my escort. Thanh Hoa was known for its bridge that we were never able to completely destroy. The weather was marginal with low ceilings and rain. As I approached the city, my electronic counter measures equipment gave me a missile launch warning. I went into a hard descending turn and headed back out to sea. The low cloud cover had me concerned and the warning convinced me to abort. I never saw the SAM.

Len Johnson ready for flight

I headed for Nam Dinh hoping for better conditions. I flew across the coast at 500 ft. to stay below the clouds. For the first time flying over NVN I saw extensive ground activity – trains and truck convoys moving about. Due to the bad weather there were no bombing missions being flown and the NVN were taking advantage of the situation. I had coasted in more to the west than I thought. Instead of being south of Nam Dinh I was north of Thanh Hoa, and had picked up Route One, the main artery that runs from Saigon to Hanoi.

I was surprised to see the extensive truck and train activity and proceeded to activate my cameras. The film moves through the cameras like movie film to compensate for the high speed of the aircraft. By looking through a scope in the cockpit and timing the speed of the film to that of the ground passing beneath, each opening of the aperture, in effect, captures a "still" image, where the subject is not moving.

Maneuvering the aircraft over the trains and trucks and monitoring the camera operation kept me busy. I was lower than normal, which was definitely not a good idea. Each time I was about to quit and head home I would spot another train or truck convoy. AAA was starting to catch up with me. I had been overland longer than usual and I was dangerously low, flying in and out of rain showers. The heavy AAA increased so much that I had to break off my mission.

I thought I was in the vicinity of Nam Dinh, so I turned to the east. This heading would be the shortest route to the Gulf of Tonkin and safety. After about ten minutes with no water in sight, it was clear that my position had been a lot further inland and to the north of Nam Dinh. "I should be out of here by now," I thought. Finally, in about another ten minutes I was over the coast.

That night at dinner in the *Hancock* Ward Room, our two photo interpreters walked in with a large map and laid it on the table where six of us were seated. This was a bit unusual.

Al Lipskey, one of the PIs asked me in an accusingly, exasperated tone, "Do you know where you were this afternoon?" It had taken them several hours of looking at film to match the images to points on the chart. My debriefing had not helped them any, for in fact, I did not know where I had been that afternoon.

"Somewhere north of Thanh Hoa," I had told them.

The route that I had flown with the cameras on was highlighted on the map of NVN. I had flown right up to the outskirts of Hanoi. No wonder the AAA was so heavy.

John Allen, sitting to my left, commented sarcastically, "Rocky the Flying Squirrel."

For the next eleven years my name was *Rocky*. I did not mind being identified with the squirrel. We each had our share of adventures and we were both harmless.

The Navy gave me a medal for that flight. There was probably some debate on whether to give me a medal or a reprimand. The citation stated that the intelligence obtained from my film was valuable to the war effort. A few days later Denny's (my fighter escort) VF-24 squadron mates gave us a more meaningful remembrance of that day – a flower in a cup. They called it the "Steeped in S___ but Smelling Like a Rose" award. Denny told me recently that he got a chewing out from his CO. Not sure why, he was just following my lead, doing his job.

THE FIGHTER ESCORT

The fighter pilot who was assigned recce escort duty would meet me in Air Intelligence to brief the upcoming flight. I enjoyed watching their reaction when I answered the big question, "Where are we going?" If it was a simple road recce mission in a lightly protected area, relief could be seen on their faces. Concern could be read in their eyes if the mission was a BDA (bomb damage assessment) flight in North Vietnam near the Haiphong Hanoi area. When it was the latter, they would become grave and very interested in my planned route and tactics. Otherwise, it would be a joy ride for the escort.

Supersonic Fighter Pilot

SIGHTSEEING OVER LAOS

The Skipper of VF-24, Harry Post, was my escort on one of those "easy" road recces in the southern part of NVN. I decided on a back door entry – entering NVN airspace from Laos to the west. I naively thought that I would surprise the enemy by coming in that way. Anyway, it was a different challenge and new territory to see.

I learned to fly from one landmark that I recognized to another that I could pick out in the distance. My course over the ground was a series of misshapen "Ss." Straight lines were a no-no.

When we arrived in Laos over my letdown point, there was an extensive cloud layer below us. We were over mountainous terrain. The Skipper was rightfully hesitant about descending into that cloud layer over unknown territory, on the wing of a very junior pilot known as *Squirrel*.

I was hesitant, too, but I was not going to let him know that. I told him to stay high; I would go down and see if we had enough room under the cloud cover to operate. I descended into the dark clouds, trusting in the terrain elevations on my chart. I would descend no lower than the highest peak in the area. I was confident that I would break out well above the ground and call the Skipper down, and we would continue the low level portion of our mission east into NVN.

The cloud cover was thicker and lower to the ground than I had counted on. I broke out of the clouds into a valley with the ground less than 1000 feet below me. Mountain peaks rose above me into the clouds surrounded the valley. That was not good!

I briefed the Skipper about the conditions. He suggested

that I abort the mission. That was fine with me, since he suggested it. When you are twenty-two years old you know by observation that guys get killed in this profession, but you don't believe it will happen to you. When you reach the mature age of thirty you know that it will happen to you, and it will be sooner than later, if one isn't very careful. The Skipper had reached that age.

HOW I CAME TO LOVE THE PRATT & WHITNEY J-57

On a later mission I was over the Gulf headed for Haiphong, when my escort told me he saw what looked like a film of fluid on the lower fuselage of my *Crusader*. I checked my gauges and saw nothing amiss. "It was probably some excess hydraulic fluid that had pooled in the engine bay and was now leaking out," I thought. F-8s are well known for bleeding hydraulic fluid. I continued the mission.

Just before my planned pop up the red engine warning light illuminated brightly. This was not a good sign. My gaze dropped quickly to the small oil pressure gauge. The needle was as far left as it could go – zero! Now I knew what that fluid was. It was the lifeblood of my Pratt & Whitney J-57 turbojet engine. I pulled the throttle back to 86% where, according to the F-8 manual, the engine might, if you were lucky, continue to run for up to fifteen minutes before seizing. I set my course for the nearest airfield, which was the USS *Hancock*. It was thirty minutes flying time away.

There was no way I could make it back to the ship so I prepared for ejection, stowing my gear, lowering the seat, checking my equipment, and mentally went through the procedures I had practiced months before, back in San

Supersonic Fighter Pilot

Diego. But the engine miraculously kept running.

The flight deck of the *Hancock* was crowded with aircraft. The Captain decided to take me aboard and ordered an emergency pull-forward. The huge ship turned into the wind. The green lights on the glide slope lens signaled a ready deck upon my arrival two miles aft and three thousand feet above her wake. The ship was ready for me. Unfortunately, I was not quite ready to land.

I had not even considered the possibility of landing aboard. The engine couldn't run that long without oil! As events quickly unfolded I had to shift gears in my thinking. I realized that I was above maximum landing weight. Dump fuel! Quick! Where is that switch?

Unable to move the throttle to IDLE for fear the engine would seize and overweight with unused fuel, I "called the ball" high and fast in the "groove."

The LSO acknowledged my call with what was painfully obvious, "You are high and fast. Keep it coming!" Ordinarily, he would have waved me off immediately, but we both knew that this might be my only shot at getting aboard. He let me continue the approach.

I hit the landing area but did not catch a wire, and continued off the angle into the air again. My nose attitude was wrong due to the excess airspeed. The tailhook bounced over the four steel cables lying across the deck waiting to grab my tailhook. I had planned for the aircraft to come to a quick, violent stop. It did not. I had blown it!

Now came the moment of truth. I had to climb back to 600 feet, turn downwind and try it again. This meant that I would have to MOVE THE THROTTLE, which almost certainly would cause the engine bearings to seize. Then I would have to eject and plunge into the ocean. That J-57 had already run twenty minutes longer than I dared hope it would. I hesitated to move the throttle. The aircraft almost stalled due to the low airspeed, the low power setting in the climb, and my hesitation to add power. I was willing it back into the air following the bolter, but I had no choice. I shoved the throttle forward knowing that my next action would probably be pulling the seat ejection curtain. Unbelievably, the engine kept running.

I saw myself at the "long green table" trying to explain to the accident board why I hadn't gotten aboard the first time. I had a greater fear of failing there in front of my contemporaries than I did of dying. So instead of doing the smart thing and ejecting when I had the opportunity to safely do so, I again opted to continue. *Squirrels* never learn.

I turned the corner and one more time called "*Crusader* ball." This time I made sure that I was on speed and on glide slope. The LSOs like to say that a good start results in a good finish. And sure enough, it did.

After I was safely aboard the Air Boss said, "Shut it down," as I came to a stop. They were in a hurry to get me out of the way and get on with launching the other aircraft.

The engine froze as soon as I shut down it down. It had run for forty minutes without oil, which is impossible. The Lord God Almighty was again looking after the S*quirrel*.

THE DAY I DISCOVERED ANGELS REALLY DO EXIST

I was on my second *Hancock* deployment to the Tonkin Gulf when I was assigned a BDA (bomb damage assessment) mission following an ALFA strike (a major air wing bombing effort) on the MiG airfield at Kep. This area

Supersonic Fighter Pilot

had a lot of AAA and SAMs.

By this time I had given up on my "sneak up and surprise 'em" tactics. The enemy knew we were coming and tracked us all the way. I came in high, staying out of SAM and AAA envelopes as long as possible. I could then trade my altitude for speed.

With the J-57 engine in afterburner, descending from 20,000 ft., I could easily come across the target supersonic. The quickly changing altitude, speed acceleration, and continual lateral movement had to make tracking me very difficult. The only time I kept all these variables constant was when I leveled out over the target. I usually came across the target at 3,000 ft. for the twenty seconds necessary to get the pictures. When I passed the target I would pull for the sky and turn for the water.

It was a beautiful sunny day with a scattered layer of cumulus clouds around 5,000 ft. I came in high from the northeast paralleling the Chinese border as the Air Wing Strike Group commenced their attack on the airfield fifty miles away. I could see everything; the whole panorama of the country lay before me. It was a rare day. The blues, greens, and whites were vivid. It was a beautiful day for golf or a picnic with the family. Yet, I was at war.

As I was on the descent twenty miles from the airfield, the strike leader, Moose Meyers, suggested that I abort. The ground fire was very heavy. But I didn't feel like coming back a second time and having to go through the preparation and emotion again.

"Nah," I thought, "let's get it over with now." This is the same kind of thinking that caused me to volunteer for detachment LIMA eighteen months earlier.

Accelerating through 700 knots the warble sound of a

251

SAM launch got my attention. I turned harder as the aircraft flashed through the cloud layer and I looked quickly for the missile. I never saw it. The airfield came into sight two miles away. In just a few seconds I would be over the target. I completely forgot the missile threat and concentrated on my approach and the operation of the cameras. I was very tense.

Incendiary shells called tracers are used by gunners to visually follow the path of their fire power. For every tracer one can see, there are twenty shells one can't see. I will say again, I learned early on that tracers have the right-of-way. I knew that I couldn't outrun those tracers. They were in front and behind my left wing, close enough to touch. There was no way that the 20mm shells could not be striking my aircraft. I hoped if they hit my wings that the fuel would not ignite or that the stick would not freeze, if they bashed a hydraulic line. I glanced at the engine fire warning light. Everything was good. Maybe I could make it to the water if I got hit. I was getting that old longing for blue water again. I'd had enough sightseeing for today. It has been said, *"Courage is being the only one who knows you're afraid."*

Kep is only about five minutes from the Gulf when flying at 600 knots. Thank goodness there were no warning lights and the stick remained firm and responsive. When I finally got out and over the water a great feeling of relief flooded over me. The tension drained. Wow! I was out of there. I noticed again how bright and vivid the day was. Still, the sight of those tracers surrounding my left wing stayed with me. Thirty years later, I still have that picture in my mind – it was an ominous sight.

As I was heading toward the ship, the next forty minutes of flight were thoroughly enjoyable. I was alive and loving it.

The day was beautiful! What a pleasure to be flying this wonderful machine. I wanted to prolong the feeling but finally, I had to return to that old wooden flight deck and land on the *Hancock*.

After landing I taxied forward and shut the engine down. I climbed out of the aircraft and headed for the left wing. For five minutes I stood under the wing and enjoyed the 20 knots of warm wind bathing my face. I was surprised that there were no bullet holes anywhere on my aircraft. How could that be? Only one explanation – my plane had been surrounded by shielding angels. Later I was to read, *"If I rise on the wings of dawn, if I settle on the far side of the sea, even there your hand will guide me" (Psalms 139: 9-10 NIV).*

EPILOGUE

In 1972 I became a Christian. I had been raised in a Methodist church but never got the real message. I did receive a King James Bible in sixth grade Sunday school, which I never opened. But I religiously held on to it for twenty years. When I was attached to VF-102 flying the F-4 *Phantom* on the USS *Independence* I had a nagging feeling that it was time to read the Bible. I did and it changed my life, forever.

After leaving Vietnam my flying career was pretty much routine. I did have a few notable exceptions, such as flying the 747-400 into the old Hong Kong airport on a dark, stormy, windy, and rainy night after a sixteen-hour flight from New York. All this changed in 2003 when I received an unsolicited email out of the blue from Mission Aviation Fellowship asking if I might have any interest in flying a *King-*

Air in Africa and Afghanistan. Then things got exciting again for the S*quirrel*.

The challenges that I had experienced flying in Vietnam were back! For example: finding and landing on a small snow covered field up in the Hindu Kush mountains in the winter; landing and taking off on a 3000 ft. dirt road at 9000 ft. elevation, surrounded by peaks towering over 10,000 ft.; operating out of a desert field on the border of Iran where the temperatures averaged over one hundred degrees and the visibility was often reduced to a quarter mile in blowing sand.

In Afghanistan in 2004 there was no radar or Air Traffic Control. There were no minimums and no rules, except the ones we set for ourselves. Fortunately for the S*quirrel*, we had GPS. We designed our own approaches to get in these small airports when the ceiling and visibility were low.

Aircraft and aircrew from all over the world did their own thing. Sometimes they flew into the mountains and all aboard would be killed. I witnessed a huge Russian freighter land, gear up at Kabul. I saw an Ariana 727 break out of a low overcast and make a hard, sixty degree bank at a hundred feet to get back on centerline. It was the Wild West as far as the rules were concerned!

On some of the fields there was the real possibility of Taliban attack. We used code words with the folks on the ground, stayed high as long as possible, parked in remote areas, and didn't waste any time on the ground.

The ride from the airport in Kabul to our rented homes in Carte Seh was often more arduous and scary then that day's flights. Traffic jams were like nothing I have ever seen. They were worse than the traffic in Paris. Folks maneuvered their carts, cars, goats, bikes, and bodies wherever there was a space, be it on the sidewalk or the wrong side of the road.

Supersonic Fighter Pilot

We live in a great country. We are truly blessed. There is no place in the world like America. When the *Hancock* departed San Francisco in December 1967, I stood on the flight deck looking up at the Golden Gate Bridge and wondered if I would ever see it again. God not only preserved me but He allowed me to see that sight over and over, when years later I flew United Airlines' Asia routes.

The flights were timed to return to SFO just after sunrise. An hour out we would see the sun coming up over the west coast of the USA. That magnificent sight filled me with thanksgiving every time I saw it. It was always a thrill to see the USA rushing toward me at 500 mph with arms open, welcoming me home. Then I would recall my feelings back in December 1967 when I was standing alone on the flight deck of the *Hancock* steaming west. We were on our way to the Tonkin Gulf and the unfriendly sky over North Vietnam. It is sad to say that many of my comrades never returned to their homeland.

The contrast between that California coastline and every other I have ever seen is startling. The air is clear and bright. The deep blues, greens and purple of the Pacific Ocean, the dark blue of the night sky turning to light, the yellows and gold on the horizon, a few lingering stars, the puffy white clouds, the green vegetation, the brown earth, the white sand, the surf pounding against the dark rocky coast, still in the cliffs' shadow – it is beautiful to behold. But above all there is the realization that this is America. I am alive and I am home!

I don't know why He brought me through the flak over Kep, or kept my engine running when it had no oil. Maybe it was so we could meet Pastor Nouh in Timbuktu and help in the humanitarian projects. I still remember Tom Waltser at the Detachment LIMA departure party. He was a young father and a loving husband with a sweet wife. He too should have lived. But he gave it all up in the Tonkin Gulf because of that stupid war.

"We want to be in a situation under maximum pressure, maximum intensity, and maximum danger. When it's shared with others it provides a bond which is stronger than any tie that can exist." – SEAL Team Officer

CHAPTER TWENTY-SEVEN

CRUSADERS VS PHANTOM

CHARLIE SNELL

"Where are those old guys who are flying those antiques outside?" Bob, the lead F-4 pilot, shouted this insulting remark from the back of the Ready Room.

These "old guys" were Marine Reserve Pilots from Navy Dallas and the "antiques" were the F-8 *Crusaders* that we had flown to Yuma to act as aggressors against their F-4 *Phantoms*.

Our F-8 squadron, VMF (AW)-112, based at Navy Dallas had been invited to Yuma, AZ to act as MiGs against the *Phantoms* to sharpen their air-to-air fighting skills. Since all our pilots had "day jobs" we had to schedule our Yuma flight around their availability.

The *Phantom* Squadron needed two *Crusaders* each day to complete the exercise. In order to meet their needs we would send two planes and pilots out for a two-day training period. Those two planes and pilots would return home as another team replaced them in Yuma. This would continue until the training was finished.

The *Phantom* was the latest and greatest fighter, so many folks thought. It had two big engines; the F-8 had one. The *Phantom* had missiles; the F-8 had guns. The *Phantom* had a big, powerful radar that could see halfway across Texas; the F-8 pilots needed no radar. The *Phantom* required two crewmembers; the F-8 only needed one fighter pilot.

The Dallas boys had been challenged and so had their F-8 *Gunslinger*.

Marine Reserve F-8 pilot, Major Pete Fromman and I practiced Air Combat Maneuvers before the fight. We just wanted to sharpen our air-to-air skills before taking on "big mouth Bob and the boys."

Bob, the *Phantom* pilot leader, made more brags than anyone else in the briefing. You could hear him saying, "I will lock you up on radar at thirty miles for a missile kill. You can't get close enough to us to use your guns or S*idewinders* with those old antiques you are flying!" And, "When it's time to end the fight I'll call 'Bug Out' and we *Phantom* drivers will make a high speed run back to Yuma. I will see you in the Ready Room since you don't have the speed to keep up with us!" he would confidently conclude.

We had three engagements that day. The fights started at forty miles separation. We turned into each other and the call "Fights-on!" was transmitted. We called Tally-Ho almost immediately by seeing their black smoke. We dumped the nose, increased speed, flew very low under them, and at the precise moment did a loop ending up at their 6 o'clock position. They never saw us with their big bad radar sweeping Arizona, or their eight eyeballs scanning the world.

The second engagement was about the same. By the third engagement Pete and I were bored, so we told them where we were. They finally spotted us and started to do something other than cruise across the desert. The old antique *Sader* was on their tail only after a couple turns. Their section tactics were terrible.

I called the leader, "Bob," and asked, "Is it time to Bug Out?"

As we were parking on the ramp, I am sure that I saw a quick smile coming from the intake area of my *Sader*.

We waited for *Phantom* drivers in the Ready Room. Needless to say, "NEVER underestimate the capability of your adversary – especially when they are flying *Crusaders*."

[Author's Note: On a North Atlantic cruise aboard the USS *Independence* (CVA 62) there were two Fighter Squadrons on board. One Squadron had the new and mighty *Phantoms* (VF-41) and we had the F-8E *Crusaders* (VF-62). Our mission was to intercept the Russian bombers north of the Arctic Circle. The *Phantoms* were launched first to make the 250-mile intercept of the incoming bomber. A minute or so later two F-8s were launched. When the *Phantoms* intercepted the Russian bomber they were surprised to find the two F-8s, who were launched last, flying wing on the Russian bomber.

If the *Phantom* had external tanks we could out run them, out climb them, and out fight them. Without the tanks they were very limited on range!]

CHAPTER TWENTY-EIGHT

PADDLES

RICHARD "HOT-DOG" NELSON

Being a Landing Signal Officer (LSO) was a great job. Unlike many of the onerous collateral duties that normally were assigned to junior officers, the LSO job made you feel that you were doing something that counted – like keeping your buddies in the Air Wing safe. On the small carriers used in the Vietnam era (*Ticonderoga, Bonhomme Richard, Oriskany, Hancock, Intrepid*), to which the F-8s were assigned, that was easier said than done.

On a perfect pass the F-8 *Crusader* tailhook crossed the fearsome ramp or flight deck edge, at only 10.1 ft. At night, with a pitching deck and minimum fuel even the best pilots were at risk. A good LSO could significantly add to safety and improve the odds. I got into the business after almost hitting the ramp at night as a nugget (new pilot) and then getting reamed by my squadron mates, including *"Buzzard"* Jewell, the current squadron LSO.

I remember his words to this day, *"Hot Dog*, the best way to learn something is to teach it."

Wow – if I had known *that*, my grades at the Naval Academy would have been better.

Our squadron Skipper also observed, *"Hot Dog*, you will either become a great F-8 pilot or you will be dead. At this point I'm not sure which will occur."

It was a serious wakeup call. I was not sure either.

So I started tagging along with the *"Buzzard"* and watched how he did things. Soon, he let me "wave" field carrier landing practice sessions, and then the squadron sent me to LSO School. By the end of the first cruise I was Air Wing qualified, day and night, which is a big deal to LSOs. This means you can "wave" all of the carrier's aircraft types without supervision.

Usually there were only about three LSOs (including the Air Wing LSO) that were fully qualified, primarily because of the unusual landing difficulties with the F-8 and the A-3 tanker, known as the *whale.* Every third day I went off the flight schedule and manned the LSO platform.

There were usually about twelve "cycles" of launches and recoveries during the carrier's daily operating schedule, both day and night. After each recovery of aircraft the LSO visited each pilot Ready Room and debriefed the pilots on their landings. It was one of those rare situations where a junior officer had the authority to criticize a senior officer's performance. Obviously, a wise LSO would be as tactful as possible when telling a senior officer that his landing was terrible.

Typical LSO duty

On approach a carrier pilot must worry about three factors simultaneously: glide slope, airspeed, and lineup. More than a small deviation from the correct parameters will result in potential disaster. Being more than a few feet above glide slope means a "bolter," or missed arrestment. Below the glide slope you risk a ramp strike and fatal crash.

The airspeed must be kept very close to ideal approach speed (around 140 knots for the F-8) or an arrestment can break the tailhook or the arresting cable. This often proves to be fatal. Lineup is also critical because an off-center arrestment can put the aircraft either over the side of the ship, or into parked aircraft on the right side.

The best LSOs developed almost a psychic ability to sense when a landing aircraft was going to deviate from the glide slope. This came from knowing the proper sound of the engine, the ability to sense motion, and knowledge of the aircraft. This enabled them to talk to the pilot with preventive guidance before problems developed, such as "Little power ... don't go low." Or, "Don't climb," and "Check your lineup." This was enormously helpful to new or below-average pilots who needed all the help they could get – especially after a stressful combat mission.

When a pilot got in real trouble the LSO had the responsibility, *and* authority, to make an instantaneous, independent decision whether to allow him to land or to "wave off" the aircraft and make him go around. Only the Air Boss or Air Operations Officer also had the power to "wave off" the aircraft.

The LSO's responsibility to control landings efficiently, but safely, is crucially important to the carrier's operations. The carrier has only limited time to recover aircraft from the previous launch, "re-spot" the deck, and arm and fuel aircraft for the next launch. Thus, a pilot that has problems catching an arresting gear wire, and makes multiple landing attempts will impact the entire carrier combat operation. Although it was sometimes overwhelming, I enjoyed having this responsibility as an LSO and meeting this challenge.

The second cruise (1967-68) on the *Ticonderoga* brought a new look to Fighter Squadron 194 and the Air Wing in general. Compared to my first cruise we were like one of those great college football teams that loses its entire senior varsity. Instead of our cadre of experienced pilots (there were only three nuggets the first cruise) we had a massive rotation of east coast pilots joining the Air Wing, including almost every senior officer slot. This produced a really dysfunctional situation. The flight division leaders had no combat experience while the junior officers knew more about flying over "Indian Country" in North Vietnam than the senior guys. This is bad for politics and survival. Nevertheless, these east coast guys were generally *very* smooth around the boat, including at night. Any LSO has to love that.

One night I was the duty, or primary LSO running the platform. Just before dawn the Air Wing LSO showed up even though he was not on duty. We were having trouble getting the last aircraft of the cycle on board – a *Queer Spad,* due to a fouled deck. The Spad also had electrical trouble with his lights, including the one that indicates "gear down." The Air Wing LSO said he wanted to wave the last bird, and took the lights and radio. "Okay, you got it," I said. What the hell; he was senior to me.

As he gave the "cut lights," the *Spad's* power came off and he swooped down for the wires. As he passed the platform in the dark, I mumbled, "No gear!" It was too late. He caught the number three wire, landing gear up, with his prop carving divots in the flight deck. I remember wondering if I would have caught the problem. Nevertheless, my "cherry" was intact – still no accidents or ramp strikes on *my* watch. I remember thinking, "That's what the Air Wing LSO gets for hogging the pickle."

A few weeks later I was waving the day shift. Two F-8s hit the break and the first one turned on approach and called the ball.

"*Redflash* 402, *Crusader*, ball, two point zero." It was one of my squadron's birds, but I did not recognize the voice or know who the pilot was. I assumed it was one of our nuggets.

At the in-close position he started to rise because of the updraft of the ship and dropped his nose. Since he was in APC, the power came smartly off. He failed to anticipate his needed correction and then jerked the nose up at the ramp, while still settling.I needed to bust him out of APC, so I yelled, "Power, power!" in order to flatten him and prevent an in-flight wire engagement and broken nose gear. He complied, and boltered.

Just as I was dictating a nasty grade on his pass to the log writer, the radio crackled, "Don't *ever* do that to me again!"

I replied, "Don't honk your nose up at the ramp and I *won't!*" A few minutes later he successfully landed. Suddenly, I saw the Air Wing LSO sprinting across the deck between passes.

"*Hot Dog*, you've done it this time. That was the CAG (Air Wing Commander) in that F-8. You are to report to his office immediately. I have the paddles."

Upon entering CAG's office I was ordered, "Brace up, *Hot Dog*! I am sick and tired of your insubordinate and disrespectful behavior! What you did today was unprofessional. You are GROUNDED! Now get out!"

I then located the Air Wing LSO. I told him CAG had grounded me. I also told him as a result, that I was retiring my paddles until the grounding order was rescinded.

I said, "If I'm not fit to fly then I'm not fit to wave. Sorry about that."

That does not sound very threatening, until you learn that this meant double duty for the other LSOs, especially the Air Wing LSO. So, I stood the Ready Room watch duty every day, ran a very spiffy watch, and I got to be pretty good at it! My telephone etiquette improved dramatically and there was always plenty of chalk for the Heavies to write on the blackboard. I was kind of like the equipment guy on a football team, making sure that there was enough Gatorade and towels for the players.

After about four days of this diplomatic impasse the Air Wing LSO came into the ready room, and said, "Okay, *Hot Dog* – you've made your point. CAG says you are no longer grounded."

I told him, "Put it in writing. And there better not be anything about this incident in my file."

I was one of those characters that the senior officers simultaneously loved and hated. I was one of the pilots that they wanted on their wing in combat, or acting as the LSO when they returned to the ship.

However, as my squadron XO told me at the end of the combat cruise, "*Hot Dog*, if I had been the Skipper you would have been court-martialed for insubordination."

I replied, "Well, XO, I guess that's why you were not the Skipper."

CHAPTER TWENTY-NINE

NIGHT CARRIER QUALIFYING

LARRY DURBIN

I had made 118 FCLP (Field Landing Carrier Practices) under the watchful eye of LT John "*Pirate*" Nichols. He was a great LSO (Landing Signal Officer) and he knew how to get most of his students qualified.

Finally he said, "Congratulations, you're field qualified and ready for night carrier landings."

To which I immediately answered, "Even me?"

"Yes," he said, "You didn't have a good flight tonight but when I told you to do something you did it. That's the most important part; you'll do fine."

Talk about mixed emotions. Elation at passing but I also knew my next landing would be on the USS *Shangri-La* (CVA-38) in this supersonic F-8 *Crusader*. I was fifty percent thrilled and fifty percent scared to death.

One dear friend who was top in academics and flight grades in his class just could not handle the stress of making a night landing on the ship. Jimmy successfully field qualified but when the time came to go to the ship, at night, he turned his wings in. A Navy pilot can DOR (Drop on Request) at anytime he feels inadequate or fearful about his performance.

While I don't think my body was actually shaking, it was at least tingling. There was a full moon but we wouldn't be able to see it because of an overcast sky. It would be a very black hole in the landing pattern, so we were told.

The LSO said, "That will be good," he went on, "You won't be distracted and will focus on the job at hand." That was baloney and I knew it.

F-8 landing on the USS Shangri-La

"I am a real Navy fighter pilot. I am a real Navy fighter pilot. I can do this, and, I can do this!" These thoughts were rebounding inside my head.

A voice somewhere in my jittery stomach answered, "Are you sure?"

Suddenly stupid logic came to me and for some unexplainable reason, it helped. I hadn't thought about this logical solution before but just before I grabbed my helmet and headed for the flight deck it came to me loud and clear again. If I could just get through this evening and make my

Supersonic Fighter Pilot

six traps (night arrested landings), shaking as I was, I could be assured that for the rest of my life, no matter what bad events came my way, I could handle any crisis with ease. Nothing in my future could compare to this night experience. If I completed this assigned task I would prove to myself and the world, that I was not a coward!

For some reason this type of logic helped calm my apprehension. I was now ready to take on this tremendous task, both mentally and physically. I knew then and there that I was going to be a real Navy fighter pilot.

I made one short stop in the head (bathroom) before manning my airplane, where I vomited profusely. I threw some cold water on my face and resumed my walk up to my aircraft. I climbed up the steps, hoisted my right leg into the seat, and sat down with a resigned plop. The plane captain (pilot's assistant) helped me strap into the ejection seat. He did not have a clue about my apprehension. My muscle memory, as we call it, took over.

G. Warren Hall had said on his first night catapult, "I tried to push the night's blackness to the back of my mind and set about preparing for my first night catapult launch. Still, the inky blackness continued to flood my consciousness. A quiet private conversation with GOD, 'Lord, if this is the end – may I please come to be with You?' was my final consolation."

The Air Boss commanded, "Start the jets!"

My personal test of fire was about to begin. I was next in line for the port (left) catapult. My nerves steadied somewhat as my brain tried to assimilate all the activity around me.

I was directed to the catapult by the eerie lighted wands in the hands of the aircraft director. There was total blackness in front of me. The catapult officer's green wand flashed to life; rapidly twirling in a small diameter circular motion was the signal for me to apply full power. I advanced the throttle. The airplane squatted somewhat on its nose gear like a bird about too leap into the air. After I checked my engine instruments, I carefully turned on my wing lights. This was my signal that the airplane and I were ready to be launched. The "Shooter" (Catapult Officer) touched the deck with his wand in a graceful movement that would have made a ballet dancer envious.

In less than a second the entire airplane hit me in back of the head like a sledgehammer. I had forgotten to place my head firm against the headrest before the shot, and WHAM, it hit me hard. I was now flying 170 mph. My life depended on accurate performance – could I do it? The dark black night was all over my airplane. I could only see a few dimly lit instruments in the cockpit. I was directed to make a left turn downwind. I could count every heartbeat. My heart sounded like a bouncing basketball!

"Nightcapper 102, turn downwind."

I replied, "Roger." Still, nothing but darkness!

"Nightcapper 102, turn to ship's heading."

"Roger." My reply was short. My brain was overloaded.

In another moment I heard the voice say, "New guy, three miles, call the ball."

He didn't really call me 'new guy,' but that's what he was thinking. The "call" meant I was at the point where I should see the ship and it was time to switch to the LSO frequency. Without even moving my head I switched frequencies with the hand dangling nervously at the end of my arm.

I checked in by saying, "*Sader* ball, 2.9." That indicated I was flying a *Crusader*; that I could see the meatball, and my fuel state was 2,900 lbs. Manhood was only three miles and 600 feet away.

Supersonic Fighter Pilot

"Steady with the nose, just relax, speed is good, going slightly high," came the LSO's comforting call. "Still slightly high, ease it down just a little, you're doing fine, no big corrections, hang in there," the LSO said.

I was at three hundred feet and the ship was getting bigger very fast. "Meatball-lineup-airspeed; meatball-lineup-airspeed; meatball line-up-airspeed," was going through my head.

"On glideslope, looking good, stay right in there, check your lineup."

The end of the ship was now coming up fast. My blood was rushing to my head; the meatball started to climb just a little. I knew I was too close to push the stick down, the ramp (back end of the ship) zipped by me, BAM! I slammed in on the deck. Out of the corner of my eye, I saw red illuminated blurred images for an instant as I slammed the throttle full forward and pulled back on the stick. "Darn, Darn, Darn!" I had missed all landing wires. I was the world's fastest tricycle running down the angle flight deck, and I was about to be thrown into the dark night air again.

Now I am trying for a second attempt to make an arrested landing. As you would expect, the LSO's voice was perfectly calm and professional.

"You're doing fine, relax; keep it coming."

Like I had a choice! This time I flew better, still keyed up, but not quite as uptight. I saw the meatball coming up, caught it in the middle and started down. Speed was good, lineup good. I wiggled the fingers in both hands and took a deep breath. "Meatball – lineup – airspeed. Meatball lineup – airspeed. Concentrate! Meatball – lineup – airspeed," I repeated to myself.

The LSO said, "Going a little high again, not bad, ease the nose over just a touch."

"Concentrate, dummy," I told myself. I was right-on a second ago, and now the ball was a little high. I eased the nose over and then back up again to stop it.

"Good catch, you're doing fine, check your lineup, looking good," the LSO said.

He was trying to help me as much as he could, and I felt it through his radio calls. I needed it.

"Okay, don't let it go high-in close this time, hold it in the middle, looking good."

Once again, the end of the ship passed under me and the meatball went zooming past. This time it stayed in the middle. The next thing I knew was a loud BAM and I was thrown full forward in the cockpit. The tailhook had caught a wire! I had made my first night arrested landing.

A quarter of a second later, the Air Boss said, "Off with the power, let us pull you back."

When a pilot is safely aboard the ship things happen very fast. Once I was sure I had caught a wire I had to reduce the power so the tailhook would release the arresting wire.

Now I had to taxi to the catapult and do it all over again. I needed five more landings before I was night qualified. I added power to go up to the catapult for the next shot into the black night. In just a few minutes, I was again thrown into the gloomy black night.

Although I was already beginning to tire, the elation over having made my first night landing inspired me to get another successful landing on my next pass. But, I boltered again! "Dumb, dumb, dumb," I thought.

Supersonic Fighter Pilot

The ship's Flight Control Officer was concerned about my performance and so was I. He knew that if I boltered again I would not have enough fuel to fly to the divert field. This could result in the loss of an airplane.

He gave the command "*Nightcapper* 102, your signal *bingo*, proceed to Cecil Field, refuel and return."

"*Bingo*" means fly to the assigned land base airport. This was not funny – not even a little. As anyone can imagine, pilots are not allowed to argue or vote with the commanders. Everyone on the ship knew that I had screwed up and was sent to the divert field. Yes, I felt terrible about my performance, but I knew that I could do it.

By now, it was almost midnight. I had been up many hours. I was sweaty, tired, half excited, and half depressed as I landed on the 12,000 ft. of concrete at Cecil Field, FL.

I called the tower and asked them to notify the duty officer that I needed some fuel quickly to fly back to the ship. In about fifteen minutes I was flying back out to the ship for the remainder of my night landings.

I was cleared into the landing pattern about 1 AM.

Nick, the LSO said, "Glad to have you back. Let's finish this up and go to bed. You are looking good; just keep it coming."

I trapped two minutes later, headed for the cat, got shot off, and was immediately cleared downwind. I got another bolter and then another trap. I had four traps and five bolters so far! I had guessed correctly; I wasn't going to be student of the week at the *Shangri-La*. Still I didn't give a darn. I was still sweaty and tired, but I had to prove my bravery to myself and my shipmates. I just wanted to finish.

I trapped the fifth time, went to full power, came back to idle, looked to the right, and raised the hook, getting ready for my final launch and landing. Then a call came over the radio that delivered the sweetest, kindest, most wonderful news I have ever heard in my entire life.

The seasoned Air Boss said, "Congratulations, 102. On one of your many bolters, you actually should have caught a wire, but you got a hook skip (my tailhook jumped over # 4 wire). We are going to count that as number six. Your signal *bingo* to Cecil (go back to the land base). Bravo Zulu (well done in Navy lingo)."

My friend, Pete Easterling, was standing next to the Air Boss in Primary Flight Control when the command was given. He still likes to tell the story of what happened next.

The way he tells it there was a slight pause and then this distant voice replied unbelievingly, "You mean I don't have to do it again?"

"No, son, head for home. You've had a long day," answered the Air Boss.

I was yelling in my oxygen mask all the way home that night. I rolled that airplane over and over. I yelled and screamed. I even took my mask off so I could hear myself yell. I don't think winning the lottery would have made me feel any better. God, I was happy! First, I had made it through flight school and won the coveted *Wings of Gold*. And now I had qualified as a Night Carrier Fighter Pilot. My entire life was already a success. Everything else would be downhill. I made it! *I made it!* Scared as hell, but I made it! I felt great. I couldn't wait to call my folks. Their son was a fighter pilot and tonight he had proven it. He was a man. YIPPEE!! HOT DAMN!!

He who conquers himself is strong.

CHAPTER THIRTY

CROSS COUNTRY

LARIE CLARK

While on a cross country flying from NAS Cecil to McChord AFB in Washington, my friend and squadron mate, Al Moore and I, landed at Hill AFB in Utah for fuel. On the ground at Hill AFB we were informed they would be closing the field at 1 PM for their annual air show. We were asked to stick around for static display, or leave before the field was closed. I chose the latter as I had family waiting for me in Seattle.

We were informed we could depart just before the field closed and could make a section afterburner takeoff. What the heck, a little pre-show effort seemed fine on our part. I was in the lead with Al on my starboard wing. We lined up and were cleared for the takeoff. I nodded, released the brakes, and continued the power to one hundred percent, and then called for burner. We accelerated nicely down the runway. I could see Al tucked in very tight on my right wing. This was going to look good for the air show crowd.

Just as we reached rotation speed I heard an explosion and felt extreme vibration in the aircraft. We were airborne in a split second, and I knew the *Crusader* was flying well, and I had it under control. I eased the power back a little and asked Al to give me a good inspection, which he did in minimum time.

He reported that all appeared good except I had blown a starboard tire. He said, "The wheel is still attached and appears to be in good shape, but your tire is completely gone."

I had no idea what had caused the tire to go. My heels had been on the deck and I didn't have size fifteen boots.

A quick decision was made to continue to McChord AFB as returning to Hill AFB would disrupt their show. The aircraft appeared to have no damage and at the speed we were going the plane was flying well. We informed Hill tower that we were on our way.

As the aircraft approached 300 knots indicated airspeed I felt the need for more nose up trim. I had been trimming during the climb so I thought, but the nose trim was not working for some reason. The trim wheel indicated full nose up trim, but that was not the case. I mentally recorded the fact that the trim was apparently inoperative. I told my wingman about this and we continued climbing for our cruise altitude. As we climbed the back pressure on the stick increased tremendously. Finally, at about 30,000 ft., I told Al and ATC that I needed to level at this altitude.

I had to place both of my knees on the lower instrument panel with my hands locked around the stick to hold the aircraft half way level. Otherwise, it would be proposing all over the sky. I flew this way for the next two hours.

On arrival at McChord AFB we informed the tower of my problem. We decided that Al should land first in case I had problems on the runway. I requested that the crash crew be standing by the runway when I landed. McCord requested that I burn down to minimum fuel and said they had a fire helicopter airborne for my arrival. The helicopter was a multi-rotor type with a huge water bucket swinging below. I was happy to see the preparation the Air Force weenies had made for my arrival.

As I landed the helicopter was hovering over me on the roll-out just in case a fire broke out. Thank goodness there were no problems on landing.

After arriving at Base Operations a LT Colonel (Safety Office) demanded to know why we would come to his airbase with a known emergency. Why hadn't we gone to Whidbey Island, or NAS Seattle? He asked me if I knew the procedure for aircraft landing with a blown tire and then proceeded to tell me.

He said, "The gear would have to be removed from the aircraft, dye checked, and X-rayed before going back on the airplane. The tire, which we don't have, when mounted, needed to be put in a room for twenty-four hours to insure no pressure is loss and to top it off and we don't have the personnel to do all this. And to make matters worse, where in the HELL are we going to get a tire for a *Crusader*?"

I was then reminded what Ron Knott said the word Air Force meant. Ron said, "Air Force is what you have when you eat too many beans or blow your nose; that is Air Force!" How true!

When I finally calmed the LT COL I told him I'd make arrangements for the tire. We wouldn't pull the gear and we came into McChord, as that was our approved and filed destination. He didn't care.

He said, "You should have gone elsewhere, and we will pull the landing gear for inspection before you can depart my airport."

I told him we blew tires on carrier landings occasionally from cable cuts, and the gear was designed for such. I also told him to call our Carrier Air Group Commander and he would tell him where to go. He then backed off of his big threat. I suppose you can say we won!

Long story shorter, I called our squadron maintenance folks at Cecil and they had no idea what had caused the control problem. I called NAS JAX AMD and they referred me to North Island AMD. I finally found a Chief there who told me it might be a spring that came off the bob-weight, which is located in the vertical tail behind one of many, maybe twenty, stress panels. These calls had taken the better part of the day.

Al and I had noticed the UHT was way off its normal static engine shutdown position. In fact it was showing just the opposite on the fuselage marks. So being two brilliant Naval *raziators,* we started the aircraft and adjusted the pitch trim knob. We were unable to get it in the correct position.

With a small handled, straight Phillips head screwdriver in hand, and at the suggestion of North Island AMD, I started unscrewing panels. I believe there were a jillion screws in each of the three panels that I removed. Finally, I spotted a spring that was obviously not in its correct position.

The vibration I'd experienced with the blown tire on take off at Hill AFB had literally moved the spring out of the detents on the bob weight for the UHT. The spring was literally, laying there doing nothing. It was a fairly simple operation to reinstall the spring and screw the stress panels back onto the aircraft. I paid for that with a sore wrist for weeks with all the twisting of that screwdriver. Where was the speed driver or electric/battery powered drill?

On start up the following day, the UHT with a zero reading trim wheel, showed a nose down of four or five degrees on the fuselage side. I elected to have my brother watch while I place the trim wheel to whatever it took to get the aircraft trim to the Take Off mark on the fuselage. With the trim set and a clearance received, I taxied out headed for Hill AFB, my intermediate stop for fuel.

On arrival at Hill, I had the aircraft fueled and filed a flight plan for my home base of Cecil Field, FL. As I was taxiing out for take off, I had to make a ninety degree turn on the taxiway to get to the runway. As I made that turn I heard and felt another tire blow. "Wow! *What* is going on?" I thought.

I notified the Tower and a car was sent out for me. The maintenance crew at Hill was fabulous. They pulled the aircraft back to the ramp and had it tied down and chocked in just a few minutes.

My wingman, Al Moore, had gone back to Cecil a couple days earlier. Our Skipper, Hal Terry, dispatched Al back to Hill AFB with a new *Crusader* tire. My three-day cross country turned out to be a seven day fiasco.

We learned later that the Navy had received a batch of bad tires. In fact, there were over one hundred *Crusaders* tire blowouts across the fleet in a short time. That's my trim story and I'm sticking to it.

CHAPTER THIRTY-ONE

CARRIER QUALIFICATIONS

WAYNE SKAGGS

In early 1965 I was a newly designated Naval Aviator assigned to Fighter Squadron 124. This squadron was called the RAG (Replacement Air Group). The primary purpose of the RAG was to train new *Crusader* pilots in all aspects of flying this supersonic aircraft before being assigned to a fleet squadron. The final test was that of landing the *Crusader* on board an aircraft carrier. We needed ten day arrested landings and six night arrested landings to qualify. After what seemed like months of many FCLPs (Field Carrier Landing Practice) we were authorized to fly out to the big ship to make our arrested landings.

When the day came for our carrier qualifications (CQ), we flew out to the USS *Kittyhawk*. The *Kittyhawk* was operating southwest of San Clemente Island off the California coast. Upon arrival overhead of the gigantic ship I was directed to fly to a holding pattern due to a crash on the flight deck. I was told I would be given a *Charlie Time* as soon as possible. (*Charlie Time* is the planned landing time aboard a carrier.)

The ship's Air Operations Officer (Air Ops) was monitoring the carrier's location in reference to emergency landing airports on the coast. He also kept up with the amount of fuel each aircraft had remaining so he would know instantly if we could reach these airports without running out of fuel in case there was a problem on the flight deck. If the pilot was directed to *bingo* that meant that he was to fly to the assigned airfield and land.

***Crusader* being hooked up to the catapult**

After an extended period of time in the holding pattern, I was directed to *bingo* to San Clemente. This was a big surprise to me because I had enough fuel to fly to Miramar Naval Station where the runways were much longer.

When I questioned Air Ops I was told, "You have insufficient fuel to fly to Miramar. Land at San Clemente."

I was struggling to get my feet on the brakes as I fumbled to find the G suit sensor for relief. Somewhere during this fiasco both of my main tires blew, due to my abuse of the brake pedals. The F-8 and I were now sliding on two hot rims toward pending disaster; but God was gracious. My speed was slowing and nose gear steering was working, so I folded my wings and skidded up neatly next to

Supersonic Fighter Pilot

the other F-8. I shut down the engine, climbed out of the cockpit, and ran to a pickup truck parked on the taxiway. There, I found the station duty officer taking notice of what had happened to his airport.

I tried to explain to the duty officer that there was an additional problem developing. I told him there was another F-8 coming in behind me that was also directed to land at his airport. I suggested that he clear the taxiway and tell the tower to inform the other F-8 to land on the taxiway. This duty officer was not a pilot and did not understand the danger approaching.

He said, "You can't land on a taxiway."

After a short, heated discussion on the merits of landing on a taxiway that was as wide and long as the runway, and not having two F-8s sitting in the middle of it, he called the tower with my request. Alas, it was too late. The other F-8 landed on the same runway – not the taxi way, blew both main tires, and skidded down the runway on the rims. Suddenly the wings folded, the nose yawed to starboard, and he skidded to a stop right next to my bird.

This was an awesome sight. There were now three F-8 *Crusaders*, parked neatly aligned in the middle of the runway with about three feet between the folded wings. The wheels on all three aircraft were ground off to the point that a jack could not be placed under the jack pad at the axle. It was going to take a Cherry Picker to lift the planes in order to install new wheels and move them off the runway. At this point it seemed the only reasonable thing to do was go to the Officers Club. We did!

Mysteriously, during the night all three aircraft received new brakes, wheels and tires. The next morning we all strapped in these aircraft and blasted off for Miramar Naval

Air Station. There we exchanged these birds for fresh ones and returned to *Kittyhawk* to complete the carrier qualification mission. Thank goodness, I never heard another word about the incident.

RUSSIAN BOMBERS

Later that year I joined Fighter Squadron 51 and we deployed to Vietnam on board the USS *Ticonderoga* (CVA-14). On our way home after a long and demanding cruise, we ran into some really bad weather about halfway between Japan and Hawaii. In fact, there was little visibility in any direction.

We were placed on alert, Condition One, because of the threat of Soviet bombers flying over the fleet. This was part of the Cold War tactics by the enemy. Our primary purpose was to antagonize the Russian bomber fleet of aircraft, namely the Bear, Bison, and Badger. We would intercept them and fly on their wing any time they crossed an imaginary line 250 miles from the fleet. And of course, they were antagonizing us as well. The Navy did not want a picture of a Russian bomber flying over the fleet, appearing in US newspapers without the escort of Navy fighters.

I was strapped in the cockpit of my *Crusader* and placed on the catapult ready to launch, while we were in Condition One. That is, we could be launched within minutes if the bombers started toward the fleet. But the weather was so bad this day I thought; "Surely they are not going to launch us in this mess."

Suddenly there was a lot of activity on the flight deck. I was getting the crank signal from the deck crew to start my engine. The orders were to launch the CAP (Combat Air

Patrol) aircraft. The weather was going to make this day very interesting.

I was launched off the *Ticonderoga* and they shot off two additional F-8s behind me. We joined up overhead the ship and were vectored by *Ticonderoga* radar to intercept the Soviet bombers. It is interesting to note that I was the lead aircraft with no radar working, and the junior pilot in the group. The ship's vector to the bombers was accurate and we soon were flying wing on the Russian bombers. It was exciting to be flying on the wing of the enemy Bear, Bison, and Badger bomber aircraft. They took our picture and we took their picture with our hand held cameras, as well. They stayed at high altitude, probably due to the low ceilings until crossing over the *Ticonderoga,* and then turned away from the fleet. At 250 miles away from the ship we waved goodbye to each other and the enemy bombers headed for home. Although we were enemies there was a kind of feeling of fraternal flying friendliness between us – I suppose only a pilot would understand that feeling. The real fun for us was about to begin.

We had no idea how much the weather had deteriorated while we were airborne, but we were about to find out just how bad it was. No one from the ship gave us any weather information. My first indication of the weather conditions around the ship was when I was on the Carrier Controlled Approach (CCA). I descended to 500 feet and was still in heavy weather with zero visibility. Then suddenly I was vectored to go around and make another approach. I heard them vectoring the number two wingman on final approach. Then there was a commotion on the radio, which was totally unreadable.

The first thing I understood after that was, "Angel, proceed two miles ahead of the ship."

My first thought was, "What the hell are they thinking? Are they going to have us eject two miles ahead of the ship?"

I found out later that the number two aircraft broke out of the overcast below 200 feet and nearly hit the helicopter (Angel) on the starboard side of the ship. The number three wingman was vectored for another approach as well. On my second pass I continued to descend until I could see the water. My radar altimeter read about 170 feet and the ship was so far to the left that I had no chance of making a safe landing. I applied power and went back into the clag for another approach.

It seemed that the ships CCA azimuth was off about 30 degrees and as a result of this we were being vectored right of the correct course. The ships TACAN was down and so was my radar. There was no way that I could find the ship on my own. I was getting low on fuel. This added to the tension that was already in the cockpit. There was no tanker airborne to give me more fuel and the divert fields were beyond flying range. As the old saying goes, "The pucker factor engaged."

The number two aircraft was now on his second approach. The ship's radar again vectored him right, but he sighted the ship soon enough to go for it and landed. On my third approach I also descended below glide slope early, expecting to see the ship to my left. No, it was to the right! I made a hard right turn, then a hard left turn, rolled out over the landing area and touched down on the deck only to get a hook skip and have to do it all over again.

Supersonic Fighter Pilot

On my fourth approach, with fuel running low, I had lost all faith in the ship's radar, and told them that I had the ship in view when actually I did not see anything. I stayed at about 160 feet radar altimeter while I dead reckoned my way around the pattern. I picked up the ship's wake and followed it inbound. As I learned later, I duplicated number three's landing technique with a quick step right while popping up over the ramp to an arrested landing. What a relief. There were three happy pilots aboard the *Ticonderoga* that day.

Later we observed the approaches on the PLAT (recorded video) and it went like this: Nothing, nothing, F-8 suddenly appears coming off the side of the PLAT display, just aft of the fantail in about 70 degrees right bank, rolls wings level and traps. Then number three pops up over the ramp and traps.

While in the Ready Room, watching this circus over and over again with the LSOs, someone noted that there was never a radio transmission from an LSO during the whole fiasco.

The response of the LSO was, "By the time we could see them it was too late to say anything."

Like they say in Naval Aviation, "If you don't scare yourself at least once a day you are not doing your job right." And so it was.

CHAPTER THIRTY-TWO

PHOTO MISSION

WILL GRAY

I returned to Vietnam in 1972, on the USS *Midway*, assigned to VFP-63 Detachment 3. I was the replacement Officer in Charge (OINC) for Lieutenant Commander Gordie Paige, who was my roommate during my first two cruises. Gordie had had been shot down on 22 July and captured. I think he was the last F-8 POW captured during the war.

The war was just about the same as it had been in 1967. If I had saved my maps I could have used them all over again since we were flying in the same area. I always used charts even though I knew the country like my own farm in Louisiana. I had a full set of charts in every scale (1:5,000,000, 1:1,000,000, 1:250,000, and 1:50,000) for the target areas. There was no storage place for all that in the *Crusader's* cockpit so I sat on the pile and kept the one I needed up in the windscreen.

The only difference between my 1967 cruise on the *Coral Sea* and the 1972 cruise on the *Midway* was time and a few minor equipment changes. I still flew the RF-8G, but with different cameras and newer ECM (Electronic Countermeasures) gear. The escorts were still F-4s with the same fuel problems.

The F-4 was a hindrance to the mission since it was short on fuel. Also, it had a large radar cross-section that made it easy for the enemy to see them on their scopes. It produced heavy black exhaust smoke that allowed the enemy to see it for miles. When we had photo-on-photo escorts, we drew little fire. We flew erratically and fast, and our small radar cross-section did not present an offensive threat to the enemy so he could not always come after us with his best shot.

There were three carriers in the Gulf of Tonkin that had RF-8 detachments. I used a new call-sign for my detachment called *Baby Giant*. And our familiar *Papa Papa* (PP) tail-code letters were replaced with November Foxtrot (NF).

The North Vietnamese defenses were virtually the same. However, I did encounter a ZSU-23, which is a 23mm AAA and is capable of acquiring, tracking, and engaging low-flying aircraft.

I was running a section of railroad that crossed the Thanh Hoa Bridge. I approached the bridge from the north moving about 600 knots and 4500 feet altitude. I had my eyes on the viewfinder following the rail line. I just happened to look up and saw a stream of red coming right at me from a point near the railroad. It looked like a solid red line. I just about broke my right leg getting in rudder to break away. It missed! The excitement was over in a second but I was impressed. It took me a couple of miles to get back on the route and continue south until my *Phantom* escort ran low on fuel.

One of the nicest features of the RF-8G was its great fuel load. With 10,152 pounds of JP-5 and a very low drag airframe it was the perfect combination for photo work. However, the maximum landing weight you could land with was about 2000 pounds of fuel due to landing gear problems.

Supersonic Fighter Pilot

The RF-8 was always the last to launch. Saving fuel was our philosophy. We met our escorts on the KA-3 tanker (the greatest tanker ever built) and waited for the F-4 to take on about 2000 pounds of fuel to top off. The cruise out to the coast-in point was made at about 31,000 feet at max endurance speed to save fuel. When we had the coast-in point located we pushed up the power and dumped the noses to gain speed before entering any SAM envelopes.

The *Crusader* would run right up to Mach One at full military power. The F-4 would generally have to go in and out of burner and play the inside of our turns in order to keep in position.

Flying combat is the ultimate experience you can have in an aircraft. Being allowed to perform a mission you have trained very hard for is extremely satisfying. It is a mixture of sickening fear and satisfaction. I know what it feels like to be a dove in a corn field on the opening day of hunting season, and after flying to the end of the field safely calling, "*Corktip, feet wet.*"

And that is a general description of the photo mission, how we flew it, and how we survived. Like they used to tell us, "You can't buy experience like this on the outside." And we would say, "And you can't give it away either."

CHAPTER THIRTY-THREE

UNEXPECTED EJECTION

MICHAEL HANLEY

It is reported that Captain Michael Hanley was taking one of the VMF (AW)-235 birds on a test hop at NAS Atsugi in 1963. Shortly after he started his take off roll he reported fumes or bad odor in the oxygen. He then told the tower that he was aborting the take off and proceeded to drop his hook for the mid-field arresting gear. The tower reported a "hook skip" and Mike shut down the engine but continued towards the end of the duty runway and the fence at the bottom of the picture.

Note: hook down and canopy gone

Seeing he could not get the *Crusader* stopped prior to the end of the runway, Mike popped the canopy (per procedures).

Mike in the ejection seat

The F-8 nose gear collapsed and the bird slid forward, through the barbed-wire fence. In doing so, the nose cone went under the top strand of barbed wire. The fence's top wire, under tension, slid up; over the nose, over the windscreen, and into the cockpit just inches above Mike's head. The wire got caught on and pulled the Martin-Baker face curtain – starting the ejection sequence. Mike is shown just after he was ejected. Note his hands are at his knees, neither on the ejection handle nor on the face curtain.

Here, Mike has managed to put his hands up to protect his face as the seat is pulled away by its drogue chute.

Supersonic Fighter Pilot

Mike separating from the ejection seat

Mike landing without a full parachute

This picture was snapped just prior to Mike's return to earth. He is probably no more than three to six feet above the deck. As you can see, only the extraction and drogue chutes had time to fully deploy. The main chute was just beginning to fill.

We are pleased to report that Mike did survive. Best recollection is that his most significant injury was a shattered pelvis.

[Author's Note: As you can tell these pictures are not the best quality, but I doubt that we could get the pilot to go through the process again just to get better photographs.]

CHAPTER THIRTY-FOUR

A NUGGET'S LUCKY DAY

TOM MYERS

The weather was perfect for a nugget (first tour pilot) flying off the carrier. The blue of the sky and sea were beautiful. The sea state was calm and there was only about ten knots of Caribbean wind. The aircraft was an RF-8A, and the date was 30 January 1964 on the USS *Roosevelt* (CVA-42).

We were on an operational workup cruise off Leeward Point, Cuba, getting ready for my first Med Cruise. I was pumped, finally in the fleet, and part of Light Photographic Squadron Sixty-Two, Det-42. We had three aircraft, four pilots, a Photo Intelligence Officer, and twenty-six enlisted maintenance troops to maintain the aircraft. We shared the Ready Room with the famous *Red Rippers* of VF-11 flying the F-8 *Crusader*. Of course, that sharing for our detachment meant four Ready Room chairs in the back for the movie and only up front for flight briefings.

That day's flight was going to be my fourth arrested landing on the *Roosevelt*. As a LTJG, the "new" part of the expression "photo weenie" had not even lost its luster. The excitement about being shot off the front end of the boat, completing the tactical reconnaissance around Cuba, and making an arrested landing is what I signed up for two and one half years earlier. Like I said, I was pumped and ready for anything.

The catapult was normal; your breathing stops as you wait for that long second that nothing happens as the cat officer touches the deck. Then you get instant mega Gs of force that pushes you back in the seat, as down the track you go. The force is a comfort as you know you will fly for a few seconds even if the engine quits.

As soon as you're off the cat you've got two things to do, well, actually six: breath, gear up, wing down, slight turn, keep climbing, and level off below the incoming air traffic. That day it all worked just fine.

There are things in flight that you don't want to hear from your wingman. One at the top of my list is, "You're on fire!" Well, he didn't say that. The second thing you might have on your top five would be, "You're leaking fluid"! He did say that.

The trick now was to determine what is leaking and how bad is the leak. In an aircraft there are three fluids, not including cold sweat at exciting times, streaming from the pilot's body in various places. Luckily all of them are different colors. The leak wasn't red so it wasn't hydraulic, and it wasn't tan like engine oil. That left the only possibility, a fuel leak.

The engine was running fine but I could see the fuel gauge decreasing in quantity. I had lost 4,000 pounds of fuel in ten minutes. I knew that this was a really bad leak.

From the cockpit the aircraft seemed to operate normally in terms of power and flight performance. There were no warning indications except the fuel gauge showing the excessive fuel loss. Without my wingman's warning of a fuel leak it could have gone unnoticed for awhile and would have put me too far from the ship to return.

Supersonic Fighter Pilot

As soon as I told the Air Boss on the ship of my problem they started a "Pull Forward" of all aircraft on board to clear the landing area for me as soon as possible.

The approach and touchdown was uneventful; no comments from the Landing Signal Officer other than the comfort of the "Roger Ball-leaking" response to the ball call.

As luck would have it, I picked up the number two wire. On rollout the nose gear compressed normally causing the F-8 to come up the deck looking like it was trying to vacuum up the rest of the flight deck with that small condensed moisture cloud in the intake.

The next two seconds was where one "situation" turned into a "true emergency." All of the fuel that had pooled in the various places of the airframe came sloshing forward as the aircraft decelerated on arrestment. When this happened about ten feet of flame came out the intake and about fifteen feet of flame came out of the tail section. And raw fuel was leaking onto the flight deck. I heard a big "Boom!"

With the explosion in the face of the engine, all the raw fuel fumes came through the air conditioning and defrost system in the cockpit and into a very wide-eyed pilot as a result of the "Boom." I must tell you that when you put fuel into eyelids, the muscles that control them lose their ability to be voluntary. My eyes closed tightly and refused to open.

The Air Boss said, "Shut your engine off!"

After a bit of fumbling around I managed to get the power off and the canopy open.

Two corpsmen lifted me out of the cockpit and took me to sickbay. It took considerable eye flushing with an eye solution before any kind of blink motion returned to my eyes.

I was lucky due to the fact that there was no fire in-flight. The engine operated normally. I had a wingman to provide external monitoring of the failure. The ship recognized the only alternative to an ejection was an emergency pull forward and a recovery, and they did it. The explosion occurred after the wire was engaged and it put fumes, not fire into the cockpit.

The material failure occurred on the cat stroke and was a fuel cell line connection separation. The aircraft required an engine change and repair of the fuel cell line.

What would I have done differently? Nothing! But if it happened again I would be quick to turn off the Air Conditioning and put my visor down.

The LT and I did gain a new appreciation of each other's abilities, and we learned from one another the rest of the cruise. However, it did take some time when I trapped onboard that my eyes didn't close automatically for an extended "blink" on deceleration. I believe that a significant number of body parts do have their own memory of events. I believe that aircraft emergencies and certain liberty calls confirm that.

The old axiom has an addition to it now, "When you're out of F-8s you're out of fighters, and just prior to any explosion, close your eyes!"

CHAPTER THIRTY-FIVE

NON – SHOT CAT – SHOT

BILL BRANDEL

One of the most dangerous jobs in the United States Navy is to sit in an aircraft and be launched off the ship by a catapult. The catapult is designed to accelerate the aircraft to flying speed within just a few hundred feet (about 250'). As with any piece of machinery things can go wrong with the catapult that will place the pilot and plane in danger.

A "Cold Cat Shot" results when the catapult malfunctions for some reason and does not provide enough power to accelerate the aircraft to flying speed as it leaves the carrier. When this happens, the aircraft stalls and falls into the water in front of the ship. The pilot either rides the airplane into the water or ejects from the aircraft.

There is also a "Hot Cat Shot." This is when the catapult exerts excessive power on the launch and rips the launching harness off the aircraft. Again, the pilot may go into the water or eject from the aircraft if he can't get it stopped before going overboard.

Then there is the "Non Cat Shot" misfortune, which is an unsuccessful deck launch due to hookup or hold back failure. Unfortunately, many catapult malfunctions will result in the death of the pilot.

The following is the story of my "Non Cat Shot" that forced me and my F-8 *Crusader* to make a high-dive into the

Atlantic Ocean from the deck of USS *Independence*, during a very dark night on February 28, 1962.

I was on board the USS *Independence* to complete my carrier landing qualifications that was required by the Navy when a pilot is transitioning into a new type of aircraft. My requirements were to make ten day arrested landings and six night arrested landings.

I had made all my day landings and now was in the process of completing the night requirements. This night I was secured to the holdback, so I thought, on the catapult, with full power applied and ready for the launch.

It's late, pitch black, raining, and the director signals me to watch the cat officer. The cat officer (the Shooter), with one amber wand held over his head is waiting for me to signal him that I am ready to go. At night this signal is to turn on my wing lights. I felt the tensioning on the holdback and was taking the final look at the engine gauges. Quickly, I shifted my gaze out the left side to pick up the catapult officer, when I felt an unexpected and unfamiliar slight jostle. It felt like the airplane was starting to move. Within a few milliseconds I knew that it was moving. I knew immediately something was bad wrong in the catapult sequence.

Things started to happen quickly. I saw the director giving me the crossed wands signal for brakes. I stood on the brakes for an instant with no apparent effect. I didn't want to pull back the power, because I had no way of knowing for sure that I wasn't still hooked to the shuttle with it doing the "slow pull" of the classical "cold cat shot." I didn't think the bridle had come off the shuttle or had broken, because I felt certain I would have felt the jolt of the shuttle passing under the nose wheel.

Supersonic Fighter Pilot

Since stopping seemed out of the question I was down to the following options: the first was to try maximum braking. I tried that and it did not work. The second option was to eject from the aircraft; I was much too low and slow for a successful ejection. Third option was to gain enough speed to fly the airplane. I was much too slow to accelerate to flying speed. The fourth option was to "ride it in." Riding it in was my only logical choice.

As I was slipping and sliding down the deck many procedures ran through my mind. I lit the afterburner to give me a little more thrust that would result in a nose-up attitude when hitting the water. Also, I jettisoned the canopy to make egress easier once I landed in the ocean.

I noted a short pause during the sixty foot fall, followed by a bright flash ("seeing stars" like when I was hit when boxing). Then I realized that the cockpit was full of water; I am alive because I can see the canopy outline lighted by the light green phosphorescence of the warm Gulf Stream water; and (bad news) my oxygen mask, had come off. I pulled the ditching handle (release) and it worked as advertised. I was able to get clear of the cockpit quickly.

The nose of the aircraft pops up for a few seconds, and I got a welcome big gulp of air before it started down again. I inflated my flotation gear and was able to stay on the surface of the eight foot swells.

I was pleased to see that I was in no danger of being hit by the carrier due to the excellent evasive action taken by the ship's captain. I did see the plane guard destroyer, USS *Manley*, in the distance and fired a couple flares to get his attention. The *Manley* was quick to pick me up and the corpsman on board treated my minor injuries.

The weather was too rough to transfer me back to the carrier until two days later. On the second day a helicopter picked me up from the fantail of the *Manley* and brought me back to the *Independence*.

Due to this accident there was a great "procedure modification" for launching the *Crusaders*. The catapult crew had been presented with a dumb design, which almost cost me my life. They did everything correctly as they had been taught, so I find no fault with them. I am thankful that I was able to survive this accident and had the pleasure of flying the *Crusader* many more hours.

CHAPTER THIRTY-SIX

BARRICADE ENGAGEMENT

STEWART SEAMAN

It was a beautiful day on the 19th of May 1965 as I was flying along in my F-8E *Crusader* just north of Messina, Sicily. My mission was practicing intercepts along the Italian coast. As I was flying I observed Mt. Etna, which was only about fifty miles southwest of my flight. Mt. Etna is one of the world's most impressive and active volcanoes. The volcano dominates the landscape of northeastern Sicily. It has the longest period of documented eruptions in the world. Many times when flying over Mt. Etna at night, I would look down into the boiling inferno and cringe at the thought of ejecting over such a place.

My squadron, VF-62, had been operating in the Mediterranean area for about three months. This was my third Med Cruise. I felt very comfortable operating off the USS *Shangri-La* although this was one of the smaller carriers in the Navy at that time. And I was really enjoying visiting the different ports in the Mediterranean. These liberty ports made the Med Cruises worthwhile.

After completion of the training flight my wingman and I headed back to the ship. Everything was working normal and I felt secure on my approach for landing. I made a good landing but could sense that something was not as it should be. According to procedures I went to full power when I landed just in case I did not make an arrested landing for some reason.

"Bolter! Bolter! Bolter!" Jim Brady, the LSO was shouting.

As frequently happens in Naval Aviation, my life was about to get a little more exciting. It appears that I had in fact caught an arresting wire, which should have stopped my aircraft. In fact, I felt the aircraft slowing down somewhat but the tailhook spit out the arresting wire and I went staggering down the deck at a very low speed. I didn't have enough flying speed so the only thing for me to do was to light the afterburner for full power and try to gain extra speed before going off the angle deck.

I rotated the aircraft to optimum angle-of-attack to stop the sink rate and to keep me out of the ocean. I am sure my high angle-of-attack looked aggressive from the flight deck but it was working and I was not about to release backpressure until the bird started climbing.

The aircraft started to climb as I left the ship. I finally came out of afterburner at 2,500 feet and was wondering what in the heck had gone wrong during my landing. I still had my gear down and the wing up and I was flying at about 200 knots.

The Air Boss called me and said something had happened to my starboard landing gear on the landing. He asked me to check my hydraulic pressure and other gauges to see if there were any problems.

I told him that everything looked good from the cockpit.

Then he told me to orbit overhead and another aircraft would join me to see if there were any damages.

The ready tanker, an A-4 *Skyhawk*, was directed by the Air Boss to inspect my landing gear. He joined my right wing and confirmed that my starboard main landing gear was still attached, but that one of the stabilizer struts was broken and the wheel was just dangling in the wind. I thought, "Okay, at least we know what the problem is now. What are my options?"

The least costly resolve to this problem would be to fly the crippled aircraft to a shore-based runway and make an arrested landing. That option was out because I did not have enough fuel to fly to the "bingo" field and I could not take on fuel due to my configuration.

Another option was to eject and make a nylon descent into the Mediterranean Sea. I sure did not like that possibility. I could make a normal approach and landing with the damaged right landing gear but the broken landing gear stub might catch on the arresting wire and cartwheel me into the ocean. My only choice was to bring the aircraft back to the ship and make a barricade engagement.

The carrier deck crew rigged the barricade in about two minutes. Jim Brady, our LSO, gave me great comfort on the approach and directed me to land between the # 2 and # 3 arresting cables.

The airplane flew great down the glide slope. As I touched down I again added full power, just in case the barricade broke. As I looked ahead, I saw the net coming my way very fast.

The tailhook caught the # 2 wire and that slowed me a bit before I went through the barricade. The vertical straps quickly curved around my wings. The airplane swerved to the right and tipped toward the deck. The airplane stopped just like an arrested landing. I shut the engine down, opened the canopy, and climbed out of my sick *Crusader*.

It was later determined that the shock strut on the right main gear had exploded. Analysis later determined that corrosion had caused weakness in that area. The airplane suffered no major damage and was flying again in a few days.

I actually flew another hop that afternoon. In those days we had a lot of incidents and just felt like this was part of the territory. Thank goodness for the barricade. It worked as advertised.

As the old saying goes, "Experience is often what you get when you were expecting something else."

CHAPTER THIRTY-SEVEN

THE SERMON ON THE RAMP

DAVE "FIREBALL" JOHNSON

A few guys have asked why I haven't added my tale to the sea stories. Here it is in a nutshell: I screwed up a night approach, blew up my F-8 on the ramp, flopped in the water, and was picked up by a destroyer. I'm not particularly proud of wrecking a machine I loved to fly.

By rights I should have been fish food; that I wasn't, I firmly believe is because there is a God who employs guardian angels (those assigned to nugget *Crusader* pilots that have really racked up the overtime), and who listens to those little pre-catapult prayers. Read on; count the screw ups, count the dang-nears, and then you decide. It sure as heck wasn't skill on my part that cheated the fish.

When I was shot off the ship the Angle of Attack (AOA) stopped working. Pretty soon it came back on and appeared to be working fine. I suggested to my fearless flight leader that we join up before coming back to the ship to check the accuracy of the AOA. However, as the flight progressed we both forgot about checking my AOA.

When I started my approach the AOA again stopped working for a few seconds but it came back on. I figured it was too late to bother anyone about this problem and continued my approach.

Ron Knott

After I transitioned into the landing configuration I determined that the airspeed indicator did not match the AOA. I knew that the AOA had been calibrated just before the flight and other squadrons also had had problems with the airspeed indicators, so I elected to rely on the AOA instead of the airspeed indication. Navy carrier pilots are taught from day one to rely on the AOA and the primary instrument for speed and the airspeed indicator as the secondary instrument.

We had Automatic Throttle (APC) on the F-8 that would adjust the power to hold the correct airspeed on approach. When I turned on the APC I found that it was inoperative as well. That meant I would be making a manual approach (controlling the throttle by hand) to landing. This was no real problem but did add work load on the pilot.

Now, I had *two malfunctions*; the discrepancy between the Angle of Attack and the airspeed indicator, *and* the auto throttle was not working.

I remember it being a really dark night on this approach. I noticed that the wing lights were inoperative as well. This is the *third* failure on this bird on this black night. So to overcome that malfunction I turned on the rotating beacon (normally off on landing) and opened the in-flight refueling door, just a small amount so another light would come on for the Landing Signals Officer to see (at night those lights give the LSO his clues as to the aircraft's position relative to the ship).

When I called the ball the AOA appeared to be working normal from the cockpit. However, the LSO only saw a "fast" approach light indicator and it was giving him false information about my speed. This is failure number *four*.

Supersonic Fighter Pilot

As a back up for checking my approach speed the LSO will rely on the SPN-12 (approach speed radar) readout. The SPN-12 was down. This is failure number *five*.

The LSO now has no way to judge my distance, glide path or altitude (which is directly related to AOA and therefore, airspeed). By all of the LSO indications I appeared to be approaching the ship really fast, when in fact I was very slow on the approach. This is false indication number *six!*

I continued the approach and appeared to be going a little high as I approached the ship. I made a small downward correction and the aircraft started coming down very fast. In fact it was coming down so fast that I could not stop the descent. I knew then I was in serious trouble and rotated the nose up while simultaneously going to full throttle and selecting afterburner in an attempt to stop the rate of descent.

The LSO stated that the aircraft dropped really fast, but was still showing a fast indication (because of the AOA error). Obviously, it was very slow in a nose high attitude.

Just as the afterburner lit, my aircraft hit the round down of the ship and broke up. The aircraft's fuel tanks erupted and a huge fireball enveloped the back half of the fuselage, which was doing a somersault behind the forward half of the airplane. The guys who were on the flight deck told me it was the most glorious explosion they had ever seen.

My brain may have been a bit scrambled from the impact but something told me that it was too quiet in the cockpit, too bright outside, and besides this, I shouldn't be going sideways across the # 4 wire. I knew immediately that it was time to leave the aircraft.

Ron Knott

I knew that I needed to sit up straight before I pulled the ejection seat face curtain. I had raised the seat very high for the approach. My head was too high to reach the ejection face curtain (the B-ring). Therefore, I had to duck my head to be able to get to the ejection handle. This permitted my hands to get past my helmet and allowed me to straighten up my neck prior to the ejection. That delay probably prevented my neck from being broken and also cut down on the time left for egress.

I didn't feel a thing when the ejection seat fired but I heard a loud bang and saw a bright flash below. I figured this was caused by the ejection seat. I quickly grabbed the toggles on my Mae West flotation gear. Then I heard another loud "crack" and felt a real jolt that yanked my hands off the Mae West toggles. Then I blacked out.

Remnants of the airplane had left the angle deck, rolled left, and entered the water inverted. Apparently the ejection seat fired at 90 degrees of bank, because no one saw the canopy, or the seat leave the cockpit (There was no photograph of the accident taken because the PLAT was down as well. This was malfunction number *seven* for the evening.)

It was later determined that the tremendous jolt that I experienced was the ejection seat hitting the water with me still attached to it. The "crack" was the drogue gun firing. One of the CO_2 cartridges had been activated so only one cell of the Mae West had inflated.

I soon regained consciousness and noticed an odd view of the ship. It was getting smaller and appearing and disappearing behind large waves. Then I saw the wing nearby, so I grabbed on to it. I cut my hand in the gap between the outer wing panel and main panel droops.

I heard someone yelling nearby but I could not determine from whence it came. About that time I noticed another ship near my position. It was a "plane guard destroyer" that is usually stationed about 1000 yards behind the carrier during air operations to rescue pilots in the water.

The crew was dropping me a horse collar (rescue sling). They tried to lift me up but I could not hang on to the collar due to the weight of my flight gear. I fell back in the water and went under. I was sucking in a lot of sea water and suddenly became aware that, "HEY, MAN! I'M DROWNING HERE!!!"

The destroyer crew had been yelling at me to grab the horse collar. They could see that the wing was sinking with the parachute. It sank just as they pulled me clear.

On the second attempt to hoist me aboard, ENS Bob Hendricks came over the side to hold my head out of the water. SN Snodgrass (duty swimmer) placed me into the horse collar again. The parachute was still about to pull me under. The crew could not get it released. Finally, the Executive Officer of the ship, LCDR Furey, climbed down the cargo net (which was hung over the side for just such events) with a knife in hand and cut the shroud lines to free me.

It still took five men to haul me in because of my weight. The vent hose to the poopy suit (rubber flight suit) had ripped out instead of disconnecting on ejection. The poopy suit was full of water. It probably held fifty extra pounds of the ocean. My flight gear weighed another fifty pounds. Add my body weight to that hundred pounds and you understand why it took five sailors to lift me aboard.

The crew laid me on a Ward Room table and began cutting off my flight gear. That is when it finally dawned on me what had happened.

I got really upset and was worried about the men on the carrier. I was afraid that some of them had been hurt when the aircraft crashed. The flight deck had been strewn with fire and flying aircraft debris. The plane captains and others were near the accident. I had to know if they were okay.

I insisted that the destroyer radio the carrier to see if anyone on the flight deck had been injured. The word came back that no one had been hurt. That relaxed me somewhat, then I promptly passed out again.

The most frightening part of the event was when the helicopter crew picked me up from the destroyer the next morning. They hoisted me up like a turkey in a wire basket. They winched me to the hovering chopper and after pulling the stretcher just halfway into the helicopter's cabin they went flying off to the *Shang*. I was sure that I was going to slide right out of the door and fly back into the water.

So instead of becoming *"Charlie the Tuna's Revenge,"* I became *"Fireball."* From then on my handle was *"Fireball."*

At the time I was sure my Naval Aviation days were over. My Skipper Stolly Stollenwerck and our XO Pete Easterling came to sick bay to hear my side of the story.

I can hear Stolly to this day: "Well, Dave, are you going to stay with us?"

"I couldn't believe it. I have a choice?" I thought. So I said, "Yes, Sir, if you'll let me."

He said, "Oh, sure, Dave," in that fatherly manner of his.

As a sidebar, after recuperating for about thirty days, my first flight after getting my "up medical chit" had an inauspicious beginning.

Supersonic Fighter Pilot

First, the aircraft went down on start. I was rescheduled for the next launch. That next bird went down with a hydraulic leak. I was rescheduled again as a spare for the next launch. Finally, they decided to launch me as a spare.

I was ready for the catapult. The catapult officer (Shooter) gave his signal to launch me by touching the deck. Nothing happened.

They suspended the catapult and tried again, and again, and again, and again, but still no cat shot.

I was finally fired off the ship on the fifth try. By that time I had developed a morbid curiosity. After going into the water on the back end of the ship, was a defective catapult going to put me into the water on the front end? Once the catapult fired it was just like old times again.

This was my nugget (first) cruise and I only had about fifty arrested landings at that time. By the time I left VF-13, I had over 300 more traps on the *Shang*. I sure didn't enjoy any of the night ones; not even a little bit. Most carrier pilots will say the same about the night landings. The daytime landings were a blast. For what it's worth I have never had bad dreams, or nightmares, or anything like that about that accident.

I found out after leaving the Navy that the aircraft I was flying the night of the accident had been in the hangar deck a few days before the accident. For some unknown reason the canopy was left open, and someone set off the fire suppression foam that filled the cockpit. This could explain the multiple glitches that I had that night trying to bring that aircraft aboard the ship.

This fact has made it a little easier for me to accept what happened that night. So in retrospect, I survived by the grace of God and am thankful that I was in the damaged bird instead of one of my squadron mates.

Larry Durbin, one of my squadron mates said, "As I remember, this was the last recovery of the night. The Skipper, Stolly Stollenwerck, and I were the only ones in the Ready Room watching the recovery on the monitor. When Stolly saw the fireball, he turned to me and said, '"Get out the next of kin report. We just lost Dave.'"

CHAPTER THIRTY-EIGHT

MEMORIES OF NIGHTS GONE BY

TOM MYER

[Author's Note: This very well written narrative is not about the *Crusader*; Tom Myers paints a picture of "memories" that all carrier pilots know so well. Thanks, Tom.]

It's the middle of the Pacific. It's flat black dark, and flitting around like fireflies are colored flashlight wands in mute silence, but with life changing directions for huge shadows lumbering slowly at times, sliding around a damp flight deck.

As your turn comes you slow up your forward movement as you go over the shuttle and slip off the front, then carefully another few critical inches, then "clunk" all movement stops.

You breathe again and now that nose gear extends slowly and the needle nose of the RA-5C comes up like a sprinter in the blocks at the "get set command." Then a low growl sound of incredible power starts and builds to a level that vibrates your soul. The two J-79 engines sound angry to be restrained by a stubby leash of steel against their willingness to fly.

A small cloud of condensation forms in the intake of each engine. Then with the flash opening of the fist of the

Catapult Officer, the growing light from the afterburners turns night into day.

In the cockpit a scan of the gauges, a checklist completed, and a salute given in hope to the Catapult Officer, and returned with his respect. He gracefully touches the deck, followed by one second of nothing. Then with a click of the breaking of the holdback fitting, your world accelerates to 170 knots in a blink and with a grunt of comforting acceleration forces, your world has become unique. It's the beginning of a night of both beauty and a breath holding flight. This cat shot me into a formless black night, where sea and sky are one and only mechanical gauges point to altitude and towards continued life.

In the day when it's hot, you're heavy and the sea is so still you can see the carrier's hull well under water; lift sometimes seems but a theory. You find yourself leaning forward when the cat releases you, straining against the straps, willing it with promises of future good behavior on liberty, to climb and accelerate. Yet in the day you're a bird; you can do and see what they do.

Now that its night you feel different. You're quieter; the business at hand is all business. The jokes have been left in the Ready Room and it is time to do the job and get back aboard safely. Now it is two hours strapped to a hard seat, mask pressed into your face; you navigate to the target trying to be invisible, willing to pay a month's flight pay to have that cloaking device of Star Trek fame, seemingly alone in the universe but knowing you're not.

You coast in, lights off, super droops, minimum afterburner to get rid of the exhaust smoke, and then all the knots you can muster. You focus your eyes out of the cockpit hunting for the sensors "on" point and anything that doesn't want to smile. Your RAN and the navigational system earn their low pay and price now.

Somehow, you jink and change headings and take directions from the backseat to arrive over the target, sensors on, viewfinder tracking. You need wings level for some night sensors longer than you want. What's there, what's been there, and what's hiding there, is the question? Then it's off target, a hard turn to an outbound heading looking for the safety of sea, the beautiful sea. Then when safe, climb, and your breath becomes normal again.

Now stretching for home, fuel balanced against Charlie time. Then the worst happens, a "Delta max conserve" call. You continue to hold, second guessing the reason for a pushover delay, trying to borrow lift, save fuel and speed up precious time from God himself. Can sweat replace fuel? They say that the only time you have too much fuel is when you're on fire. You think about the need for in-flight refueling and whether it's available tonight. The thought is a comfort for its availability, but you're not looking forward to a low fuel need to do it, especially at night. It is not natural to hit something hanging from another aircraft with your aircraft when you are still flying at night, in the dark, marginal weather, with the alternative if it doesn't work, being the sea.

Finally, it's your turn, a pushover on the exact second, at an exact place, and a no turning back commitment to an approach through the muck. Getting to that point on that second is an art form of no small amount of skill. We have all had them work smoothly and professionally and other times with 4G turns at 90-degree bank angle into that point, then idle power, speed brakes, and some smart remark from the back seat.

Some nights the nose is bathed in St. Elmo's ghostly glow, with the occasional trickle off of electric rivulets. You wonder about the visibility at the ship and the distance to the closest "bingo" land base. Sometimes that distance means only one chance at the deck in the *Vigi*, most times it was two, or when lucky, three passes at night.

Once you're pushed over, you're now heart and soul focused on the gauges, keeping airspeed and tracking to the inbound heading under control. Your Radar Attack Navigator (RAN) backs up the approach details, checklists, and altitude bases hoping for you to see the wake of the plane guard DD. He knows when you want to hear details from him and when you don't. You both know your lives have never been in greater peril than it will be in these next few minutes but you never even hint to it. You don't live to fight but now you do fly to live. Fate teaches that we were born and trained to develop safe, walk-away-from carrier landings. The aviator's lore is that fate gives us a bag of safe carrier landings and each time we do one we take one safe one out. We just don't know how many are in the bag, and a bolter takes one out, too. That's why bolters are "no damn good." It's like a mulligan in golf ... you don't want to do one; walk away traps are so much better.

Now we're at five miles and we level off, slow down, gear down, flaps at fifty, hook down, APC on. Last chance to balance fuel, then it's look outside at a half-mile and call the ball *Peacemaker*, *Hooter,* or just *Vigi* "Ball" with your fuel remaining. And if you're a seasoned carrier pilot you look at that down hook handle *one more time*. It's not that you would hate to owe the LSO a bottle for forgetting your hook ... you want to land and stop NOW.

Supersonic Fighter Pilot

You find that pin point of orange and the two green bars. The sea is not always a friend and the deck is moving. You don't chase it, Angle of Attack, lineup, and keep that ball in the center. At this point you are convinced beyond a shadow of a doubt that your RAN in the back because he can't see anything, has the mental ability and character, to be a religious zealot during these approaches. It's at this point you stop breathing and blinking for fear you'll miss something.

In close now, you feel every gust of burble coming over the deck, you want to be smooth and yet your grip on the stick slowly grows tighter. You don't look at the deck; your survival depends on every skill you have at this moment. You can't let your mind break your scan and say "Oh, there is the deck" or "Oh, there is the ramp." You listen for the LSO to say something, anything, that just might save your life or someone else's. I do believe you are so focused of what he might say on the radio started with the letter "P" for power or "W" for wave off, your body would respond before the sentence was complete. Then it's a rush of deck lights as you seem to settle into a black hole, then a jarring hit and a scraping hook. You jam that power back to 100%, try to get the nose up, make it fly again, just in case.

Then with the joy of your rebirth with earth-people, you're thrown forward into the straps. Yes! Then you wait a fearful one second for a wire break or hook release before you're stopped. Then throttles back, hit the nose gear steering, keep it straight, little left rudder on rollback to swing the nose right, hook up, flaps up, lights off, wing fold, find your director, power back on, and taxi clear of the foul line, thumbs up for an "up" aircraft and all in 3-4 seconds.

Now the exacting mimed chaos of the flight deck, aircraft movements of inches, at times with the cockpit over the water, with no sound but a head nod or a light wand flick from a young seaman in his early twenties who is working twelve hour days leaning backward into 30 knots of wind on a wet moving dark deck, jet engines ready to pull you in or blow you over. Your life is totally in that one yellow shirted director's hands for those moments that you are still moving on deck. He knows that and you know that, but you never hear his voice, see much of his face, nor know his name. But there is a trust, a bond of respect for what each of you do together. To do your job you need him.

Finally you're in your final spot, you complete system shut down check list, twelve tie down chains that holds the aircraft to the deck and then the canopy is opened. Then that mask comes off for the first wonderful breath of fresh night air and sea breeze that releases all of the tension you've had since the approach pushover. Steel pins on red flags are put in the seat so you cannot accidentally eject and then you realize your legs are shaking and are still pressing hard, holding the brakes.

Then you pick your way around tie down chains and duck under wings finding your way off the deck, into the cat walks and passageways of your city, your home. The LSO, one of your own, finds you and in front of friends and peers, you hear your landing grade, accepting, feeling either vindicated or just lucky. Then you debrief the mission and see the hardcopy of your risks and the profile and attempts on your life, the threat you didn't see in flight. Your ego takes some comfort that your mission supports the Air Wing and the battle of the day to come and the risks are the same, but

Supersonic Fighter Pilot

your soul takes comfort in not having to dream of the destruction to consider the human loss in all wars.

And then there were joys that never grew old, like busting out on top of the sun-blessed clouds, a blue that you live for on rainy days; or a night of a billion stars humbling the soul and then doing the hardest part, the landing, at the end of the flight; or low level at the speed of heat when the world is a blur depending on where you look and your whole body is alive as never before for any movement, even an inch lower or tree a foot higher.

Then there are those special days: "liberty call," a boating exercise, fun when sober, into adventures of the youth in us all, shore based in Cubi Point with San Miguels, the fragrant river, and the risk of monkey on a stick, the cat shot in the Cubi Officers Club, Hong Kong suits, beautiful sites, in a land of the strange and exotic. There are Thailand's wonderful treasures and Philippine friends, then Pollywog's becoming Shellback's on crossing the line not politically correct, down under where past sacrifices and times still bring respect and rewards, the USO shows and performers to remember. Then on the other side of the world, Cannes, Palma, Barcelona, Beirut, Athens, Rhodes, Sicily, and for many Christmas's and New Years at Naples, Italy.

Aviation on the edge brings soaring highs and frustrations of things that go wrong and turn out okay and things that turn out bad and crushing lows that follow. Families apart, with expressions of love only in letters or tapes. Then the time comes where friends, wingmen, GIBs (Guys in Back), so full of life, are gone. Ready Room empty chairs, fly-offs with empty seats bring the sad truth: Fatherless kids, wives now widows and men who, in our memories, will never grow old. Each one serves, some only in wishing for others. Neither contributes more for the mission.

CHAPTER THIRTY-NINE

WASTE IN SPACE

RON KNOTT

One of the most humorous stories in Naval Aviation happened to a friend of mine while he was assigned to a flying squadron on board one of the Navy's aircraft carriers. The complications he encountered flying his Douglass A-1 (*Spad*) was enough to make anyone extremely nauseated, to say the least. I will identify him only as Don since this could be embarrassing to him although this event happened many years ago.

Don was flying the *Spad* from the deck of an aircraft carrier operating in the Mediterranean Sea. He was a seasoned fighter pilot on his second seven-month (Med Cruise) when this calamity took place. Don, like most Navy fighter pilots thought he was the "best of the best" as far as flying off and on the boat was concerned. Somehow the Navy instilled that characteristic into all its pilots. The old saying of, "You can always tell a Navy fighter pilot, but you can't tell him much," was especially true in Don's way of thinking.

The A-1 that Don was flying had many epithets. It was called the *Skyraider*, the *Spad*, the *Queen,* and many other choice names. The A-1's mission was usually long and tiring, especially when flown from the deck of an aircraft carrier. The *Spad* would normally be launched on the first mission of the day and fly for five or six hours before returning to the ship. The airplane had the capability of carrying a tremendous amount of ordnance composed of bombs, rockets, and 20mm cannons. It was a very stable weapons platform thereby allowing the pilots to pulverize the assigned target.

A-1 *Spad*

The reciprocating engine of the A-1 consumed fuel at a much slower rate than jet fighters. Therefore, they could stay airborne much longer than the jets. When returning to the ship after these long missions the A-1s would normally be placed in a holding pattern to allow the jets to land first. There was much heated discussion about this dilemma within the Air Group. The jets were rather thirsty and had a high rate of fuel consumption and had to get on deck as soon as possible. Their mission was usually over in less than two hours while the A-1's mission lasted several hours.

A-1 drivers would make remarks to the jet jocks to the effect that, "You were low fuel state when you took off and we had to hold for you to land after flying for six long hours. You'll never win a war like this."

Supersonic Fighter Pilot

The jet jocks would respond, "You flew so slow that the war would be over before you arrived at the target." And so this friendly squabble continued between the prop pilots and the jet pilots during the cruise.

Each group had "Esprit de Corps" when it came to their mission. The Navy instilled into each and every squadron that they were the best. This pride is really what made the system work. Our carrier, the old rusty *Shangri-La* (CVA-38), would stand up against the new nuclear powered *Enterprise* (CVN-65) by exaggerating her capabilities. The *Spad* (A-1) driver was as proud of his aircraft as the supersonic F-8 driver was of his bird and rightly so.

Don had flown many missions in the A-1 and was well familiar with the long scheduled flights for his squadron. In fact, he really enjoyed being on the longer missions just to get away from the confines of the ship for a while.

During the cruise he had developed a constipation problem. He explained his predicament to the friendly Flight Surgeon and was given a laxative to resolve his difficulty. These small pills looked so powerless to Don. He said, "What the heck, I'll take a couple of them just to follow the doctor's orders." After he waited a few hours nothing happened. In pain and disgust he elected to take a handful more of these little innocent looking capsules. With one big gulp he swallowed several more pills.

Don was not scheduled to fly during this period due to his difficulty in defecating. However, the Scheduling Officer asked if he would consider standing by as a spare pilot for the next launch. It was normal operating procedure for all squadrons to man a spare aircraft in case a scheduled aircraft had a maintenance problem at the time of launch. The spare pilot and plane would be spotted on the deck ready to be launched if needed. The A-1 had a good reputation for making the scheduled flight so the spare pilot and plane were seldom launched. Don, being aware of this fact accepted the spare position, thinking that there was no chance for him to be shot off the front end of the big boat.

As luck would have it one A-1 had a maintenance problem. Don was taxied forward and catapulted off the boat on a 5-hour mission. The excitement of the launch and the joy of flying took Don's mind off the little pills he had taken earlier in the day. Things were going great for the first thirty minutes of this five hour mission. Then suddenly, like a shot in the dark a sharp pain hit him in the pit of his stomach. The little pills were working after all. They seemed to have the impact on his paunch equal to the force of a 500-pound bomb. He had to go, but where???

This critical problem needed attention, now! Desperately looking around in the cockpit he saw the only receptacle that could be used to contain his waste. His oxygen mask bag would be just the precise container for this job. This large nylon bag had the capacity to hold about one gallon of anything and was somewhat waterproof. Urgency was upon him.

The A-1 has a large cockpit compared to most fighter type aircraft, yet it's still a tightly confined area. With the coordination of a fighter pilot and the agility of a monkey, Don assumed the position of the cave man. He hunkered on the aircraft seat to relieve himself of this excruciating impasse.

Don had scored "expert" on hitting the target at a recent bombing exercise but he was having terrific difficulty hitting the small oxygen bag bouncing around in the cockpit. He had assumed a crouched position on the edge of the seat, cave man style, with his flight suit pushed down around his knees for this delicate delivery. His position was such that he did not have good target acquisition. To add to his complication he had only one hand to spare for this unimaginative operation. The other hand was necessary to keep the aircraft as smooth as possible since the A-1 lacked an autopilot. You can imagine his challenge of trying to hold this nylon bag and fly hunkered on the seat. The top of the bag had to be stretched open with his left hand, while flying the airplane with his right hand. This is one emergency that standard Naval operating procedures had not considered.

Finally he let go. He filled the bag with about 40% liquid, about 40% solids, and a 20% mixture of the two. He was able to score about an 80% hit in the target area. The other 20% ran down his left arm and the side of the bag onto the seat. "Well you can't have everything," he said to himself. "It's in the bag," took on a new meaning for Don that day.

The relief of the bowel movement felt great. Now a much greater problem was at hand, in hand, and on hand. "What am I going to do with this bag full of crap," he thought to himself. He couldn't hold the bag for the remaining four-and-half hours of flight. Yet, he dared not let loose of this darling little pouch because the only thing that held its contents secure was a tiny drawstring at the top. This drawstring would work loose easily if the bag bounced around in the cockpit and would allow the bag's ingredients to spill all over the place. This was not a very comforting thought to say the least.

Don thought ahead of the arrested landing that he must make at the end of the flight. He said to himself, "That will be a disaster. This sack full of goodies will be propelled through the cockpit like a five-inch rocket gone stupid when I land.

The extreme gravity forces encountered from such an arrested landing will cause the bag to explode in my face. I have got to get rid of this potential threat before landing, but how?"

The fragrance was so strong. He could hardly endure his captivity. Somehow he must get rid of his bag full of human waste before landing. He even considered ditching at sea, but soon changed his mind when he remembered the water temperature was so cold that he would expire from exposure in a short time. He knew that sharks would be attracted to such a scent in the water as well. Also, he knew this act would be terribly hard to explain to an accident investigation board, should he survive all other perils. He had to stick it out with his waste in space.

Don's wingman was unaware of the problems his leader was having. He could see unusual movement taking place in his leader's cockpit and he noticed the airplane was really unstable. He flew close aboard to investigate the mystery.

Don saw the wingman flying near. Immediately he knew what he must do with his dirty diaper. He said to himself, "I'll open my canopy and throw this bag on my wingman's airplane. This garbage will smear all over his canopy." Don got so excited about his new plan of action that he almost flew into the water. "This would be the greatest joke of the cruise," he said to himself. He could hardly wait until landing on board the boat to tell his squadron mates what he had done to his wingman. "He who laughs first ...."

The older Navy aircraft had the capability of opening their canopy in flight. Standard Naval operating procedure for the A-1 aircraft was to take-off and land aboard the Aircraft Carrier with the canopy open. This procedure would give the pilot a better chance of survival in case the aircraft

Supersonic Fighter Pilot

went into the drink. This procedure was used until the invention of the ejection seat that was standard equipment on the faster jets.

Don opened his canopy and got ready for action. Using hand signals he signaled his wingman to move into tight parade formation. The wingman moved into the proper position. Don mentally calculated the trajectory needed to score a hit on his wingman. With a smile on his face and determination in his mind he pitched the bag full of crap with all his strength, toward his wingman.

Don had forgotten only one small detail. That is, it is almost impossible to throw anything out of a flying aircraft, without it returning to the point of departure. The air pressure around the canopy is extremely high. This condition is created by prop wash and the airspeed of the aircraft. Therefore, trying to throw an object overboard in flight is like trying to sweep leaves into the face of a hurricane. It just can't be done. The oxygen bag full of his waste was no different. When the tremendous force of wind hit the little bag it turned inside out and came flying right back into the cockpit. The contents of the bag were all over the inside of the cockpit and Don. His waste was in his face; it was all over his clothes; it was smeared over everything. He had to wipe it out of his eyes just to see. The control stick and throttle were so slick he could hardly grip them. He became nauseated very quickly and regurgitated all over himself and the poor airplane. He soon had dry heaves. He had four more hours in this messy airplane before he could land. No divert fields were available and no way to come back on board the ship prior to the scheduled recovery time. He just had to set it out and watch the little oxygen bag flopping on the side of his canopy. It lodged there by the drawstring, and just flopped in the breeze as a reminder of what had taken place.

The brown streak down the inside of Don's canopy got his wingman's attention. He thought Don's aircraft had developed a bad oil leak. Don was unable to talk to him, to tell the real story because his mouth microphone was coated with the ingredients from the oxygen bag. He was not about to put that messy little mike just kissing distance from his lips. He was *not* laughing. His trick had worked great; not on his wingman as he had planned, but on himself. He was thoroughly disgusted. Finally, after what seemed like an eternity it was time for him to return to the ship for landing.

Each Naval Aircraft has a Plane Captain assigned. The Plane Captain is usually a young enlisted man and his duties are to keep the aircraft serviced, cleaned, and ready for flight (In the Air Force they are called Crew Chiefs). He also aids the pilot in strapping into the aircraft and assists him with his flight gear before and after the flight. When the flight is completed and the aircraft is parked on the deck the Plane Captain climbs up the steps and aids the pilot in getting out of the cockpit. He normally will take the pilot's helmet, kneeboard, navigation gear, and other items so the exit from the cockpit won't be so burdensome on the pilot.

Don's Plane Captain was trained very well and would be at his side as soon as possible after landing. This flight was no exception. As he taxied forward and secured the engine the Plane Captain mounted the side of the aircraft in haste, to aid the exhausted pilot. The poor fellow was not aware of the conditions in the cockpit. When he stuck his head in the cockpit to assist the pilot he started heaving uncontrollably. He emptied his lunch on Don, on the aircraft, and on himself.

Supersonic Fighter Pilot

This poor sailor had to be taken to sickbay for medical attention.

After Don got out of his airplane he signaled the crash crew to come immediately. They thought the aircraft was on fire. Don finally was able to persuade them that he was the real emergency and he needed a fresh water wash down. They turned the water hose on him and spent several thousand gallons of water on this poor pilot. Finally, he took off his flight suit and helmet, walked to the edge of the flight deck, and threw them as far as he could into the deep ocean, never to be seen again. He walked down to his stateroom in his shorts. He found what remained of the little bottle of pills and threw them overboard.

This unlucky old *Spad* was placed in the aft end of the hangar bay behind all other aircraft. It sat there for many days before flying again. Most of the ships supply of deodorant was sprayed in the cockpit to get rid of the awful smell. The stink finally went away but the story remains in the minds of everyone that knew of Don and the little pills. Don is known as the "poor pill-popping prop pilot with a puckering potty problem." As a joke his squadron mates gave him a bag of corks, of assorted sizes, for emergency use in the future.

[Author's Note: of course this is a subsonic story but one that many *Supersonic Fighter Pilots* have enjoyed.]

CHAPTER FORTY

SOLDIER OF THE YEAR

LARRY FLENNIKEN

Blood was gushing from the large wound in my back. The medic said, "Larry, every time your heart beats blood squirts about two feet high!" I could feel myself getting weaker and weaker with every heartbeat.

"Am I going to make it, Doc?"

His honest reply was, "I don't know."

The helicopter had just dropped a group of us Army Infantrymen in a hot battle zone in the Republic of Vietnam. Our squad had been on the ground for only about forty-five seconds when I took a round in my back. The blast knocked me about fifteen feet. I knew I was badly injured, but I just didn't know how serious.

Spiritually, I was not ready to die. I had been raised a Christian but in my teenage years I had gotten away from that teaching and was doing my own thing. Many of my friends had been drafted and sent to Vietnam. Then I got my greeting card from Uncle Sam and I was soon headed for Vietnam with the U.S. Army as well. The Army treated me well and I was honored to be selected "Soldier of the Year" by my peers. However, this honor didn't keep me off the front lines of battle.

As I lay there bleeding I prayed and asked God to let me live. I also asked the Lord to have others back home pray for me. I recall as a kid that intercessory prayer would get results. I was deeply fearful and needed a quick miracle or I would die in that far-away country. I was not ready to die!

The area we were fighting in was so hostile that helicopters assigned to Medical Evacuation units were told not to enter our region. In fact, the Army had lost fifty-seven helicopters and crews in the past few days on such rescues. Therefore, my chances of getting flown out of that dangerous area to a field hospital were slim to none. In fact, I did not want another chopper crew shot up just to rescue me. The area was just too unsafe.

Little did I know that halfway around the world the Lord placed my need on a group of Christians who were having a Tuesday night Bible study. In fact, my mother was in that group of believers in Flint, Michigan.

She interrupted the Bible study by saying, "Something is very wrong with my son, Larry! We need to pray for him right now!"

The little group entered into intercessory pray for me most of the night. They didn't have a clue that I had been wounded and was in very grave condition. But the Holy Spirit placed me on their hearts and let them know that I needed prayer. I am so glad that He did.

Their prayers were amplified in heaven that night, louder than any "give-me" type prayer you could ever imagine, and God responded. One of my favorite sayings now is, "Prayer commands heaven."

There was a chopper flying high overhead of our operating area. The pilot could see there was a big firefight going on below him. He also overheard radio transmissions about a seriously wounded soldier that needed to be taken to the field hospital. He was not part of the Medical Evacuation group. He was returning from another mission and just happened to be in our area. Something told him to drop in for my rescue. Our commanders said, "No, it is much too dangerous." He kept coming.

The door gunners of the chopper were awfully upset because their pilot had put them in harm's way to save me. They kept their machine guns blazing in all directions, while the pilot hovered for the rescue. I was loaded on board quickly and we lifted off. The chopper was hit several times while climbing out. I thought I would be killed for sure before we got out of that area. But somehow we made it to the field hospital. I was told later that the helicopter was damaged so much in the rescue attempt that it never flew again.

After Vietnam I came back home and tried to live a good life. I had several jobs but seemed to be really unstable because of the trauma I experienced in the war. I worked for General Motors for a while but I just was not happy there. I quit that job and started working at a health club.

One day I saw a man pass the club that resembled one of my fellow soldiers in Vietnam. I said, "Jimmy, is that you?" He wheeled around and recognized me on the spot.

My wife and I had Jimmy over to our home many times in the next few months. He knew almost nothing about Christianity. He was the kind of guy that went all out for whatever he was doing. My wife invited him to our church. And Jimmy found what he had been missing all these years.

Jimmy became a mature Christian very quickly. He bought a beautiful new suit to wear to church. My way of bragging on the suit was to say jokingly, "Jimmy when you die I want you to leave me that suit!"

He said, "That's a deal Larry!"

It was only a short time later that Jimmy said, "Larry, it looks like you are going to get my suit soon."

I said, "What do you mean?"

He said, "I just came from the doctor and they tell me I have less than ninety days to live." I was crushed.

It appears that he was a victim of *Agent Orange* that was used to defoliate the trees in Vietnam. Many servicemen and women died after leaving Vietnam who were exposed to *Agent Orange* while serving in that country. Their names are not on the great wall in Washington, DC.

Jimmy's weight dropped from 170 pounds to 80 pounds in just a few weeks. He lost his hearing and became blind. As I was walking down the hall of the hospital to visit Jimmy, I could hear him singing.

He was singing, "*If God Is Dead (Who's This Living In My Soul)?*"

I suppose a tear dropped on his arm as I leaned over his bed. He said, "Larry, is that you? Don't cry. I had a dream last night and the Lord said that He is taking me home today!" Jimmy died just a few hours later.

I started giving my testimony to Christian groups across the nation. A few years later I was speaking at a Christian men's group in Chicago. I noticed a fellow in the back of the building that seemed to be really excited about something. Finally, when there was a break in the service he came up front and said, "I am the helicopter pilot who rescued you on February 4, 1967 in Vietnam!" We both were completely flabbergasted. I had not seen or heard from him since that dreadful day in Vietnam.

He had been shot down a couple months after my rescue and was discharged from the Army due to injuries he received during the crash. After leaving the Army he moved to Odessa, TX. His company had transferred him to Chicago and he just walked into this service as a visitor that night. We both were shocked when he found me. And he was especially overwhelmed that I was speaking to a Christian group. By the way, the title of my talk that night was, *Not by Chance, but by Divine Appointment.*

I had the honor of being president of *Rolling Thunder.* This is a group of 250,000 motorcyclists who ride from California to Arlington, VA each Memorial Day to lay a wreath on the grave of the Unknown Soldier.

As you can tell by my testimony that prayer is the only reason that I am here. We often think that we are human beings with a small spiritual experience, when in fact we are spiritual beings with a short human experience. But what we do during our human experience will determine our spiritual address forever!

Thanks for allowing me to share this true story with you. Also, I want to thank you "fast movers" for coming to the aid of us soldiers on the ground in Vietnam. Several times when we were about to be over-run by the enemy our commander would call for close-air-support. In just a few minutes the whole world would be exploding around us. You *jet-jocks* would pound our enemy into eternity in just a few fly-bys. I would always say, "Here comes Big Brother to help in our fight." Thanks!

CHAPTER FORTY-ONE

THE LOST MODEL

RON KNOTT

Chance Vought Aircraft Company had a beautiful scale model of the F-8 *Crusader* made and presented to one of the first F-8 Squadrons. No one seems to know, nor can I find records of, which squadron was first given this beautiful model. It was about eight feet long and six feet from wing tip to wing tip. Made from the finest wood and painted Navy colors it was a beauty to behold.

Somehow VF-32 (Fighter Squadron 32) had this model in their possession. I first came in contact with the model on a Mediterranean cruise in 1964. I was in VF-62, Air Group 10, aboard the USS *Shangri-La* operating in the Mediterranean. VF-32 was on board the USS *Saratoga* in the Mediterranean at the same time. There was a Fleet Conference called for the Task Force aboard the *Saratoga*. Therefore, officers from other ships would take the small personnel boats, over to the *Saratoga* for the meeting. It was decided that all fighter types would meet in the Ready Room of VF-32 on board the *Saratoga*.

As we walked into VF-32 Ready Room we observed that big, beautiful F-8 *Crusader* model suspended in the overhead. It was secured by a large cable hanging from the ceiling. The model was banked in about a thirty degree left turn about seven feet above the deck. It looked stunning.

Ron Knott

The skipper of VF-32 was the host skipper for the conference and he told everyone present, with delight, how his squadron had stolen this model from another F-8 squadron and that no one, no way, would ever be able to take it from them.

I was sitting next to my Skipper, CDR Phil Craven, when this boast was made. I leaned over to CDR Craven and said, "Skipper, I'll get that model tonight if you will give me the okay."

He just grinned and said, "Get it, Ron."

Soon the conference was over and we all headed back to our respective ships. We had used the officer's liberty boat to make the journey from the *Shangri-La* to the *Saratoga*. This boat was covered and not really suitable for carrying large objects. However, the enlisted whaleboats were open and very large. As we came along side our home, the USS *Shangri-La*, the thought hit me that we needed one of these whale boats to bring the F-8 model back to our squadron once we had relieved VF-32 of their prized possession.

After arriving back on board the *Shangri-La* I told my plan to three other Lieutenants in my squadron. Al Moore, Bill Worley, Jim Brady, and I set the plan in motion. At midnight we went to the Quarter Deck watch officer of the *Shang* and told him there was talk of an emergency sortie being called before daybreak. We desperately needed a whaleboat to take us over to the *Saratoga* to pick up some essential aircraft parts so that we would be ready for this emergency sortie. He was more than accommodating. He gave us the boat and a good crew to make the journey.

When we arrived at the *Saratoga*, we requested permission to come aboard and told the same story to that watch officer. He was very cooperative and let us come on board with our toolbox. No one knew we had a large lock cutter in that box. This was the very thing we needed to cut the large cable holding the F-8 model in the ceiling.

L to R: Bill Worley, Ron Knott, and Jim Brady

Ready Room Commandos man the Ready Room at all times. VF-32 was no exception. These young enlisted men answer the phone, pick-up messages, and are used as security guards for the Ready Room after flight operations are secured. We positioned ourselves near the Ready Room and found a phone to make the call.

I called these Ready Room Commandos and told them that I was the Main Communications Officer of the ship and their squadron had received an emergency message. It must be picked up immediately. We knew there were two men in

Ron Knott

the Ready Room so I requested that at least two men were required to sign for this high priority message.

These poor fellows almost ran over us en route to Main Communications, which was several decks away from the Ready Room. As soon as they departed we went into the Ready Room with the lock cutters armed for action. In a very few minutes the beautiful F-8 model was in the hands of the Fighting Sixty-Two.

We wrapped a large white sheet around the model and departed in haste. The Officer of the Deck asked no questions when we hurried by his station. We quickly ran down the ladder, jumped into our whaleboat, and headed back to the *Shangri-La*. The mission was completed by 0200.

The next morning when everyone arrived for the All Officers Meeting, there were shouts of cheer in our Ready Room. This F-8 model looked more stunning anchored overhead Fighter Squadron Sixty-Two's Ready Room than in the spaces of Fighter Squadron Thirty-Two. CDR Craven was ecstatic; that is, until he received a call from CAG.

It became very apparent that the Commanding Officer of Fighting Thirty-Two found no amusement in this exercise whatsoever. He was hot. Changing the home address of this model was not at all favorable with the good Commander. The Commander started an investigation on just how this immoveable object could have possibly departed his quarters.

The Quarter Deck watch said, "Some pilots from the *Shangri-La* took something off during the night wrapped in a white sheet that looked like a cross."

"Finders keepers," was not so in this case. The CO of VF-32 was having a change of Command in Naples, Italy in a few weeks and he had told everyone, including several Admirals that this model was going to be displayed at that event. Now the poor Commander had no model to display.

Embarrassment was the predicament of the day. The message traffic continued for several days for the embezzled model. Finally, CDR Craven elected to return the model, but he did so in style. It was placed on the port CAT of the *Shang* and photographed. CDR Craven acted as the CAT Officer in this dramatic scene. The model was then placed on board a COD (freight aircraft) and flown back to the *Saratoga*.

In later years it was taken again by VF-62 at Cecil Field, Florida. Then I planned another mission and took it from VF-62 to my new squadron, VF-174, the F-8 RAG. VF-62 stole it back from VF-174 and it was never seen again.

Ron Knott

CHAPTER FORTY-TWO

FIRE IN FLIGHT

BOB BEAVIS

"You're on fire!"

My wingman shouted loud and clear and then promptly broke away from me.

I must say that transmission got my attention immediately, if not sooner, as my heart rate accelerated and pounded louder than an M-16 at rapid fire. I started looking for the announced fire.

This fire was not part of the fun package that my wingman and I had planned for the Chicago area. I had just been promoted to section leader as was my wingman Marine pilot, John Shaw. We were out for a fun flight in the supersonic *Crusaders*. The flight was planned to be a leisurely cross-country training journey. We had departed Beaufort Marine Air Station, South Carolina, on this cold, cloudy, and windy November night for Naval Air Station, Glenview, which is located near Chicago.

The *Crusaders* climbed to cruising altitude quickly. The high flight above all the weather was a real joy. The *Crusader* and I were one. It seemed to react to my thoughts; it was a beauty to fly. Although there was no moon the stars seemed much brighter above all the haze and smog. I was very proud to be a Marine fighter pilot zooming through the atmosphere at 600 mph. At that moment I would not have traded jobs with any earth-bound executive. I had trained for months to be in this position of authority and flight.

When we arrived in the Glenview area it was dark and cold. During our descent we were engulfed in the towering clouds. These clouds went all the way down to about 400 feet, and there were high surface winds.

Descending through 4000 feet John called me and said, 'You're on fire!"

He immediately broke away from me. I glanced down into the cockpit and all my instruments looked fine. Then I adjusted my rearview mirrors away from my pretty face and jockeyed around in the seat so I could see behind me. Sure as heck, the left wing was burning! I thought about ejecting. But, I was in a summer flying suit and I said to myself, "Boy, it would really be bad to be floating in Lake Michigan on this cold and windy night. I may not be rescued until daylight if I eject."

O'Hare airport was the nearest landing field. I declared an emergency for priority handling by the controllers and set up for a straight-in approach to O'Hare airport. On my approach I spotted Glenview Naval Air Station off to the right. Immediately, I headed for this military landing field, because they had runway foam and were familiar with military aircraft.

Actually, my airplane was still flying very well. It did not appear to be affected by the fire at all, but I was. I didn't observe any problems flying the bird but I may have been too scared to notice.

The approach to Glenview was uneventful. I expedited it, and made a long straight-in approach at high speed. The gear came down and the wing went up normally but when I touched down I discovered I didn't have any brakes.

The runway that I landed on was short compared to military standards and less than 8000 feet long. That is long enough if you have brakes, but with no brakes it becomes very short. The engine at idle rpm still puts out a small amount of thrust. I did not need that extra push. Therefore, to stop my forward motion I shut the engine down immediately after landing when I realized that my brakes were inoperative. The airplane decelerated quickly. However, by this time the airplane was really burning and the tower repeatedly told me that I was on fire!

As I was rolling to the end of the runway, I raised the canopy and started to climb out. I felt a slight tug when one of my leg restraint garters stopped my progress. These garters are used to keep your legs from flailing around during a high-speed ejection. It was a good thing that I felt the tug otherwise I might have been hanging upside down dangling outside the cockpit. I quickly released the garters and jumped out the right side of the cockpit while the airplane was still moving. I cleared the wing and started running away from the burning airplane. The airplane came to a stop in just a few feet. I sprinted for a stand of trees alongside the runway and turned around to watch the *Crusader* burn. Fortunately, the base crash crew was on the scene and extinguished the fire very quickly.

I was not injured but I sure hated to lose a great airplane. As soon as I could get to a telephone I called my Commanding Officer. I asked him if he was sitting down and how many airplanes he owned. He seemed to be in shock. I told him, "You now have one less tonight." He was pleased that I was not injured.

Later on I was told that the flames were from a hydraulic fire, which probably originated in either the left wheel well or between the wing and the left wheel well. I never did find out the cause of the fire.

The next day they flew a T-33 up from Beaufort to take me home. I was back on the flight schedule in a couple of days.

DA NANG INITIATION

In the fall of 1966 my squadron, VMF (AW) 235, was operating from Da Nang Air Base. I was scheduled for my first mission the day after we arrived. The squadron was located in an old hangar on the east side of the field, which was adjacent to a fuel farm. The operation of the fuel farm was directed from a simple tent. Our aircraft were fueled from hoses dragged out from the tent. It was an old Marine system for setting up expeditionary airfields in a hurry.

I had just finished pre-fighting my airplane and was climbing into the cockpit when a mortar or rocket hit the fuel farm. There was one hell of an explosion. It hit about 200 feet from my location. *Boom!!!* It knocked me off the airplane and I dropped to the ground like a rag doll. The canopy glass of my airplane was destroyed.

After a moment, I picked myself up and regrouped. I looked at my airplane and it scared the crap out of me!

As I was standing there the Gunny Sergeant walked up to me and said, "C'mon, Lieutenant, I've got another airplane for you."

That kind of made my day, you know? The whole thing didn't faze him at all. Just a few days before a similar explosion killed several Marines in the fuel farm. But true to form, the Sergeant's attitude was, "Hey, the mission must go on." He assigned me another *Crusader* and I took off. That was my initiation into the Da Nang routine.

LOW ON FUEL

One day in June I was coming back from a mission from North Vietnam and I was almost out of gas and ideas. Everything on the left side of the airplane had been released but the ordnance on the right side would not release – I had Mk 82 bombs hung on my right wing. I was coming back from an Air Force controlled flight known as DAS (Direct Air Support) mission. I tried several times to get rid of the ordnance but it wouldn't come off the wing. The hung bomb reduced my flying range due to the extra drag on the airplane.

On my approach to Da Nang airport I lowered the landing gear and tried to raise the wing but it would not budge. Great, one more thing to worry about! My flight lead, Major Don Dilley, was even lower on fuel than I was.

He said, "I'm going in to land. Good luck, Beaver."

I again tried to get rid of the bombs, but I could not release them. All my options were gone and I had to land before the aircraft flamed out due to fuel starvation.

I knew that I would need the entire Da Nang runway to stop the fast moving Crusader. Since the wing would not come up, the flaps would not come down, and the leading edge droops would not extend. That meant that my landing speed would be about 200 knots instead of the normal 150 knots.

As I crossed the approach end of the runway I chopped the power and flared. I touched down on the main gear, but the airplane was an absolute squirrel because of the ground effect. It was skipping all over the runway.

I caught the mid-field arresting gear as planned. But I was going so fast that the tailhook broke the cable. Now, I've got less than 4,000 feet of runway left and I was still going like a bat out of hell. My thought then turned to the mine-field off the end of the runway. I told the tower that if I didn't catch the BAC-12 gear (the emergency arresting gear at the end of the runway) that I was going to eject.

Fortunately, I caught the BAC-12 gear and it jerked the airplane to a stop. Once I had stopped the airplane I put all the emergency stuff behind me because I had to prepare for the next mission. This was just another day of operations at Da Nang.

I flew more than 150 missions during this war.

I am thankful to be alive and well many years later. Flying fast airplanes in the U.S. Marine Corps has filled my memory book with lots of exciting events. I am thankful to all the Marines who taught flying skills and the maintenance folks who worked on the airplane to keep me safe and provide our country with a force in readiness. Semper Fi!

"Airpower is the supreme expression of military might, and fleets and armour no matter how vital, must accept a subordinate role." – Winston Churchill

CHAPTER FORTY-THREE

SHORT STORIES OF VALOR

EDWIN F. MILLER JR.

My RF-8 photo *Crusader* was shot down on May 22, 1968 and I was captured by the enemy. I was not released until March 14, 1973. However, as a POW in North Vietnam, I was called one of the "new guys" by the other prisoners because I was shot down in the latter part of the first stage of the air war. The POWs with whom I lived were captured before I was. This "new guy" appellation became ironic after three or four years.

I was born in New York in 1940 and grew up in Franklin Lakes, New Jersey. This is a small town in the New York metropolitan area. I entered the Navy in 1964 after attending Cornell University.

Several comments about my POW experiences: some people have expressed concern about "brain washing." It was my experience, and I believe I can generalize, that life in the prisons of North Vietnam made me more patriotic, more aware, and more thankful for the liberties of life in the United States.

A great source of strength and comfort during my imprisonment was the friendship of the other prisoners. I would like to use this forum to thank the citizens of this country for their support and particularly for their actions in helping to obtain better treatment for the POWs and our release.

Also, I would like to remind the reader that there were significant casualties in the war, leaving 75,000 children fatherless. These American children deserve your thoughts and support.

DON RESSEL, VF-62

We were night re-qualifying on the USS *Shangri-La* with only one wire in the landing area, and that happened to be the number one wire. This meant that a perfect approach would result in a bolter. The LSO briefed us that when we heard the word "aboard" that meant it was too late to hit the ramp and we could do whatever we thought appropriate to try to grab that "one" wire. We went for the "one" wire and were all re-qualified. There was really no need for the pilots to be put in such a dangerous situation.

ALAN WRIGHT

As a nugget going through the RAG (VF-174), one of my instructors on an ACM hop was Duke Hernandez. In the briefing he told me the way to shake a bad guy off your tail was a high G barrel roll.

He said, "It is impossible for anyone to follow you through a high G barrel roll."

I thought, "That may be true for the average fighter pilot, but I would show him that I could do it."

To make a long story short I tried to fly the high G barrel roll against Duke. I departed and ended up beside Duke going backwards. Duke later said there was smoke coming out of my intake.

The airplane then started flopping around and eventually ended up going straight down doing some sort of snap rolls. We had been taught that spin recovery involved blowing the droops. If you think you are spinning but aren't, DON'T blow the droops or you may never recover. I didn't think the airplane was spinning because the nose wasn't rising and falling so I sat there doing nothing.

Eventually, I decided it wasn't going to recover by itself; therefore it must be spinning, so I better blow the droops now. I raised the guard and had my hand on the lever to blow the droops when at that exact moment, a voice like the voice of God came over the radio saying, "You aren't spinning." I took my hand off the handle and the airplane eventually recovered on its own. Great mind reading and timing, Duke. Thanks.

The other story involves our Air Wing Six CAG, Jack Christiansen. I was a first tour LTJG and idolized him. He liked to fly the F-8s in our squadron and he liked to do touch-and-goes on the boat. He thought it was great fun to light the burner and boom the bridge when he went around. Whoever was flying with him also did touch-and-goes when CAG did.

When I was flying with him I would copy him and also boom the bridge. I had no way of knowing that eventually the Admiral got sick of the noise and when he learned that GAG was responsible, he dressed him down. Later that same day, I boltered, and boomed the bridge like always.

Apparently the Admiral thought it was GAG again and he got his second dressing down of the day. It seems funny now but it wasn't at the time.

Ron Knott

DAVID C. CORBETT

During the 1968 Siege of Khe Sanh, VMF (AW) 235 flew in support of Operation Niagara, the massive air operation which included Navy, Marine, and Air Force aircraft in a continuous attack against communist positions.

Tet '68 had just started, and to read the US newspapers, we were losing our butts. In reality, the Marines in I Corps were destroying the enemy. The F-8 was the only aircraft which could carry the monster 2000-pounders and we did a lot of helicopter landing zone clearing with this destructive weapon.

During a three week period we worked very closely with the ground units defending Khe Sanh. They were in a tough position because it was difficult to re-supply them. The bad guys were attacking them in every possible way. The most effective method of the enemy was to tunnel toward the perimeter wire, pop-up, and attack the Marine positions. This had to be stopped. Someone decided to use our F-8s to stop the enemy.

We flew mission after mission, dropping our big bombs only about 300 feet from our own positions. The bombs had delayed fuses which allowed them to penetrate two or three feet into the ground before they exploded. When they went off whole sections of the tunnels would collapse. The plan worked better than we expected and the enemy's drive to take Khe Sanh was squashed. I can't imagine how the ground troops felt about us dropping the bombs so close. They apparently had a lot of confidence in the pilots and it paid off for them.

With four *Crusaders* loaded with two Mk 84s each, fused with 36-inch *Daisy Cutters*, the devastation to the landscape was incredible, to say the least. On one mission I remember that with a total of eight 2000-pounders, we completely leveled an entire mountain. I was so impressed that I actually went down low and slow to see the results. It was terrible, but very effective.

Another time, I dropped these same weapons on enemy troops in the open. The enemy was literally cut in half. The *Daisy Cutter* exploded 36 inches above the ground. In my opinion, this was the most effective weapon against the enemy. Sometimes it is entirely appropriate to kill a fly with a sledge hammer.

PETER MICHALE

During the spring of 1965 the training aircraft carrier, USS *Lexington* was in the shipyard. This required another ship to be assigned to allow advanced flight students to complete their landings. By sundown on that windy Florida day, we had accidentally shut down Jacksonville's military runways. I was sure my naval aviation days were over.

We had flown from Beeville, Texas to Cecil Field Naval Air Station in Jacksonville, Florida, to find CV-9, the USS *Essex*, a decorated World War II carrier renowned as "the Oldest and the Boldest."

We were flying the Grumman F-9 *Cougar*. At Cecil, we were again briefed on our carrier procedures and were escorted to the ship by our instructors. In spite of the ship's losing both its radio and its glide-slope datum lights, we landed aboard successfully; however, our triumph began to unravel during our return to Jacksonville.

Back at Cecil Field, Steve Longo hooked the emergency field arresting gear, rigged to stop planes without brakes.

The arresting gear has a cable stretched across the runway to catch a plane's tailhook, much like the wires on an aircraft carrier's deck. Heavy anchor chains are attached to each end of the cable. The anchor chain links deploy sequentially to slow and stop a plane making an emergency landing.

I followed Steve into the landing pattern and was cleared to land on an alternate runway with a strong crosswind. I had a harder than normal landing and blew a tire. Our tires had been boosted to 300 psi for carrier landings. Within seconds, there we were: Steve hooked to the anchor chain and Pete sitting in a pile of smoke. Cecil is closed!

In the meantime, Al Nease had been flying in the landing pattern back at the ship, but his *Cougar* had lost hydraulic pressure and he could not retract his tailhook. He was sent to Jacksonville Naval Air Station, where he was faced with bad choices: land downwind with the hook down, take the arresting gear in the wrong direction, and tear the Cougar into pieces; land past the arresting gear with little runway remaining; or, try to land upwind in the proper direction but run out of runway and crash. Al flew the downwind approach. He landed past the arresting gear, but with very little runway remaining he used his emergency brakes. Al's tires blew and he skidded off the end of the runway. JAX is closed!

On that day we had shut down Naval Aviation in Jacksonville. Nonetheless, everyone walked away and the planes were not damaged. The debriefing was not pleasant but we learned how quickly bad situations develop and why everyone needs a Plan B.

The three of us completed flight training and went on to fly the exciting F8 *Crusader*.

Supersonic Fighter Pilot

TOM IRWIN

LTJG Tom Irwin, a young F-8 pilot with VF-24 flew De Soto Patrols in December and January, and participated in the 17 February 1965 strike into North Vietnam, followed four days later by another raid on the Chan Hoa barracks near Dong Hoi airfield. He recalled the early days of the war.

As the SAM sites began to multiply, they became a big threat to the F-8s as the early ECM (Electronic Counter Measures) equipment went first to the A-4s.

I remember a jury-rigged set in 1966 which consisted of a D-cell battery powered receiver with an antenna attached to the canopy with suction cups. You couldn't turn it on to test it until you were airborne because the ship's radar would burn it up on deck. The antenna came down around you like a spider web during the catapult stroke. This was our anti-SAM protection device. Where there is a will, there is a way! "It is better to live one day as a lion than a hundred years as a sheep." – Italian proverb

PAUL FORREST

We had two types of aircraft at *Gitmo*; about 10 F-8Es and a half dozen U-2F two-engine utility aircraft. There were about a dozen pilots assigned to VC-10, not including the CO and the XO. We all flew both aircraft on a wide variety of missions.

There were two F-8s on the hot pad at all times and two others armed as back-ups. Depending on what was going on, two pilots were suited up ready to go within a five minute launch time, and two others in the general vicinity to become the primary hot pad pilots if the first two aircraft were launched.

The F8s were also used for fleet training – basically radar intercept training for controllers on board the Navy vessels undergoing training or shake-down cruises at *Gitmo,* or high-speed target pulling for the crews to practice their artillery.

On a beautiful Caribbean day I was flying a *Crusader* on practice radar intercepts with one of the destroyers. It just so happened that my VC-10 Skipper was on board that destroyer for a little enlightenment on how the black-shoe Navy operated. When I completed the intercepts the air controller asked me to make a couple of attack passes at the destroyer so they could practice evasive maneuvering.

I would roll in with the ship broadside to me and they would attempt to turn into my pass so I would fly over their bow. I made a few routine passes and decided to see how they would do with a high speed pass. I accelerated to Mach 1.2 and flew over the ship at 10,000 feet.

The air controller on board proudly announced, "We have you in our sights on two batteries …."

He didn't finish his sentence as my sonic boom hit the ship. I pulled off to do a series of slow rolls climbing back to altitude. This cost me a couple days in hack for the rolls but it was worth it. Those were the good ole days!

JIM WHITE

In early January 1968 we arrived on Yankee Station. Our first operating day was a disaster. Pete Cherney launched on one of the first missions and his aircraft developed a severe oil pressure problem just after he got airborne.

Supersonic Fighter Pilot

I was one of the LSOs on the platform. We told Pete to jettison all of his ordnance and return to the ship ASAP. It only took him about ten minutes to drop all his weapons and start his approach for landing.

As he was turning in behind the ship for landing his engine failed.

We called "EJECT, EJECT," and he punched out at about 200 yards aft of the carrier. The ejection seat worked normally and he got a fully inflated parachute. The helicopter was over him in seconds and deployed a swimmer to help him in the water. Somehow Pete got hung up in the shroud lines of the parachute and it was taking him under. The swimmer tried to help Pete get untangled from the sinking chute but he almost went under as well and had to back away. Tragically, Pete drowned.

The chopper was finally able to pick up Pete's lifeless body and parachute and laid him on the deck just in front of me. Without question, this was horribly nerve racking for me and a terrible way to start a cruise.

A few days later my Skipper and I were flying a Barcap mission when *Red Crown* (the combat air controller) notified us that two *Bandits* (MiGs) were fifteen miles ahead of us and were heading our way at very high speed.

Red Crown then reported that the *Bandits* were only three miles from us.

The next thing I knew is the two MiG-17s flew past us head on. The Skipper never saw the MiGs. I call the MiGs and we make a hard left turn pulling about 8 Gs. I was about to black out due to the high Gs so I pulled up to stay in the fight. As I went high the Skipper was still trying to out turn the MiGs, which was useless. I flew over the top trying to set up for a shot at them on the down hill run. But when I came back down the MiGs were on the opposite side of the circle, and there was no way I could out turn them.

The Skipper still did not have the MiGs in sight. I was calling the MiGs position and telling the Skipper that they are gaining on us. Finally, I told the Skipper that we should exit the fight or he was going to get shot down. He agreed.

We dived for the deck at supersonic speed and headed for the coast. I was sucking oxygen all the way to the ship. It is interesting to note that the Skipper was shot down on the next cruise flying the A-7. His eye sight was terrible!

The next day I was on a bombing mission to Vinh, and six SAMs were fired at my flight. One hit an aircraft of VF-194 flown by Bob McCann that was close to me. The explosion almost destroyed my aircraft as well. WOW! What a life of adventure.

After Vietnam I was blessed to fly the *Crusader* in the Reserve squadron at Navy Dallas. Then I flew the F-100 and the A-7D with the Air Force. At the same time I was flying commercial jets for Delta Airlines. Now I am flying in movie stunt work and flying *Citations.* I have been blessed because many of my peers did not return from Vietnam and I am still on the green side of the grass.

BROOKS DYER

I was checked out in the *Crusader* with the famous Fighter Squadron of VMF-251 located at Beaufort, SC in June 1963. On my second flight in the F-8 I was headed for outer space to earn my 1000 mph pin. Pete Tumillo was my chase pilot.

Supersonic Fighter Pilot

I completed the check list prior to taking off. The canopy locking lever seemed a bit stiff but appeared to seat normally, and the canopy indicated closed and locked.

As I was zooming through 17,000 feet at 450 knots the canopy departed the aircraft. Wow! That got my attention loud and clear. I ducked down in the cockpit to get out of the wind blast. This caused me to induce some negative Gs on the aircraft which resulted in fuel venting from my wing tip. Pete saw the fuel venting and knew that something was wrong with my aircraft.

Immediately, I reduced power to reduce the wind blast and slow the aircraft down. Then I looked at the ejection handle and noticed that it had been pulled out and was facing upwards at a 45 degree angle. This was not normal and could cause the ejection seat to fire at any moment.

I had been briefed that the ejection seat's handle had a modification installed that prevented inadvertent firing of the seat in just such a circumstance as I was in. I had also been briefed that a pilot trying to stow the handle properly in a similar incident, had resulted in a severely dislocated shoulder. Nevertheless, I made a slow move to properly stow the handle. I soon discovered this was not a good idea.

Pete joined on my wing and gave me hand signals on what to do. The noise level was so high that I could not hear anything on my radio. He gave me the landing gear signal to get me slowed below 220 knots. Then he signaled me to raise the wing which slowed me even more. It was still very noisy, a bit cool and windy, but not at all unpleasant (except for the anxiety).

He led me back to Beaufort for a relatively uneventful landing and a larger than normal welcoming reception, as he had radioed the squadron of our situation.

Ron Knott

I flew an uneventful FAM-2 the next day and was awarded the 1000 mph pin. I was always very forceful with the canopy lock handle afterwards!

AL NEASE

I was a junior 2nd LT (Gold Bar) flying with VMF (AW)-235 out of Da Nang in April of 1966. We got word one morning that a famous general officer would be accompanying us on a deep strike into Laos. This was a low level, nape/strafe/high drag bomb run with only two passes allowed due to anticipated enemy ground fire.

The famous General Officer was none other than Marion Carl. At that point he was F-8 qualified but as far as I knew did not have a lot of time in the F-8. I thought, "Oh, brother, this is going to be a real goat rope experience."

General Carl, by far being the senior officer present, could have asserted his authority and demanded to lead the flight. But General Carl was too much of a gentleman and too knowledgeable of combat air operations to assume that he would be a competent flight leader. Our Skipper, LCOL George Gibson led the flight with General Carl on his wing. One of our senior company grade officers led the second section and I was number four, flying Ron Foreman's wing.

The flight went flawlessly. We dropped our nape and high drag bombs on the first run, took the bad guys totally by surprise, and made a second pass with our guns. We had dropped down to about 500 ft. in order to surprise the enemy. Four F-8s coming in at treetop level at about 400 knots had to have a demoralizing effect on the bad guys.

The only negative side of the whole experience was that General Carl wrote me up for a low pass on my strafing run.

Supersonic Fighter Pilot

Obviously, he was lower than I was on his run but a 2nd LT cannot argue with a two-star General.

Bottom line: I gained a tremendous amount of respect for General Carl that day. It was amazing to me from my twenty-three year old perspective to see an "old guy," (i.e., anyone over forty), do so well and be so unassuming.

JAY MILLER

Ron Sonniksen and I flew two F-8s across the Pacific with only a wet compass for navigation. We took off from San Diego and were scheduled to in-flight refuel 600 miles west from a Marine KC-130. The KC-130's radar was in error and they kept giving us wrong heading information for the join-up. Finally, as we were getting low on fuel we found the tanker with our ADF and got the life saving fuel that we needed.

The next 400 miles were again by ourselves until we joined another KC-130 for fuel. We are now 1000 miles from San Diego and are very tired, but we still had a long way to go.

After five hours in the cockpit we arrived over Hawaii. Ron's wife had packed a lunch for us, which we appreciated very much. We used garbage bags that we had brought as portable toilets. I was numb and frustrated, and badly wanted out of that airplane.

The air traffic controllers started giving us vectors that would add many minutes to our flight. I was tired and ready to land. I told the controller that I was single engine and needed to land ASAP. The controller, thinking we had lost an engine cleared us straight in to land.

After landing, my legs were so numb from the cold and the long flight that I collapsed on the tarmac. When the plane captain arrived I told him there was a bag under my seat. Even in the heat the bag was still frozen, which shows how cold it had been during the flight.

We *still* had a long way to go. We took off from Barber's and halfway from there to Wake we found an A-3 tanker; but we left him while he was tanking someone else and went into Wake. Then from Wake to Guam we were supposed to have A-3s for tanking, but an F-4, which desperately needed the A-3s, was having problems with the tanker so we decided to press on. That was kind of scary. Guam isn't a big place and we had to rely on those old F-8 TACANs but we found it. Finally, after a ten day journey we joined our ship. I learned the true meaning of the statement, "Adapt or perish."

LOU PRITCHETT

After doing fleet tours (one in the Far East) in ADs and in A4s, I had just completed a two-year tour with the Navy as an Aircraft Accident Investigator. There was very little flight time to be had. We were limited to four hours a month (for flight pay purposes) in old and worn T-28s (Trainer) and SNBs (small twin engine). So my flight skills were rusty.

It was great to be back in the Fleet Marine Force, stationed at Beaufort, S.C. I was assigned to Marine All-Weather Fighter Squadron 451, flying the F-8 *Crusader*.

I had known and was old friends with some of the 451 Squadron Pilots from my previous six years in the FMF. Each one that I knew personally was a top notch pilot. The squadron had been together for over four years and had

Supersonic Fighter Pilot

logged some great flying experiences (and liberty calls), including a Med (Mediterranean) Cruise, plus some action in a flap down in the Dominican Republic. They were a tight group.

After the necessary two weeks in Ground School I was assigned to my first flight (FAM-1) in the Mach 1.9, afterburning F-8 *Crusader*. Remember, I had not touched a jet aircraft in two years and had never flown an afterburning aircraft.

I was facing my first flight in the *Crusader* with some anxiety. I was not worried about killing myself. I was totally concerned about doing a good job so I would be accepted by the squadron pilots. It was my experience in the United States Marine Corps that reputations were earned, not given, because of rank or any other reason. You had to prove yourself.

Ed (or "*Mofak*" as he was called by all) was to be my chase pilot. We had known each other briefly during my Japan tour a few years earlier. I knew that he was one of the most respected and even admired pilots in the entire Marine Corps. I knew that if Ed gave me an UP CHECK (satisfactory) grade on my first flight in the F-8, it would go a long way in earning my acceptance by the other squadron pilots.

I studied the Ground School stuff, systems and procedures, before the flight. I was as ready as I could make myself. Ed gave me a not too detailed briefing on what we were to do on the flight. He briefed for an afterburner take-off. I swallowed hard. The Briefing Guide for the FAM-1 called for a basic engine (no afterburner) take-off, which would be much less exciting. I called this to Ed's attention. He smiled, winked, and said, "Lou, you can hack it. Things just happen a little faster than in the A-4." I swallowed hard again and in my agitated mind, quickly went over the procedures for an afterburner take-off and climb.

After we took the runway I advanced the power to 100% and lit the burner. "BANG!" From there on I was just along for the ride. I was so far behind the airplane I might as well have stayed in the Ready Room. Anyone who has ever flown the F-8 will remember their first afterburner take-off. The climb out in the F-8 is near vertical. If you drop the nose even a little, you'll go through Mach 1 in a second and the noise of your shock waves on the ground make for angry citizens.

There had been a lot of complaints from the chicken and turkey farmers in South Carolina about the shock waves made by jet aircraft, which they claimed were killing their chickens and turkeys. It seemed that if I didn't keep the nose pointed straight up it would go down enough to go through the Mach. Well, I broke the Mach so many times on the climb out that I must have killed a thousand or so chickens that day.

The rest of the flight went pretty well, even the landing. During the flight I had sweated a lot, literally and figuratively, and was in a dehydrated state. I must have drunk a half dozen Cokes before I got to the Ready Room.

I got back to the Ready Room before *"Mofak."* The usual Ready Room Rats – young pilots who weren't flying at that time and had nothing better to do than "hang out" – were waiting for us – waiting for *"Mofak"* and me. They looked like the pilots who hang out on "Vultures Row" on an aircraft carrier watching landings, and just hoping someone will prang.

Supersonic Fighter Pilot

They were standing on the other side of the Ready Room and I was just inside the door – waiting for Ed, and the verdict. No one said anything to me. I was purposely being ignored and sweating a lot.

Then Ed burst into the room (Ed never just entered a room; he burst into a room). All eyes were on Ed, waiting for "the word on the new guy."

I'll never forget the next few seconds.

"Great hop! You flew like a champ but I knew you could hack it. Everyone shake hands with our newest *Crusader* pilot."

I had made it! Ed's endorsement was all I needed to grease my acceptance into the squadron.

"You can hack it," and it meant a lot me.

DEAD BUG

My wingman and I in our trusty Marine *Crusaders* were clawing our way back to home base in bad weather: after another one of those highly unsuccessful night dive bombing missions under the Blind Bat's flares, somewhere around a place called Tchepone.

These missions were labeled "Special" since they were "out of country" in either Laos or Cambodia. Remember, LBJ had told the American public that there was no American action outside of Vietnam – or something like that. But these were highly classified missions.

We were directed to divert to either Ubon or Udorn. I never could remember the difference even when I was in Vietnam. So we got a vector, were picked up by Ground Controlled Approach (GCA), and made a sterling end of runway landing. But there were no Air Force types near the runway to observe our superior landing skills. It must have been raining too hard.

After checking in with Wing Ops back at Da Nang, our Wing Ops Officer told us to stay where we were until morning. Da Nang was under another one of those semi-irregular mortar attacks. I didn't argue. It was about 0300 and I was already working on a 20-hour day. It had been a long one. We were given directions to the Transient Pilots quarters.

En route I heard loud noises, which only are made by genuine United States fighter pilots. There was a party going on somewhere and I was determined to find it.

My wingman elected to hit the sack so I continued solo. I finally found the noise in this sort of blacked out tent/building. I opened the door/flap and entered into what could only be a Fighter Pilot's Bar. There were guys in sweaty flight suits laughing loud like they were inebriated. There were squadron patches and pictures of airplanes all around. My kind of place! I was still in full flight gear, torso harness open, and carrying my navigation bag and hard hat (no bag cover.)

I sauntered over to the end of the bar. "What'll you have?" asked the bartender.

I remember my exact words. "Gimme the strongest thing you've got in a tall glass – with ice, if you've got it."

By this time the place was mostly quiet. All attention was on me. It was sort of like a John Wayne movie when the new gunfighter comes to town and walks through the swinging doors of the saloon for the first time.

The bartender gave me a water glass full of mostly ice and some vodka. I put it away in a couple of gulps, reached into my bottom G suit pocket, got some MPC and tossed it

Supersonic Fighter Pilot

on the bar. Whoops went up. I was a hero. Fighter pilots gathered around me. I was in fighter pilot's heaven.

They introduced themselves, asked me about where I had been that night, what was the target, what was the weather where I had been, why I had been diverted, etc. All good questions. Then, realizing I was a Marine they decided to introduce me to an Air Force game called "Dead Bug."

Now the game of Dead Bug doesn't have a lot of rules. It goes like this: a bunch of people are gathered around the bar, some sitting on stools. Someone yells "Dead Bug" and the last guy to fall off his stool (backwards) and on to the floor has to buy the next round.

Well, as the night went on they always seemed to distract me just before someone said "Dead Bug." I was usually the last to hit the floor, but hit the floor I always did. They were hospitable and never let me pay for a drink, encouraging me to do better the next time.

My only real memory of that night after making my order at the bar, was that of great fun among a great bunch of guys, and drinking drinks that had real ice. The Air Force knows how to live.

My wingman woke me the next morning with, "Captain, the Colonel just called and he wants us back at Da Nang, pronto!" When I tried to get up I took the pillow with me. The back of my head, or rather, the bloody back of my head had stuck to the pillow. I was still in complete flight gear and had no idea how I got there.

For weeks after that my wingman thoroughly enjoyed telling the troops about the Captain in the shower, in full flight gear, with his head under the water trying to get that damned pillow off his head. For the flight back I told my wingman to take the lead – good combat navigation training for a junior officer. I was in no condition to drive. I wasn't even safe for solo and my hard hat did not fit well, at all.

If any of you Air Force types read this, thanks for a great night!

WAYNE WHITTEN

The setting is Da Nang airbase in Vietnam in late August 1966, where my squadron mates and I (then a 1st Lieutenant) in Marine Composite Reconnaissance Squadron One (VMCJ-1), were in our tenth month of a thirteen month combat tour. VMCJ-1 was the "eyes and ears" of the First Marine Aircraft Wing in Vietnam flying the RF-8A photo *Crusaders* and the EF-10B *Skyknight* electronic warfare aircraft. The Douglas EF-10B, affectionately known as *Willy the Whale*, was a two-place, straight wing, subsonic aircraft that had been converted for electronic warfare duty. The EF-10Bs were soon fully committed to locating and jamming enemy air defense radars in support of Navy and USAF air operations against North Vietnam (NVN).

Our pilots were qualified in both aircraft and crewed with Naval Flight Officers like myself, with specialty training as electronic countermeasures officers (ECMOs) in the two-place EF-10B. The ECMOs basically ran the mission systems with the pilots relegated to handling communications and navigation. So at first many of the pilots saw themselves as just moonlighting in the old *Whales* from their day jobs as *Crusader* photo jocks. However, they soon realized the real action was up north where the EF-10Bs were in demand.

Things had heated up that summer with the ground war as our Marines had begun *Operation Hastings* to engage a

Supersonic Fighter Pilot

NVN division that had crossed over the DMZ. And so it was that in August we began nightly patrols along the DMZ in our trusty *Whales* watching for movement of SAMs. Ironically, our adversary chose that same month to emplace a *Cross Slot* radar normally used for coastal surface search just north of the DMZ, but a couple of miles inland. For several nights running we intercepted and reported this new *night owl* radar as it was usually all we picked up most nights and no one reported receiving it during the day time. Our intercepts were noted in daily briefs to the Wing Commander and it quickly became a topic of speculation as to its purpose and threat potential. Shortly thereafter we were asked to get a targetable fix or location on this strange radar.

Late one night two EF-10Bs went to work to try and locate the radar. Arriving on station we found our adversary was on the air and the challenge was on. Our pilots worked hard to keep accurate aircraft positions, as I used our direction finding equipment to try and get an accurate fix through triangulation. We then did some homing runs with our position over the suspected site marked by the USAF *Sky Spot* radar, which was located south of the DMZ. It was used for radar directed bombing. We created a bit of radio chatter and the section lead from a USAF F-4C *Phantoms* flight working the area under flares came up and asked what we had going. Hearing it was a radar, he got our best coordinates and made a pass dropping a string of the new CBU cluster bombs that resulted in a spectacular fireworks show underneath us. When the radar abruptly went off the air everyone was ecstatic. We reported it as likely being knocked out.

Two nights later the radar was back up and running! The Wing Commander declared it must be of some operational import to the North Vietnamese and therefore presented a threat to his aircraft that must be dealt with, forthwith.

It was clear that a photo was needed for targeting and good news was VMCJ-1 had a flight line full of RF-8As with eager pilots to go get it. Bad news was this was Vietnam and service turf battles came into play that kept our RF-8As from flying north of the DMZ, which was USAF territory. However, the Marine powers that be in Da Nang were not eager to hand this one off to the boys in light blue. It was decided to send in an EF-10B on a stealth photo mission as, unbeknownst to the USAF headquarters, the old *Whale* had a secret recon camera in its belly!

Our liaison officer in Saigon at the USAF headquarters, arranged for us to fly a special daylight reconnaissance mission the following morning. "Subs," our assistant photo officer and I, got the nod for this mission and we launched at dawn's early light. As I recall our instructions were to make only one photo pass at about 8-10,000 ft. over the suspect area. We did that with the old K-17 camera chugging along. Afterwards, "Subs" and I agreed that with it being a clear day we stood a good chance of picking up the radar, which had a large TV-like antenna if we made a low level visual run. The next thing I knew we were at treetop level looking at a bunch of AAA guns up close and personal with lots of scared natives running from this new Yankee pirate "attack" plane. On our second pass we took a hit that sounded like an artillery shell exploding. We decided that discretion being the better part of valor, we had best return to base with our prize film. Everyone gathered around on the flight line to gawk at a fist sized hole in the nose cone while the photo shop downloaded the film and ran off to process it. And yes, there were some hard questions being asked as to how we got hit

Supersonic Fighter Pilot

by a low caliber automatic weapon at the directed altitude.

We were saved from our Skipper's inquisition by a call from our liaison officer asking us to get the film down to Saigon ASAP. The USAF wanted their pros to read it out and they also wanted the flight crew to come down for a debrief. So "Subs" and I jumped into another *Whale* and went off to Saigon with the film. Turns out we had indeed captured the radar on the film albeit a bit blurry. Somehow, a couple of days later we got permission for our RF-8As to follow up with a low level high speed mission to get a nice targeting image. They not only confirmed the radar but also numerous lucrative targets around it. The Wing Commander declared it an eminent threat to his forces and the next day our Marine A-4 *Skyhawks* conducted a major strike that knocked out the demon radar and wreaked havoc on the other targets. Two of our RF-8As got the bomb damage assessment photos the next morning confirming the demise of the radar. Oh boy, it took nearly a month this time before a replacement radar was back on the air!

In retrospect, it is nice to have contributed to the "Lore of the Corps" by flying the only official photo mission flown in combat by an EF-10B, but sadly the whole episode is reminiscent of the frustrations that our military faced during the trying years of the Vietnam War.

PART III

STATICS

APPENDIX A

CHANCE – VOUGHT CRUSADER

The Chance Vought Company encountered difficulties in moving into the jet age, developing the disappointing *Pirate* fighter, and then the downright dangerous *Cutlass*. However, they were able to recover their fortunes and then some with the outstanding *Crusader* fighter, and refined the aircraft through a series of modifications.

The Navy requirement that led to the *Crusader* was difficult to meet. The third Vought jet fighter began life as a US Navy requirement issued in September 1952 for a carrier-based fighter capable of a top speed of Mach 1.2 at altitude; as well as reliability and serviceability, high maneuverability, and good carrier-landing characteristics. Vought and seven other aircraft manufacturers submitted proposals.

The first XF8U-1 was rolled out in February 1955 and took to the air on 25 March with Vought's chief test pilot John W. Konrad at the controls. The prototype broke Mach 1 during this initial flight. The second prototype made its first flight on 12 June. By this time, the new aircraft had been given the name *Crusader*.

The Vought engineers came up with a brilliant design to meet the requirement. The most unusual feature of the aircraft was the "variable-incidence" wing, which addressed the landing problems experienced by the *Cutlass*. On take-off and landing, the XF-8U-1's wing could be pivoted up seven degrees, hinging on the rear wing spar and jacked up by a hydraulic actuator. The pilot had a locking handle to ensure that the wing stayed in place in flight, and a positioning handle to raise the wing once the locking handle was released. The wing-raising system had a pneumatic backup in case the hydraulic system failed.

The armament section contained four 20mm Colt MK-12 revolver-type cannons with 144 rounds per gun. There were two guns on either side of the nose. The production aircraft were equipped with an AN/APG-30 gun-sight-ranging radar which permitted the pilot to track a target on his cockpit radar screen. When the target was within range of the guns the pilot would receive a signal to commence firing.

Behind the guns on each side of the aircraft was a launch rail for a single *Sidewinder* heat-seeking missile. (This was increased to two missiles on each launch rail on the later models.)

THE PHOTO CRUSADER

The Navy also wanted a reconnaissance variant of the *Crusader*. The 32nd production F-8U-1 was pulled off the line and modified as the "F-8U-1P" photo-reconnaissance configuration. All armament and the fire-control system were deleted and replaced by a camera array in the bottom of a redesigned forward fuselage.

The redesigned forward fuselage was big enough to allow the refueling probe to retract completely into the fuselage, eliminating the blister on the left side. The height of

Supersonic Fighter Pilot

the vertical tail was also reduced to increase speed. The first F8U-1P flew on 17 December 1957.

CRUSADER RECORDS

The Navy was eager to show the *Crusader* off. Prototype XF-8U1s were evaluated by VX-3 beginning in late 1956 with few problems noted. Weapons development was conducted at NAF China Lake and a China Lake F-8U-1 set a speed record in August 1956. CDR "Duke" Windsor set, broke, and set a new Level Flight Speed Record of 1,015.428 mph on 21 August 1956 beating the previous record of 822 mph set by a USAF F-100. This set a new National Air Speed Record.

[Authors Note: There are recorded documents that claim the British *Fairey Delta* 2 set a world speed record of 1,132 mph on March 10, 1954. (This was an experimental aircraft and only two were built.) More speed records: In December 1957 the F-101 *Voodoo* flew 1,207 mph. May, 1958 the F-104 *Star Fighter* set a record of 1,404.19 mph. In early 1959 the MiG-21 flew 1,484 mph. In December 1959 the F-106 *Delta Dart* set a world speed record of 1,525.96 mph. In 1961 the F-4 *Phantom* set a speed record of 1,606.324 mph. F-15 *Eagle,* 1979, speed of 1,650 mph later increased to 1,875 mph. YF-12A *Interceptor* flew 2,070 mph in 1965 and the SR-71 *Blackbird* flew 2194 mph in 1976.]

FOR THE RECORD

The *Crusader* had already been flown more than 1000 mph in test flights by Windsor and other test pilots. He had

Ron Knott

been told only to exceed 1,000 mph during the speed run, in order to break a record set by the Air Force with an F-100C in 1955. The Navy did not want to reveal the *Crusader's* top speed, but it still won the Navy and Vought the Thompson Trophy for that year.

The problem originated when the Navy absolutely insisted at the time that no publicity or public record of any kind would show the top speed of the F-8 until long afterward. That is why Duke got recognition a year later, when the security was downgraded.

The fact is that Captain Lynn Helms USMC was the first Naval Aviator to exceed 1000 mph.

Captain Lynn Helms,
First Naval aviator to exceed 1000 mph

Captain Lynn Helms USMC was Project Test Pilot on the original XF-8U. Duke Windsor was the senior pilot. John

Supersonic Fighter Pilot

Konrad received *Crusader* 1000 mph Certificate Number 1. Lynn Helms received *Crusader* 1000 mph Number 2, dated 24 June 1955, signed by Paul Thayer, VP of Chance Vought. Duke Windsor received 1000 mph Certificate Number 3.I also have a photo of Helms being congratulated by Duke Windsor as being the first Naval Aviator to fly 1000 mph, dated June of 1955. As many of you know, J. Lynn Helms was later appointed FAA Administrator under President Ronald Reagan.

For some reason the Navy played hide and seek with the *Crusader's* speed capability for over fourteen months.

CRUSADERS IN THE FLEET

According to the posted records the first fleet squadron to fly the *Crusader* was VF-32 at NAS Cecil Field, Florida, in 1957. They deployed to the Mediterranean later that year on the USS *Saratoga*. VF-32 renamed the squadron the *Swordsmen* in keeping with the *Crusader* theme.

The Pacific Fleet received the first *Crusaders* at NAS Moffett Field in Northern California, and the VF-154 *Grandslammers* (named in honor of the new 1000 mph jets and subsequently renamed the *Black Knights*) began their F-8 operations.

Later in 1957 in San Diego, VMF-122 accepted the first Marine Corps *Crusaders*.

On 6 June 1957, two *Crusaders* took off from the USS *Bonhomme Richard* in the Pacific with CAPT Robert G. Dose and LCDR Paul Miller at the controls. Three hours and 28 minutes later after a mid-air refueling by an AJ-2 *Savage* tanker near Dallas, Texas, the two aircraft set down on the deck of the USS *Saratoga* off the coast of Florida. The two aircraft set an unofficial speed record and performed the first carrier-to-carrier transcontinental flight in history.

Five weeks after that on 16 July 1957, an F-8U-1 and an F-8U-1P attempted to set a coast-to-coast speed record under *Project Bullet*. The F-8U-1P was to photograph the country from coast to coast during the flight from Los Angeles to New York City. The F-8U-1 was forced out of the exercise by damage to its refueling probe during a refueling attempt over Albuquerque, New Mexico. The F-8U-1P landed in New York after a flight of three hours and twenty-three minutes, with an average speed of 725.55 mph. The pilot was US Marine Major John Glenn, who a few years later would be the first American to orbit the Earth, and would then go on to be a long standing Democratic Senator from the state of Ohio.

By the end of 1957 the *Crusader* was equipping operational US Navy and Marine squadrons in numbers. In the summer of 1958 US President Eisenhower ordered a military intervention in Lebanon, with *Crusaders* from the *Saratoga* providing top cover for landings on 15 and 16 July. They encountered no opposition.

Navy pilots were happy with the *Crusader*. It was a *fighter*. Vought had promised the Navy it could do Mach 1.4, but it could actually fly faster than Mach 1.8, had a climb rate of over 30,000 feet per minute, and it was muscular in maneuvers. However, it did suffer from a number of teething problems and defects:

- It could be a handful to land, particularly on the older and smaller *Essex* or *27-Charlie* class carriers. Despite the many fixes Vought engineers had incorporated to reduce landing speed it still landed

"hot" by the standards of older Navy aircraft, and the critical landing speed tended to vary considerably with the slightest change in throttle setting.
- In some compensation the variable incidence wing made the aircraft "a joy on the catapult shot," as one pilot put it. Although retracting the wing to flight position after takeoff was a little troublesome for inexperienced pilots as the aircraft tended to drop or "porpoise" during the transition.
- At least initially, the landing gear was weak and tended to collapse on impact after steep approaches.
- Finally, recovering from a spin in the *Crusader* was difficult although it gave plenty of warning of "departure" from normal flight. One *Crusader* flight instructor said that it took a "ham-fisted ignoramus to spin the bird."

The *Crusader,* like Vought's *Corsair I*, had a high accident rate. It was about two to three times higher than that of the McDonnell F-4 *Phantom* and four times that of the later Grumman F-14 *Tomcat*. However, as had been the case with the *Corsair I*, the *Crusader's* virtues thoroughly outweighed its vices.

The *Crusader* was not an easy airplane to fly and often unforgiving in carrier landings. Not surprisingly the mishap rate was relatively high compared to its contemporaries, the A-4 *Skyhawk* and the F-4 *Phantom II*. However, the aircraft did possess some amazing capabilities, as proven when several unlucky *Crusader* pilots took off with their wings folded. The *Crusader* was capable of flying in this state with limited maneuverability.

When U.S. Navy pilots entered the Vietnam conflict in 1966, the F-8 *Crusader* saw action against North Vietnamese MiGs. By war's end in 1972 *Crusader* pilots had accounted for nineteen downed enemy aircraft.

While missiles accounted for most of the victories four enemy planes were downed in dogfights by the *Crusader's* formidable Colt Mark 12 cannons. It was an achievement that earned the pilots a place in history and the moniker *Last of the Gunfighters.*

The unarmed photo *Crusader* was operated aboard carriers as a detachment (Det) from either VFP-62 or VFP-63 to provide photo reconnaissance capability. During the Cuban Missile Crisis in 1962 RF-8s flew extremely hazardous low-level photo reconnaissance missions over Cuba.

When conflict erupted in the skies over North Vietnam it was U.S. Navy *Crusaders* that first tangled with the MiGs in August 1965. At the time the *Crusader* was the best dogfighter the United States had against the nimble North Vietnamese MiGs. Some experts believed that the era of the dogfight was over as air-to-air missiles would knock down adversaries well before they could get close enough to engage in dogfighting. As aerial combat ensued over North Vietnam from 1965 to 1968 it became apparent that the dogfight was not over and the F-8 *Crusader* and a community trained to prevail in air-to-air combat was a key ingredient to success.

The *Crusader* would be credited with the best kill ratio of any American type in the Vietnam War, 19:3. Of the 19 MiGs shot down, 16 were MiG-17s and three were MiG-21s.

The Marine Corps (USMC) *Crusaders* flew mostly in South Vietnam. However, there were some carrier based

Supersonic Fighter Pilot

Marine squadrons as well. And some of the Marines in the South flew CAP missions in North Vietnam. The US Navy *Crusaders* flew primarily from the small *Essex* class carriers. USMC *Crusaders* also operated in close air support (CAS) missions.

The last active duty Navy *Crusader* fighter variants were retired from VF-191 and VF-194 aboard USS *Oriskany* in 1976 after almost two decades of service setting a first for a Navy fighter. The photo reconnaissance variant continued to serve for yet another eleven years with VFP-63 flying RF-8Gs up to 1982 and the Naval Reserve flying their RF-8s in two squadrons (VFP-206 and VFP-306) until disestablishment of VFP-306 in 1984 and VFP-206 on March 29, 1987, when the last operational *Crusader* was turned over to the National Air and Space Museum.

Several modified F-8s were used by NASA in the early 1970s, proving the viability of both digital fly-by-wire and supercritical wings.

THE STATISTICS

All F-8 pilots will testify that the *Sader* was a delight to fly and fight in but was very hard to land, especially aboard a carrier. Therefore, deck landing accidents were not uncommon. More than a few *Crusaders* ended up in the water instead of on the carrier deck. Ramp strikes (the aircraft approaching too low and violently hitting the stern of the carrier) were not unusual, and always catastrophic. The *Crusaders* were flying from the smaller carriers. Their high landing speed left little margin for error. The F-8 with its single engine was always in big trouble when an engine failure occurred in flight.

There was a period when at least one ejection from a *Crusader* was made every month from June 1957 to February 1969, with a break for March; and then picking up again in April until May 1970! Such a loss rate would be unacceptable today and would surely result in a fleet-wide grounding but in those days it was an accepted part of life in the *Crusader* community.

APPENDIX B

CRUSADERS AT WAR

The *Crusaders* were used in several very important missions during the Vietnam War. Of course there were the air-to-air (dogfights) encounters with the enemy. The photo *Crusader* flew extremely dangerous missions of taking pictures of the enemy at low altitude before and after a mission. The Close Air Support (CAS) mission of the Marine *Crusaders* was treacherous duty, which required a high degree of accuracy to support the troops on the ground. The Marine *Crusaders* also flew Battlefield Air Interdiction (BAI) missions. That is, they used the *Crusader* to attack enemy forces before they could be deployed effectively against friendly units, and/or to degrade enemy capability by disrupting and destroying rear zone units and logistical support. A primary mission of the Marine *Crusaders* both in North and South Vietnam was the prevention or destruction of, or interference with enemy movements, communications, and lines of communication, with 20mm cannons, rockets, or bombing.

CUBA FLIGHTS

In the fall of 1962 the military was monitoring the activities of Soviet military forces in Cuba. In mid-October, a U-2 spy aircraft brought back pictures that indicated the Soviets were setting up intermediate-range ballistic missiles (IRBM) on the island of Cuba. This was a direct threat to American cities.

The military needed detailed photographs taken at low altitude, of the missile sites. The RF-8 *Crusader* was the ideal airplane for this assignment. *Crusader* over-flights of Cuba began on October 23, 1962, under the codename "Blue Moon."

Flights of RF-8As from VFP-62 based at Cecil Field, FL, departed Naval Air Station (NAS) Key West, FL twice a day to photograph the activities in Cuba. These flights would land at NAS Jacksonville, where the film was offloaded and developed, then rushed to the Pentagon. Four Marine pilots were temporarily assigned to VFP-62 for the missions although they flew Navy RF-8As.

The flights confirmed that the Soviet Union was setting up intermediate-range ballistic missiles (IRBMs) in Cuba. President John F. Kennedy ordered a naval blockade of the island and placed American strategic forces on full alert. After an intense, nerve-wracking confrontation the Soviets agreed to withdraw the missiles, in response for American reassurances that US IRBMs would eventually be withdrawn from Turkey.

Each photo *Crusader* was given a stencil of a dead chicken after an over-flight to keep score. The dead chicken was a poke at Fidel Castro, who on a visit to New York City in 1960, insisted that a chicken be killed and cooked in front of him to ensure that nobody tried to poison him.

The over-flights went on in earnest for about six weeks. The twelve Navy and four Marine pilots who flew the missions all received Distinguished Flying Crosses, while VFP-62 received the prestigious Navy Unit Commendation.

During the photo surveillance flights there were Combat Air Patrol (CAP) flights flown by Navy and Marine *Crusader* fighter pilots. Their mission was to orbit at high altitude to be ready to defend photo aircraft in case MiGs attacked them. They were also on alert duty at Key West, FL and from the decks of several aircraft carriers. They would be launched in case a MiG made a run on any friendly aircraft. In fact these fighter pilots were launched many times when MiGs flew toward the slower flying Navy and Air Force reconnaissance aircraft. These fighting *Crusaders* operated under the control of a Ground Control Intercept group (GCI) whose powerful radar could observe any aircraft operating from the island of Cuba. Somehow the MiGs knew when the fighting *Crusaders* were airborne. They would immediately rush back to Cuba as the *Crusader* was vectored toward them.

SOUTHEAST ASIA

The next arena of action for the Photo *Crusader* was in Southeast Asia. These surveillance flights were often met by anti-aircraft fire. On May 21, 1964, an RF-8A piloted by LT Charles F. Klusmann was hit and badly damaged. Klusmann managed to get the aircraft back to his carrier, the USS *Kitty Hawk*. However, on a mission over Laos on June 6, 1964, he was hit again and shot down. His POW story is recorded in this book.

Supersonic Fighter Pilot

On August 4, 1964, the destroyers USS *Maddox* and USS *Turner Joy* were supposedly attacked by North Vietnamese torpedo boats. In retrospect, it is uncertain whether any attack actually took place. Whatever the case, the incident was played up by the US government and the American press.

On August 5, 1964, retaliatory air strikes on North Vietnamese PT boat bases were launched from the carriers USS *Ticonderoga* and the USS *Constellation*. F-8 *Crusaders*, Douglas A-4 *Skyhawks*, and Douglas A-1 *Skyraiders* participated in the strikes, while RF-8As provided reconnaissance support. One *Skyhawk* was shot down with the pilot becoming a POW, and one *Skyraider* was destroyed, with the pilot killed.

On August 10, 1964, the US Congress passed the *Tonkin Gulf Resolution*, committing the US to full-scale, direct intervention in Southeast Asia. The war was now officially on. The *Crusader* would play a significant part in the conflict.

The *Crusader* participated in the strikes, providing escort for attack aircraft, performing attacks with cannons, *Zuni* rockets, and bombs, as well as performing pre-strike and post-strike intelligence on targets. F-8s suffered a number of losses due to anti-aircraft fire and surface-to-air missiles (SAMs), as well as operational accidents.

North Vietnamese MiG-17 and MiG-19 fighters began to fly against the Americans in April 1965. They shot down a number of US aircraft and damaged an F-8, while the *Crusaders* scored no kills against them in 1965. *Crusader* pilots were eager to take on the MiGs.

The *Crusaders* weren't getting shots at MiGs because the MiGs were focused on attacking the *strike packages*.

Ron Knott

Tactics were changed with the fighters sticking close to the *strike packages* and letting the MiGs come to them.

The tactic paid off in a big time fight with MiGs on June 12, 1966. CDR Harold L. Marr, a long time *Crusader* pilot, got into a dogfight with a MiG-17. His first *Sidewinder* went wide but the second *Sidewinder* destroyed the MiG.

June 21, 1966, a RF-8A was shot down. Other *Crusaders* were vectored in on the location to provide cover for the pilot, who had ejected successfully. Then MiG-17s made a run on the *Crusaders*. LT Gene Chancey hit a MiG with cannon fire tearing off his wing. However, the MiGs scored hits on the *Crusader* piloted by Chancey's flight leader, LCDR Cole Black. LCDR Black was forced to eject.

LTJG Phil Vampatella's *Crusader* had been hit by flak earlier but he was still in the fight. A MiG appeared at his rear and he out ran it. The slower MiG broke off the attack. Even though Vampatella was low on fuel and had problems turning due to his battle damage he decided to turn back and engage the MiG. His *Sidewinder* sent the MiG into the ground. Vampatella won the Navy Cross for the action.

Unfortunately, the attempt to protect the downed *Crusader* pilots failed. The SAR helicopter got lost and never showed up. LCDR Black and the RF-8A pilot became POWs. LCDR Black was one of three *Crusader* pilots known to be shot down by a MiG during the war.

July 14, 1966, a MiG shot up CDR Rick Bellinger's *Crusader*. CDR Bellinger ejected and was rescued. On October 9, 1966, CDR Bellinger evened the score. He fired two *Sidewinders* at a MiG-21 and sent it into a rice paddy. A week later US Secretary of Defense Robert McNamara visited the USS *Oriskany* and pinned the Silver Star on Bellinger's shirt.

Supersonic Fighter Pilot

The third *Crusader* was lost on September 5, 1966. The *Crusader's* pilot was USAF Captain W. K. Abbott. Captain Abbott was flying with the Navy on an exchange program. He became a POW.

A fourth *Crusader* went down under unexplained circumstances and its loss was credited to a MiG. All other *Crusaders* that were destroyed in the war were lost to flak, SAMs, and operational accidents.

The Navy *Crusaders* were used primarily for air superiority mission roles. In contrast, the Marines used the aircraft almost entirely in the strike role, supporting ground forces in South Vietnam from the air bases at Da Nang and Chu Lai. Marine *Crusaders* used cannon, *Zuni* rockets, and iron bombs attached to the stores pylons with *multiple ejector racks* (MERs).

The bombs could be fitted with long *daisy cutter* fuses to increase their effectiveness against enemy forces in the open. The big Mark 84 bombs were also sometimes fitted with delayed-action fuses to allow attacks on underground tunnel complexes. The bombs would bury themselves into the ground and then detonate, collapsing the tunnels.

The *Crusader* was designed for the air superiority mission and its pilots had been trained as dogfighters, while the *Phantom* was a big fighter-bomber and its pilots had been largely trained for intercept missions. In the first part of the war *Phantom* pilots took a back seat to *Crusader* pilots.

Although air-to-air combat got the glory, photo-reconnaissance *Crusaders* served a vital and often under-appreciated role. Photo reconnaissance was unusually dangerous, particularly for *post-strike* missions where the reconnaissance aircraft flew in to determine how much damage an attack had done. Under such circumstances the enemy would always be prepared and waiting.

A fighter, usually a *Crusader,* since that meant a good performance match to provide a second set of eyes to drive off MiGs if that became necessary, typically accompanied the RF-8s. The RF-8 pilot was always in charge of the mission and called the shots, which sometimes caused problems because the fighter pilot could be senior to him in rank.

The next *Crusader* kill was May 1, 1967, by LCDR "Moe" Wright. He was part of an escort of six *Crusaders* for A-4 *Skyhawks* on an *Iron Hand* flight. Three MiG-17s made an attack on the Navy aircraft.

One MiG got onto the tail of an A-4 but Wright blew its tail off with a *Sidewinder.* The pilot did not eject. Ironically, one of the *Skyhawk* pilots scored a kill himself. LCDR T. R. Schwartz, who had been a *Crusader* flight instructor, flew his A-4C toward the tail of a MiG. He fired three *Zuni* (unguided) rockets at the MiG and knocked it out of the sky. It was the *Skyhawk's* only air-to-air victory of the war.

May 19, 1967, LT Phillip Wood flying an F-8C, was escorting *Skyhawks.* He spotted a MiG-17 closing on a Grumman A-6 *Intruder* that was also participating in the strike. LT Wood fired a *Sidewinder* at the MiG but it missed. However, another MiG shot LT Wood's aircraft. Wood maneuvered behind the MiG and shot him down with a *Sidewinder.*

CDR Paul H. Speer and his wingman LTJG Joe Shea, were escorting A-4s carrying the new *Walleye* TV-guided glide bombs to strike a power plant in the middle of Hanoi. After the strike they were jumped by MiG-17s. CDR Speer

Supersonic Fighter Pilot

got into a dogfight with a MiG and knocked the MiG out of the sky with his second *Sidewinder*.

LTJG Shea was able to destroy a second MiG with a single *Sidewinder*. In addition, two of the carrier's F-8Cs were working over a SAM site with cannon and *Zunis* when a MiG-17 streaked in front of them. LCDR Bobby Lee fired a Sidewinder and blew the MiG-17 in half.

On July 21, 1967, F-8s were escorting A-4 *Skyhawks* on a raid when they were jumped by about ten MiG-17s. CDR *Red* Isaacks fired a *Sidewinder* at a MiG but the missile lost lock and went wide. He tried to fire the second *Sidewinder* but it would not fire. He then tried the third *Sidewinder* that knocked the MiG out of the sky. While this was going on a MiG attacked CDR Isaacks' aircraft and it was hit several times. CDR Isaacks made it back to the *"Bonny Dick"* with his damaged aircraft.

LCDR Robert Kirkwood fired a *Sidewinder* at the same MiG that CDR Isaacks knocked out of the sky. LCDR Kirkwood found another MiG and fired a *Sidewinder* at it but the missile missed. Then LCDR Kirkwood closed in on the MiG and got a *guns only* kill. The MiG pilot ejected.

LT Phil Dempewolf scored a probable kill on a MiG-17 with a *Sidewinder*. Two other MiGs jumped his *Crusader*. LT Tim Hubbard got a confirmed kill on another MiG-17. He shot a *Sidewinder*, two *Zunis*, and cannon fire to knock down the MiG. The MiG pilot ejected.

December 14, 1967, *Crusader* pilot LCDR Rich Schaffert was flying an F-8C from the USS *Oriskany*, providing escort for an A-4 piloted by LTJG Chuck Nelson on an Iron Hand mission. Schaffert's aircraft was armed with the normal four 20mm cannons and three *Sidewinders*. The A-4 was preparing to attack a radar site with one of its *Shrike* antiradar missiles when two MiG-17s appeared to converge on the A-4. Schaffert tried to sneak up on them but they got wise, dropped their drop tanks, and turned to fight. As Schaffert turned to stay with them he suddenly found two more MiG-17s attacking him from out of the sun.

Four MiGs now confronted Schaffert. He didn't like the odds. Unfortunately, his face mask had fallen down during his maneuvers, he couldn't spare the seconds to replace it, and so he couldn't call for help. Much to his own surprise he managed to turn out of the attack by the second pair.

For the next ten minutes Schaffert mixed it up with the four MiGs. He was not only badly outnumbered the North Vietnamese pilots were clearly experienced, and no pushovers. He managed to get off his three *Sidewinders*. The first should have been a kill but failed due to a defective proximity fuse; the second went wide, and he was too busy to watch what happened to the third. In response, two MiGs fired a total of four *Atoll* missiles at him but they all went wide.

His missiles gone, Schaffert then closed on a MiG to kill it with the 20mm guns. He was a good shot and felt confident. Regrettably, the guns jammed due to depletion of air pressure in the pneumatic feed system. Now all he could do was try to survive until help arrived. Chuck Nelson was coaching Schaffert on what he could see of the situation from his *Skyhawk*, and other *Crusaders* were moving in. Three of the MiGs gradually dropped out of the fight but Schaffert found himself engaged in a deadly confrontation with the last, performing a series of violent up and down scissors maneuvers. The agile MiG-17 was slowly gaining the advantage so Schaffert decided to bug out. At the top of the sixth scissors he pointed his nose down, engaged afterburner, and left the slower MiG behind, pulling out of his high-speed dive just skimming the treetops.

Schaffert got his *Crusader* back to the Oriskany with too little fuel to perform a second go round. While weapon failures had cheated him of any kills, his duel had lasted an adrenalin drenched 10 minutes 45 seconds, an eternity in a high speed dogfight. He had simply out flown his adversaries and became a legend among Navy fighter jocks.

The MiGs didn't get away unscathed that day, however. While Schaffert was trying to stay alive several other *Crusaders* had jumped into the fight, which became a wild dogfight. LT Dick Wyman found himself on the tail of a MiG-17. Wyman launched a *Sidewinder* and scored a hit, later recalling: "The wing fell off. Red fire streaked along the side of the aircraft as it cart wheeled into a rice paddy."

The *Crusaders* didn't score another kill until June 26, 1968. A MiG-21 made a head-on pass at three *Crusaders* and one of the Navy pilots, CDR "*Moose*" Myers, yanked his F-8H around and put a *Sidewinder* into the MiG blowing its tail off.

On 9 July 1968, LCDR John B. Nichols III was riding shotgun for an RF-8 on a low-level reconnaissance mission when they were bounced by two MiG-17s. Nichols fired a *Sidewinder* at one that missed. The MiG went into afterburner and that made him a perfect target for another missile. Nichols' second *Sidewinder* scored a direct hit.

July 27, 1968, four F-8Es fought with four MiG-17s and CDR Guy Cane hit one with a *Sidewinder*. He thought he'd missed until he saw part of the MiG's wing come off. The MiG then spiraled into the ground.

August 1, 1968, two *Crusaders* piloted by LT George Hise and LT Norm McCoy, were vectored against a bandit picked up on radar by a Navy vessel offshore. It turned out to be a MiG-21 that fired on them with an *Atoll*. The missile went wide and Hise got into position to retaliate with his own missile. He believed he scored a hit but the MiG disappeared into a cloud.

McCoy spotted the MiG-21 again a minute later and hit it with another *Sidewinder*. He chased it down to the ground to confirm the kill even though he was dangerously low on fuel. He managed to link up with a tanker out at sea. McCoy was credited with the kill.

September 19, 1968, two F-8Cs were on combat air patrol when they were vectored to a pair of bandits. The *Crusader* pilots climbed to meet two MiG-21s. LT Anthony G. Nargi fired a *Sidewinder* that blew the tail off one of the MiG-21s, with the pilot ejecting. Both *Crusader* pilots fired a *Sidewinder* at the second MiG-21 and one missile exploded close by the target but the North Vietnamese pilot zoomed away to safety.

April 22, 1972, two F-8Js found a MiG-17 and tried to sneak up on it for a *Sidewinder* shot. The North Vietnamese pilot, either inexperienced or rationally concluding he didn't have a chance, simply ejected safely and his aircraft plowed into the ground. It might not have been much of a kill but it was still a kill.

APPENDIX C

MiG KILLERS

The *Crusader* would be credited with the best kill ratio of any American type in the Vietnam War, 19:3. Of the 19 MiGs shot down, 16 were MiG-17s and 3 were MiG-21s.

APPENDIX D

GOD AND THE MILITARY

What does the Commander In Chief of the Universe have to say about war and warriors? Should we always turn the other cheek and let the enemy destroy our freedom and the freedom of others, when some thoughtless demonstrator taunts the military? Is the military professional considered a murderer, as some say? Or should those who have served, and are serving, be lifted up as people of distinguished valor?

Military personnel were so important in the plan of God that He commanded Moses and Aaron to count those able to fight: *"Take a census of the whole Israelite community by their clans and families, listing every man by name, one by one. You and Aaron are to number by their divisions all the men in Israel twenty years old or more who are able to serve in the army"* (Numbers 1:2-3). It is very clear that the Commander In Chief of the Universe desired a strong military on the earth.

"Go, number Israel and Judah ... Joab reported the census figures to the king: In Israel there were 800,000 able-bodied men who could serve in the army, and in Judah there were 500,000..." (2 Samuel 24: 1-9 *God's Word*). Again, fighting men were there ready to carry out the will of God.

"And there was war in heaven: Michael and his angels fought against the dragon; and the dragon fought and his angels, And prevailed not; neither was their place found any more in heaven. And the great dragon was cast out, that old serpent, called the Devil, and Satan, which deceiveth the whole world: he was cast out into the earth, and his angels

were cast out with him" (Revelation 12:7-9). The strong military of heaven will get rid of the enemy once and for all. Yes, God is love. But He will not allow His enemy to destroy His plan in heaven or earth. He has ordained the military as the primary protector of His plan on earth.

God Himself once destroyed the whole world by water, because it had become so filled with violence. In several places in Bible history it is recorded that God ordered the extermination of an entire people. This included men, women, children, and even the enemy's livestock. These were cases where there was no more talking, reasoning, or consultation. It got so bad in a few cases, it was either they kill us or we kill them. *"But thou shalt utterly destroy them; namely, the Hittites, and the Amorites, the Canaanites, and the Perizzites, the Hivites, and the Jebusites; as the LORD thy God hath commanded thee:"* (Deuteronomy 20:17).

"He teacheth my hands to war, so that a bow of steel is broken by mine arms" (Psalms 18:34).

It is clear that God uses war and the military for His purpose throughout the history of Israel. Warriors like Joshua, Samson, and David were blessed by God and raised to positions of authority in order to carry out the will of God. They were warriors!

In the New Testament the first Gentile convert is a soldier (Acts 10), and Jesus uses a Roman military officer as an example of faith greater than any he had ever seen in Israel (Matthew 8:5-13). God continues to honor our soldiers, sailors, airmen, and marines today!

A strong military is a necessity, not a luxury. Unquestionably, the stronger the military the greater the deterrent to war. The Bible is among other things, a military book.

Military life is filled with love, loneliness, and loss. Family members are part of the team as well; not just the one who wears the uniform. We all should appreciate these families who sacrifice for others.

Men and women who serve their country with character, dignity, and honor can rest assured that the civic duty they perform is condoned and respected by our Sovereign God. Those who served, and are serving in the military, deserve our respect and our gratitude as well. – Ron Knott

APPENDIX E

MEMORIAL DAY

On Memorial Day we reminisce about those who received their final "Charlie." The names are many; too many, and the numbers increase all too frequently. Those who have made that final "Trap" were competent Officers and Men, yet the "Big Air Boss" had a higher calling for them. No, it is not by luck, nor by skill that we remain, it is only by grace and mercy. We who endure should be thankful for the extra holding time allotted.

We will all have that "Final Charlie Time." Some sooner than others as we read, "Another One" on the e-mail reports. We all hope for an OK-3, but a hook skip to 4 would be delightful. I will be thankful just for the barricade. The "Boss" does not want any to perish. He has made provisions for all to be spared. He will erase our drinking and stinking, fussing and cussing, lying and dying, smoking and choking, and other fighter pilot transgressions (mine are many) if we only ask. He will remember them no more. Then He can clear the deck for our arrival. According to His Manual our departed friends will welcome us aboard that Eternal Shangri-La (not CVA 38). Our Eternal Financial Statement will be beyond calculation and the retirement is out of this world. I am looking forward to flying at the speed of light. How about you?

Please review His Guidebook to insure you are ready for the Final Inspection. If you have questions, just ask and He will direct you. Five Thousand years after the "fat lady sings" we can still be having F-8 Reunions on the other side while the Marines stand the duty, ".... the streets are guarded by the United States Marines."

Most of us only consider ourselves as human beings with a small spiritual experience when, in fact we are spiritual beings with a short human experience. What we do spiritually during our human experience will determine our spiritual address forever. The human experience is usually over in threescore and ten years (more or less) but our spiritual component will last forever. We should enjoy the former but not forget about the latter.

Today you're younger that you will be the rest of your life. So enjoy and be thankful. Ron

APPENDIX F

MY GROUND EMERGENCY

(I only include "My Ground Emergency" to inform others in case such an emergency should happen to them or their family members.)

"DayMay, DayMay, DayMay; I am hit but I am going in anyway."

Supersonic Fighter Pilot

That famous line became a reality to me some months ago. I had just returned home after a busy and demanding day when all of a sudden the world started spinning and my landing gear (legs) retracted without will. This was worse than any F-8 departure or spin I had ever experienced. I knew that something was bad wrong with my systems. I could hardly communicate. I asked the wife to call 911 immediately, if not sooner.

The bright flashers and loud siren arrived and the attendants commenced to poke and pound all over my body. In the mean time I threw up all that I had eaten in the past month, so it appeared.

I knew that I was in deep serious trouble when one of the masked men said, "His blood pressure is 235/139."

Then they hit me with a Nitro pill of some sort. I knew for sure that I was way outside the envelope and headed for a risky recovery.

I was not too concerned about making the trip to the "Eternity Fraternity" although I thought for a while I was on my way to that land of no return. I had made reservations for that destination long ago. One day we will all make that journey, no matter if we are ready or not. My primary concern was the possibility of spending the rest of my days in a vegetative state or worse.

Upon arriving at the hospital they commenced hooking me up to all sort of weird thingamajigs. They checked my BP on the port side, and then the starboard side, and determined their machine was kaput. It was not. I was having a stroke.

That dumb costume that they throw at the patient the moment one goes behind those sacred curtains in ER is a joke. It is completely void of backside coverage. And trying

403

to tie the strings in the back that no man can tie, is ridiculous to say the least. This costume is the first indication that you may be there awhile.

As always they begin with serious interrogation about my existence. I suppose they were wondering why I invaded their sanitary spaces. This must be something akin to breaking into the White House. But in my case they start with physical harm. The needle punching started on the starboard side of my body for my precious blood that they embezzled and replaced it with some unsightly fluid that percolates down the cloudy tube into my body. All the while they are pumping the BP cup so hard on my port appendage that my fingers turn blue. Finally, they put me on an automatic BP machine that pumps me up every few minutes with the monitor placed in a position that I can't see. It buzzes and snorts and makes all kind of sounds after each assault on my body. I think for sure, "it is all over."

Of course the EKG is part of the package deal that comes with the ER invasion. Normally they place a cold salve fresh from the deep freeze, on many private parts of my body. As I shiver from the frosty stuff they began placing little suction cups on the creamy substance. These little suckers attack my body like a hungry leach. Next they commence connecting 220-volt (I fear) wires to all of the above. It may not be 220-volts but I am not quite sure at this time. I lay in wait for the first surge of high voltage to my body. The little machine groans and growls and spits out adding machine like paper that reads my consequence. The technician is quick to hide the results on the adding machine paper so I am unable to determine if I am 'alive and well' or something less desirable. When I asked, "How does it look?"

They are quick to exit without saying a word never to be seen again. All the while I am wondering, "Will I make it?"

In addition to the sticky salve they had pretty little strips of colored tape that was placed all over my body. Little did I know that the removal of those little strips of tape would peel my body hair off like skinning a squirrel! Surely that tape had been soaked in super-glue before I arrived. Later I removed a few of the little monsters that were in less dense hairy places on my body with great smarting. I elected to wear the others that are in the heavy hair zones and just let them deteriorate over the next few years.

Finally the Doctor pokes his head through the curtain and introduces himself. My first reaction, "Is he a doctor?" Most of them look like they just rode their skateboard up the hall and invaded your ER room. Finally he starts punching and probing and asks the same questions the nurse asked thirty minutes ago.

"Tell me what is wrong with you?"

I say, "I hurt."

He says, "Where?"

I play the game and say, "All over more than anywhere else."

He says, "On a scale from 1 to 10 how much do you hurt?"

I say, "7.234!" That seems to get his attention and lets him know that I am a real person.

Then he asks, what I think is wrong with the Cowboys.

I said, "I think they need an ER appointment."

Finally he says, "I think you need an X-Ray and a MRI."

I cringe when I hear MRI. That is akin to being buried alive in a culvert on the Santa Monica Freeway.

Ron Knott

The trip to the X-Ray room was an experience to say the least. They strap you down on this portable bed-like object and zoom your body to the next designation of investigation. The attendant performs as if he is trying to break the speed record to the X-Ray station. There must be bets placed on his performance. All the while I am hanging on watching the ceiling zip by at the "speed of heat" noticing that much of the ceiling is in bad shape and many overhead lights need replacing. Objects whoosh by on my right and left, or is it my left and right? I don't know since I am inverted on the bed. I think I have vertigo! We hit the big double doors to enter the sanctum of no man's land with a large poster "Authorized Personnel Only." I can hear the big doors flopping back and forth as we race down the hall. Finally we make an arrested landing at the door of the X-Ray room. I think he won. The attendant must have beat the time and set a record. He was so pleased while I was still trying to determine my bearings.

He then rolled me into the cold and dark room where photos of my innards would be taken. Surely the pictures would be in living color? No such luck. My first glance at the technician was unpleasant to say the least. I thought, "This must be the morgue!" This Dracula looking figure with glasses as thick as Coke bottle bottoms, greeted me with such a cool reception.

"Lay down on the table," he barked.

I had forgotten about the backless costume that I was issued until I lay on the cold table. That cold salve for the EKG was not in the league with the freezing table top on the X-Ray slab. Wow! What a wake up call that was!

He commanded, "Take a deep breath and hoooooold it, don't breathe," and then he leaves the room, forever.

Eternities pass. I am turning blue.

He finally says, "Breeeeeathe!" What a relief.

Now that my back is frozen he says, "Turn over."

And we go through the same process again. Finally he dismissed me with a chilling goodbye. It never entered my mind that I must again be the object of a record-breaking race back to the ER room. Sure enough "Speedy" was eagerly awaiting my return trip. His fame had spread throughout the hospital. I think all departments had a bet on his return record. The hospital staff lined up along the hallway to watch the marathon. He hit every speed bump at full speed. My body bounced up like it was being ejected. He won again. After signing autographs he put me back on the ER bed.

A few hours later the blood test, black and white pictures of my innards, EKG results, MRI, and the urine investigation was returned.

I thought I heard them say, "We have a problem, Houston."

I said, "Say again?"

The Cardiologist and the Neurosurgeon said, "You have had two strokes."

"Not me. Can't be," I thought.

"Yep, you had two minor strokes but somehow there is no permanent damage!"

During all this time my wife and a host of friends world wide, were sending priority emergency messages to Admiral Almighty on High. It worked! I am doing great with no damage.

I have said all of this to say, "It can happen to you as well." Yet, I hope not. Please have a check up often. If you are taking BP medicine for God's sake take it as prescribed. If you feel faint or just think you are experiencing a stroke get to the hospital ASAP. And most importantly keep in contact with Admiral Almighty for quick emergency aid.

I have added humor to this report but I assure you it was not a fun time. Have a great future.

APPENDIX G

ABOUT THE AUTHOR

Captain Ron Knott flew Navy Fighter Aircraft from the deck of many aircraft carriers around the world. After seven years of active duty with the Navy he joined Delta Airlines as pilot, and flew for that company more than thirty years. He continued to fly in the Naval Reserve for an additional six years. He has also owned and operated several civilian aircraft over the years.

Ron says, "I have never flown an airplane that I did not like. However, after more than 20,000 accident-free hours of flying, over a fifty-year span, none could erase the thrill of flying the *Crusader*.

He has developed over twenty large real estate projects; owned and operated Ron Knott & Associates, Inc., an Oil & Gas production company. He started World Wide Imports that sold Mercedes Benz, BMW, Porsche, and other fine automobiles.

He said, "The Navy taught me multi-tasking in assigning me several duties at one time."

Ron has authored several Bible studies and Christian books. *Trophies of Heaven* was his first book and is now in its fifth printing. Next he authored *Battered Believers*, exposing legalism in the churches, plus *Born Again, the Bible Way*, a narrative on scriptural salvation. His next book was *Tithing – Fact or Fiction?* that explains the Bible way to give and error taught by many groups. And *Testimonies for the Soul* tells of mighty miracles of mercy, and recently *Jesus Christ – Who Is He?*

Ron is past president of the North Texas Chapter of International Fellowship of Christian Businessmen. He has appeared on many radio and television talk shows and had his own TV talk show for several months.

He and his wife Sharon are generous donors to the needy. They have visited and contributed to orphanages in Russia, Romania, Korea, and the Philippines. He is a true philanthropist.

Ron and Sharon have been blessed with two boys and two girls, five grandchildren, plus a host of children they support around the world.

He practices the directive, "*It is better to give than to receive.*" He says, "I had much rather be on the giving end than having to be on the receiving end."

Ron Knott

12837206R00245

Made in the USA
Lexington, KY
04 January 2012